THE RISING TIDE

Archaeology and Coastal Landscapes

Edited by
Alan Aberg and Carenza Lewis

Oxbow Books

Published by
Oxbow Books, Park End Place, Oxford OX1 1HN

© Oxbow Books and the individual authors, 2000

ISBN 1 84217 028 7

A CIP record for this book is available from The British Library

This book is available direct from

Oxbow Books, Park End Place, Oxford OX1 1HN
(Phone: 01865–241249; Fax: 01865–794449)

and

The David Brown Book Company
PO Box 511, Oakville, CT 06779, USA
(Phone: 860–945–9329; Fax: 860–945–9468)

and

via our website
www.oxbowbooks.com

*Cover: The village of Bosham, West Sussex. Looking south into Chichester Harbour.
Photograph by the University of Portsmouth Central Photographic Section*

Printed in Great Britain at
The Short Run Press, Exeter

Contents

List of Contributors iv

1. Introduction *(Alan Aberg and Carenza Lewis)* 1

2. Lost and Found: The Archaeology of the Essex Coast *(David Buckley)* 5

3. Archaeology on the North Sea Coast of Lower Saxony: Recent Research *(Erwin Strahl)* 17

4. The Archaeology of Coastal Landscape: The Cleveland Experience *(Robin Daniels)* 23

5. Maritime Fife: An Integrated Study of the Maritime Archaeological and Historical
   Resource of Fife *(Ian Oxley)* 29

6. A Maritime Landscape in East Fife *(Colin J. M. Martin)* 39

7. The Archaeological Potential of the Scottish Intertidal Zone: Some Examples
   and an Assessment *(Alex Hale)* 51

8. Intertidal Archaeology in Strangford Lough *(Brian Williams)* 61

9. Exploitation and Modification: Changing Patterns in the use of Coastal Resources
   in Southern Britain during the Roman and Medieval Periods *(Stephen Rippon)* 65

10. The Changing Landscape and Coastline of the Isles of Scilly: Recent Research
    (Jeanette Ratcliffe and Vanessa Straker) 75

11. Stress at the Seams: Assessing the Terrestrial and Submerged Archaeological Landscape
    on the Shore of the *Magnus Portus (David Tomalin)* 85

12. The Langstone Harbour Intertidal Archaeological Project: Building a GIS for Data Integration
    (Dominic Fontana, Peter Collier and Alastair Pearson) 99

13. Sea Ponds, with reference to the Solent, Hampshire *(Christopher Currie)* 107

14. The National Trust: Survey and Management in the 'Neptune' Zone *(Philip Claris)* 115

Index 119

List of Contributors

ALAN ABERG
29 Pine Walk
Liss
Hampshire GU33 7AT

DAVID BUCKLEY
Essex County Council, County Hall
Chelmsford CM1 1LF

PHILIP CLARIS
National Trust
3 Sheep Street
Cirencester GL7 1QW

CHRISTOPHER CURRIE
71 Upper Barn Copse
Fair Oak
Nr Eastleigh
Hampshire

ROBIN DANIELS
Cleveland County Council
Southlands Centre
Ormesbury Road
Middlesborough TS3 0YZ

DOMINIC FONTANA ET AL
Department of Geography
University of Portsmouth
Buckingham Building
Lion Terrace
Portsmouth PO1 3HE

ALEX HALE
Department of Archaeology
University of Edinburgh
Old High School, Infirmary Street
Edinburgh EH1 1LT

CARENZA LEWIS
Corpus Christi College
Cambridge CB2 1RH

COLIN MARTIN
Archaeological Diving Unit
Scottish Institute of Maritime Studies
University of St Andrews
Fife KY16 9AJ

IAN OXLEY
Archaeological Diving Unit
Scottish Institute of Maritime Studies
University of St Andrews
Fife KY16 9AJ

JEANETTE RATCLIFFE
Cornwall Archaeological Unit
Old County Hall
Station Road
Truro TR1 3AY

STEPHEN RIPPON
Department of History and Archaeology
University of Exeter
Queen's Building
The Queen's Drive
Exeter EX4 4RH

ERWIN STRAHL
University of Wilhelmshaven
Postfach 2062
L-2636 Wilhelmshaven
Germany

VANESSA STRAKER
Cornwall Archaeological Unit
Old County Hall
Station Road
Truro TR1 3AY

DAVID TOMALIN
Isle of Wight County Council
Clatterford School
Carisbrooke
Newport SO23 1NZ

BRIAN WILLIAMS
Department of the Environment
Northern Ireland
Historic Monuments Branch
5–33 Hill Street
Belfast BT1 3AY

1. Introduction

Alan Aberg and Carenza Lewis

The papers published in this monograph were given at a joint conference of the Nautical Archaeology Society and the Society for Landscape Studies. They were designed to review, within the limited time available, various aspects of and approaches to archaeological research in coastal landscapes. In bringing together research from two traditionally separate disciplines, namely terrestrial and maritime archaeology, this conference had two major aims. Firstly, to acknowledge and welcome the range of recent interdisciplinary research in coastal archaeology which has seen the former intellectual divisions dissolved, and secondly to pave the way for future, similarly fertile work which will lead to greater understanding and protection of this fragile historic environment. The zone where sea meets land is an active area of research by a number of different agencies, and the questions being pursued in this varied and dynamic sub-discipline reflect both research and management problems raised by the legacy of human exploitation in coastal landscapes.

This research is not confined to Britain. Erwin Strahl sets out the results of intensive interdisciplinary studies in North Germany, where periodic transgressions of the sea have created successive phases of reclamation and abandonment in the coastal marshlands. Historical geographical studies of the village patterns and vernacular architecture have been extended by excavation and environmental analysis to produce a record of change in house types and economy spanning the Neolithic to the Medieval periods providing a picture of coastal landscape evolution over a period of 5000 years. An interesting comparison to this is provided by Jeanette Ratcliffe describing research in the Isles of Scilly: here a combination of environmental sampling techniques and fieldwork has compiled a chronology of gradual submergence over those same five millennia, which has produced the present landscape of intertidal monuments between the islands. Steven Rippon contributes an equally significant study contrasting coastal landscape evolution in the Severn and Thames estuaries which reveals differing regional economic exploitation of the coastal zone. Sea-ponds are one such element in the coastal economy, and these are considered in detail by Christopher Currie, who examines the evidence for such features in the Solent Estuary.

The artificial and unhelpful nature of the demarcation of coastal research by the Medium Low Water Mark is evident in many of the papers in this volume, and is exemplified by David Tomalin in research on the Isle of Wight side of the Solent. The Wootton Creek project has embraced a coastal zone five kilometres in width extending seawards to a depth of twenty metres. This five-year project (funded mainly by English Heritage) has enabled the reconstruction of successive changes in the landscape since the Neolithic period, and has identified coastal activity by communities spanning an area ranging from the present muddy foreshore up onto the higher ground of the hinterland around Quarr Abbey. Another Solent project was carried out at Langstone Harbour, where Portsmouth University, Hampshire County Council and various voluntary agencies have made extensive use of GIS techniques, backed up by fieldwork, to map archaeological sites and topography as part of research into the evolution of the harbour system. The technical input is expensive but this paper shows that it is crucial because of the flexibility it offers in the manipulation of data, and provides a strong argument for the mustering of such resources whenever possible.

At both Wootton Creek and Langstone Harbour the county Sites and Monuments Record has been an important part of the project, and similar benefits of local authority initiative are evident in the papers of David Buckley on Essex and Robin Daniels on Cleveland. This is evident also in Scotland where Ian Oxley has initiated collaboration between the local authority, university professionals and voluntary organisations in a survey of 'Maritime Fife'. A further reminder of the high potential of the Scottish resource, with its great length of indented coastline and many islands, is provided by Alex Hale.

It is evident that research resources are not distributed evenly within the United Kingdom. If Colin Martin's local study of Pittenweem, Fife, can provide not only extensive evidence of local industrial and maritime exploitation but also of international trade in the medieval and post-medieval periods then more effort is surely justified to find the finance to accomplish similar intensive work elsewhere. This case is proved by new work in Strangford Lough in Northern Ireland, here considered by Brian Williams.

There is no evidence of any lack of public interest in the coastline, its history and environment. The enjoyment and management of the coast figures prominently in the policy documents and actions of the public agencies, whether by the creation of new access routes, such as the Pembrokeshire Coastal Path, or the setting up of quangos such as the Coastal Forum which aims to encourage collaboration between private, public and voluntary sectors. The Countryside Commission has designated as Heritage Coast some 1500 kilometres in scenic areas, and the National Trust has acquired 550 miles of coastline as part of its Enterprise Neptune programme. The value of an archaeological voice in these organisations is demonstrated for the National Trust by Philip Claris, whose paper shows how archaeological considerations can be taken into account. As a result, even when sites such as Orford Ness are accepted for primarily ecological reasons, the survey and management plans give equal weight to the human heritage in coastal environments.

Public awareness of the heritage potential of the coastal environment has been heightened by recent discoveries, including a timber circle lying between the high and low water marks of the Norfolk coastline. This monument, stranded in the tidal zone and threatened with destruction by the very sea which had protected it, rapidly caught the public imagination. Interest in this site was so high that the nick-name originally coined by the local press, 'Seahenge', became irrevocably associated with the monument, to be used by public and professionals alike. (This is in spite of the fact that the monument does not appear either to have been a henge, or to have originally lain in the sea.) Interest in the fate of the monument, fanned by the strident involvement of many non-archaeological special-interest groups, commanded local and national media headlines for days as archaeological decisions met with legal and physical challenges. Subsequently, a television documentary on the site, its excavation, analysis and reconstruction was shown during peak viewing time in Christmas week 1999 and seen by more than four million people. Consequently, it seems safe to assume that an increasingly great proportion of the general public is becoming aware of the archaeological potential of the coastal zone, and of its fragility.

Research into the archaeology of coastal landscapes is a large and growing programme, thanks in no small part to support from English Heritage and other archaeological agencies. The scope of research into the subject has changed profoundly within the last decade. There is now a general acceptance that the present Medium Low Water Mark is only a temporary boundary in the long history of advance and retreat of the coastline, and that the coastal landscape is indeed a distinct entity seamlessly integrated with both the sea and with dry land. To be understood and protected fully, the coastline must be acknowledged as a landscape of unique character, while at the same time being studied holistically within its widest context, which can include land-locked markets and distant sources of raw materials. It is still a poorly-understood zone whose archaeological potential is only beginning to be quantified, and whose historic development, both economic and physical, is only beginning to be reconstructed.

The economic and physical development of the coastal landscape, whether presently submerged or not, is still continuing apace, and the papers in this volume demonstrate the need for increased financial resources in response to current threats from development and natural erosion. At present the causes of beach erosion are still not fully understood, although it seems probable that no single reason such as changes in absolute sea level is responsible, but that a combination of factors (both natural and human) acting together causes the most damage. As 'Seahenge' demonstrated, different combinations of wind and tide can be as disastrous to archaeological monuments on the foreshore as long term changes in the relative levels of land and sea. Beach erosion of sites such as the wreck of the *Anne*, a seventeenth century warship near Rye, may also be partly due to offshore gravel extraction compromising beach replenishment.

More research is needed into the effects of dredging which removes offshore deposits of sand and gravel, and Environmental Impact Assessments need to do more than consider single licences for extraction in one limited area. The approach of the Crown Estates and Welsh Office in initiating a 'total' approach to the assessment of gravel extraction in the Bristol Channel is a step in the right direction away from piecemeal studies. But these problems are by no means diminishing. In 1993 ten million tonnes of aggregates were lifted from the seabed, while it is expected that aggregates required in the period 1992 – 2006 will total 320 million tonnes for England alone. The consequences of resultant sediment drift need to be monitored for its effects on adjacent historical environments as well as for the disturbance of sites on the seabed. A large variety of structures including harbour works, pipelines, sewer outfalls and coastal defences all cause similar disturbances: although their immediate effects are perhaps more easily seen and understood, it is still difficult to ensure that the archaeological impact is properly analysed, monitored and mitigated. Agencies, such as water authorities, still have no statutory duty to take archaeological damage into account in the intertidal and offshore zones, although others, such as the National Rivers Authority, are required by their conservation strategies to consult English Heritage and the county Sites and Monuments Records. The Joint Nautical Archaeology Policy Committee, which acts as a forum for organisations with interests in underwater archaeology, has published with the Crown Estates a *Code of Practice for Seabed Developers* (1995) However, although more than 2000 copies have been printed and distributed, and despite blanket endorsement by the British Marine Aggregate Producers Association, there is still a need to ensure that all developers receive and abide by its recommendations.

Some coastal agencies are more aware of the archaeological implications of their responsibilities. The Ministry of Agriculture and Fisheries takes care to specify which heritage bodies, both statutory and non-statutory, should be consulted in its guidelines on *Coastal Defence and the Environment* (1993), as does English Nature in its publication *Estuary Management Plans: a co-ordinated guide* (1993). Although estuary management plans are non-statutory, English Nature does recommend that all such plans include one for 'archaeology and the heritage'. The interests of English Heritage also are defined for users as encompassing landscape, historic towns, wetlands, coastal fortification, historic ports and wrecks, the last perhaps added with the Secretary of State's proposals set out in the consultation document *Protecting our Heritage* (1996) in mind. The sections in that document proposing extensions to English Heritage powers over wrecks on the foreshore still regrettably remain to be implemented, and the management of sites such as the *Anne* at Rye and the Dutch East Indiaman *Amsterdam* at Hastings exposes a loophole in the present provisions.

It is clear that awareness of the need to protect the archaeological resource of coastal landscapes still needs to be raised among agencies concerned with the natural environment, and the resources expended on other aspects of environmental conservation matched. If the National Rivers Authority can fund a survey of the 380 km of coast between the Humber and Thames to establish beach profiles and the seabed for an offshore zone 4 km in width, surely we need similar archaeological input? But only CADW in Wales has to date initiated a survey of coastal monuments, although English Heritage and the (then) Royal Commission on Historical Monuments for England produced a management statement on *England's Coastal Heritage* (1996), while Historic Scotland has a policy paper *Conserving the Underwater Heritage*.

Such national strategies require the financial resources to back them if the laudable stated aims are to be carried through to actual survey of monuments and the identification and protection of areas at risk. This cannot come from existing archaeological budgets as these are already stretched, therefore it is imperative that new finance should be provided for assessment of the coastal zone. The one encouraging sign is the growth of local forums devoted to archaeological research and management of the coast, of which the Severn Estuary Levels Research Committee is the prime example. This has recognised from the outset the need to construct a programme that examines the archaeology of both shores of the estuary as a single entity in a drowned landscape that originated as a Palaeolithic river valley and evolved thereafter as a maritime zone exploited by communities on both coasts. The Hampshire and Wight Trust for Maritime Archaeology has achieved comparable collaboration in its promotion of maritime research in the Solent and Isle of Wight areas, allied with efforts to promote public awareness of the archaeological resource through educational programmes. The Tamar Estuaries Historic Environment Advisory Forum is another initiative which is attempting to develop collaboration between universities, local authorities and voluntary agencies in identifying the archaeological resources of an estuary and the elements required for its successful management.

Here perhaps is a way forward. Regional co-operation between central and local government, universities and voluntary agencies seems to be the only logical approach to the coastal littoral where tidal effects and coastal currents do not recognise man-made boundaries, and maritime communities themselves have economic and cultural links that extend beyond local, regional and even national territories.

2. Lost and Found: The Archaeology of the Essex Coast

David Buckley

Given the county's long indented coastline, the sea forms an inseparable part of the landscape of Essex. The coast has long been both a zone of numerous maritime and industrial industries and a major routeway for people and goods. Its landscapes are both man-made and natural, an environment of continual change, and recent years have increased recognition both of its archaeological and historical importance and of the steady loss through natural and man made processes. The area has a long history of archaeological work, and this continues through a number of current initiatives, including the National Mapping Programme. Aerial photography has demonstrated the exceptional potential of the coastal and wider intertidal zone for multi-period settlement evidence, while ground survey along the intertidal zone has identified zones of interest across the coastal belt and located many sites which are of particular importance in their range of preservation compared to dry land sites. Wrecks of vessels are abundant on the Essex coast, but systematic identification and recording is only now getting under way; likewise sea walls have so far received little attention. These gaps in the record are now being addressed. Industries were numerous and varied, including those directly related to maritime trades such as wharfs and docks, and those sited for proximity to water-borne transport such as lime production. Oyster pits, wild-fowl decoy ponds and salterns were all once common along the coast, evidence for which continues to be recorded by both ground and aerial survey. Coastal defences date back to the Roman period with the shore fort at Bradwell, and although subsequently the stronger defences were located along the Thames' other coastal towns including Harwich which were protected by a series of defences.

The full range and quality of historic sites around the Essex coast has only recently been recognised. Their importance, and the need for appropriate recording and management strategies, is acknowledged both locally and nationally. These objectives are being achieved thought programmes of recording, liaison with other national and local conservation bodies, and the inclusion of archaeology within management plans.

"Essex and the sea have been antagonists for centuries. 'On the east' wrote John Norden, the Elizabethan topographer, Essex 'encountreth the mayne Ocean, an infallible bounde'. Ceaselessly the conflict born of that encounter flows backwards and forwards with the tide. The creeks, estuaries and rivers of the Essex coast – Stour and Colne, Blackwater, Crouch and Roach, Thames, Ingrebourne, Roding and Leas – are arms of the sea restlesly probing the heart of the county. To William Camden, another Elizabethan topographer, it seemed that 'the Ocean windeth itself into it'. The geographical area of the county is 1,528 square miles, but no point lies more than thirty-four miles from tidal water."

Hilda Grieve (1959)

Introduction

This extract from 'The Great Tide' (Grieve 1959) is an apt starting point for a consideration of the Essex coast. Such is the indented nature of the coastline, comprising some 480 kilometres from the River Thames at Purfleet to the Stour estuary in the north, that the sea forms an inseparable part of the landscape of the county. This interrelationship has been highlighted in the work of many writers and artists, but the interest is not just an aesthetic one. For centuries the Essex coast has been a thriving zone encompassing numerous maritime and agricultural industries while also serving as a major highway for the movement of goods and people. The present century has seen a marked decline in most of this activity and much of the evidence for it had been 'lost'. However, over the past decade a considerable amount has been rediscovered as a result of survey work co-ordinated by the Essex County Council Archaeology Section and it is the nature of the surviving archaeological evidence, the 'found', which this paper explores.

Physical basis of the region

Essex lies geologically within the London basin, a structural feature resulting from earth movements during the late Mesozoic and early Tertiary periods. Only in the

Figure 2.1 The Colne Estuary typifies the Essex coast, showing coastal exploitation both old and new: holiday caravan park on Point Clear (foreground); leisure boats in the creek; disused oyster pits on Cindery Island (centre right) and the medieval port and town of Brightlingsea beyond. (Photo: ECC).

northwest and south of the county in Thurrock does hard rock outcrop in the form of low lying chalk hills. This basin was subsequently filled with river-borne sediments from the west and marine or estuarine material from the east and these deposits underlie the coastal zone (Trueman 1971). The glacial period had a profound impact upon the landscape north of the Thames valley where the Tertiary rocks are covered by an extensive sheet of boulder clay and other outwash deposits. The Thames and other major rivers have laid down gravel beds and carved terraces, whilst the last 10,000 years have seen a gradual relative rise in sea level on the Essex coast and within the major estuaries.

In terms of its topography, the mapping exercise carried out by the Countryside Commission and English Nature (1997) to characterise the landscape of England identified the greater part of the Essex coast as being within a single Thames estuary zone. However, in detail it includes landscapes, both natural and man-made, of great contrast (Murphy and Brown forthcoming). The coast is also an environment of continual change as demonstrated by attempts to reconstruct the position of the coastline during the prehistoric period which show the movement resulting from rising sea levels since the Ice Age (Wilkinson and Murphy 1995, fig. 126; Buckley 1995, fig. 1). At Tilbury the overall change in sea level since the beginning of the Mesolithic (c. 9000 BP) is in the order of 28m.

The present day appearance of the coastal fringe of the county is also one of great variety (see Fig. 2.1). Along the Thames estuary towards London the region is urban and industrialised. This urban pattern is repeated at various points around the coast, for example at Southend and Clacton as a result of 19th century holiday resort development. The built environment is represented on a more modest scale by former small fishing ports and harbours like Maldon, local tourist locations noted for their historic buildings and attractive barges. In contrast along much of the coast the landscape comprises wide expanses of marsh with creeks and intertidal mud flats. Formerly extensively grazed, much is now ploughed with an arable farming regime. Only along parts of the northeast coastline between the Colne and Stour estuaries are there cliffs, these low lying and prone to erosion. Throughout most of its length sea walls provide a boundary, albeit temporary, between the sea and dry land.

Nature of the loss

Recent years have seen increased recognition of the uniqueness and importance of the Essex coast for its archaeological and historic sites as well as for nature conservation. There has also been a recognition of the steady loss and attrition through a range of natural and man made processes (Gilman *et al* 1995). In summary these include:

Encroachment of the sea. Being predominantly low-lying the coast has been vulnerable to erosion as a consequence of the rise in sea level which has taken place since the end of the Ice Age. This is notable in north-east Essex, for example, at Clacton and Walton on the Naze, where sea defences now attempt to prevent further retreat of the cliff line.

Erosion of grazing marshes. Figures produced by English Nature (1992) show a 73% loss of coastal grazing marshes in the Greater Thames Estuary between 1935 and 1989.

Erosion of the intertidal mud flats. Once exposed erosion is aided by such activities as construction of coastal defences, dredging of channels, recreational activities such as beaching of boats on mud flats, damage from power boat wave action, bait digging and even the survey activities of archaeologists!

Construction of sea walls and other defences. Enclosure of saltmarsh through the construction of banks and ditches has taken place since the 13th century to create grazing marsh, but subsequent drainage has enabled arable use and consequent damage to and loss of buried features.

Pressures of development. The coastal zone generally has seen much loss resulting from development for housing, infrastructure and industry, including port facilities (Buckley 1995, 5–6). In Essex there has also been extensive quarrying for chalk, sand, gravel and brickearth. The scale of loss can be clearly seen at Purfleet, Thurrock, notably in the form of large, now abandoned, chalk quarries. One of these with easy access to the M25 motorway recently saw further change when it became the site for Lakeside, a major new shopping complex.

Collectively these destructive agencies have placed, and continue to place, considerable pressure upon the historic coastal landscape. It is therefore important to rediscover and record both specific sites and areas of particular importance in order to ensure their conservation as part of constructive management proposals for the wider coast being promoted by local, regional and national authorities.

Archaeological response

History of recording

There is a long history of archaeological work along the Essex coast and both national and local museums contain many finds resulting from this work. An early instance reflecting this interest appeared in the *Gentleman's Magazine* for 1852 in the form of an engraving showing the digging of Roman remains on the Thames. The importance of Clacton for worked flints was also known in the 19th century and the full potential of the area was recognised by Hazledine Warren. He established the importance of the buried channel found in the cliff face at Clacton for the Palaeolithic period (the term Clactonian is known world wide) and also found the Neolithic Grooved Ware pottery on the foreshore at Lion Point, Clacton, which gave rise to the term Rinyo-Clacton (Warren *et al.* 1936). A brief summary of more recent work relating particularly to the Thames valley has been published (Buckley 1995 with references).

Sites and Monuments Record

The Essex Sites and Monuments Record was established in 1972 and is now the most up-to-date computerised record of archaeological sites in the county with c. 16,000 separate entries (Gilman 1996). In addition to collating existing and incidental new data, over recent years a range of specific enhancement projects have been undertaken to improve coverage of the record for particular aspects of the archaeology of Essex. This work has considerably expanded understanding of the archaeology of the coastal zone and the following summaries aim to demonstrate the range and integrated nature of this work.

Projects

National Mapping Programme

The Essex Mapping Project is the most significant enhancement initiative forming part of the RCHME funded National Mapping Programme (NMP), focusing on cropmarks and other archaeological features visible from the air. It aims to map all archaeological sites in the county visible on aerial photographs at a scale of 1:10,000 (see Buckley 1995, fig. 5 for an example of replotted cropmarks in the vicinity of Orsett, South Essex). The project encompasses both specialist archaeological photographs (including those taken by the RCHME, Cambridge University Committee for Aerial Photography and the Archaeology Section) and vertical coverage dating back to the Second World War, particularly the RAF photography of the 1940s and 1950s. It includes cropmark and earthwork features dating from the Neolithic to 1945 (Ingle and Strachan 1994; Strachan and Ingle 1996). To date almost half of the county has been completed, including most of the coastal zone. The results of this project include not only new additions to established distributions of certain types of site, but also information about whole categories of previously neglected and unknown types of site. Details of these coastal features will become more apparent in the following project summaries.

Excavation

Aerial photography has demonstrated the exceptional potential of the Essex coastal zone for multiperiod settlement evidence, a reflection of the fertility of soils in this region and the advantage of a coastal location. The high level of development in the county, and of mineral extraction in particular close to the coast, has resulted in numerous development-led excavation projects over the

Figure 2.2 Rounding up sheep on Wallasea Island: (Photo: Douglas Went).

past 30 years confirming the existence of occupation features back to the early Neolithic. It is impossible to cite all of the individual references relating to this work and attention is therefore drawn to the various period papers in *The Archaeology of Essex* (Bedwin 1996) as a lead-in to the results. Multiperiodicity and longevity of occupation is particularly clearly demonstrated by the work carried out on the Southend peninsula (Wymer and Brown 1995) while the extent of the impact upon the landscape is seen on the sands and gravels north of the Blackwater (Wallis and Waughman, forthcoming), and most recently from the excavations at Elms Farm, Heybridge (Atkinson 1995 and in prep.). Here the settlement lies adjacent to the River Blackwater close to the estuary and the coast. A plot of features produced from a geophysical survey across the site indicated the degree of complexity which could be expected, and evidence from the Neolithic to the Saxon period was revealed by excavation. The layout of a late Iron Age settlement and succeeding Roman town was established, and the excavation included much of a temple complex and associated activity areas. The vast quantity of finds from Elms Farm is still being assessed and analysed, but along with discoveries from other excavated sites, these have raised numerous questions about the inter-relationship of settlements of all periods with the coast and its associated resources.

Ground survey of the intertidal zone

Natural erosion also threatens many sites, and it was the knowledge that Mesolithic flintwork was eroding from the riverbank at Hullbridge on the Crouch estuary which helped to focus attention upon the need for research to locate and record more sites and features around the coast. A survey, known as the 'Hullbridge Survey' after the site which initiated the project, was commenced in the Crouch estuary, but was subsequently extended to the whole coast (Wilkinson and Murphy 1995). It was recognised that while various zones of interest could be identified across the coastal belt, each with a characteristic range of archaeological sites, the survey should be focused in particular upon those within the intertidal zone. Many new sites were discovered, notably several of Neolithic date, which are of particular importance when compared with dry land sites since having not been subject to ploughing they retain full soil horizons. Following the initial survey, one of these Neolithic sites, the Stumble in the Blackwater estuary, was chosen for excavation (Wilkinson and Murphy forthcoming). This required the overcoming of many problems: not least the need to programme fieldwork between high tides. Such work can be costly, but the quality of evidence for Neolithic settlement provides exceptional return on the effort put into conducting the excavation. In addition to occupation features a significant quantity of well preserved finds including pottery and flint were recovered from concentrations interpreted as *in situ* middens.

Elsewhere, there are structures, such as hurdles or trackways, which reflect encroachment by the sea; every effort is made to follow up reports of new features. One such report during 1996 was of a length of trackway discovered at Walton on the Naze north of Clacton. This was of more substantial construction than a number of the timber structures found by the Hullbridge Survey (Wilkinson and Murphy 1995), but like them is believed to be Bronze Age in date. Unfortunately this site was 'lost' again as a result of shifting sand before it could be

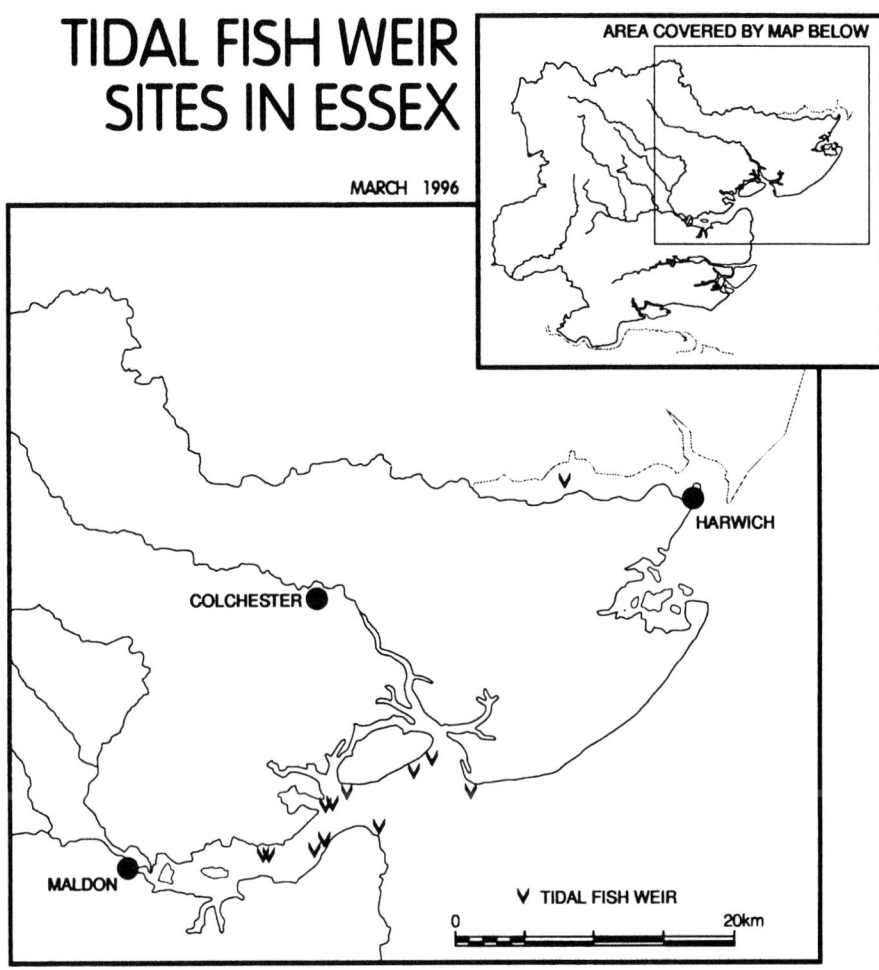

Figure 2.3 Tidal fish weir sites in Essex.

fully recorded, a further demonstration of the difficulties arising when working in the intertidal zone. These structures are a reflection of attempts to exploit the coastal marshes, one such activity long maintained being that of pasturing sheep. A photograph of Wallasea Island (Fig. 2.2) taken before the island was ploughed, published by Wentworth Day (1943), has a caption explaining that it shows rounding up sheep, qualified by the quote "A wild, flat, wide land of bleached grasses and singing winds". This view is more reminiscent of ranching in the Australian outback than the marshes of present day Essex, but it is probably typical of their appearance, and of the approach taken to farming on the marshes from the Bronze Age to the Second World War, prior to the widespread reclamation for arable cultivation.

Aerial survey of the intertidal zone

The Hullbridge Survey kept close to the present day shoreline, but appreciation of the potential of the wider intertidal zone was highlighted following a report from Ron Hall, a local boatman, that a number of timber structures were visible at low tide on the mud flats at Collins Creek out in the Blackwater estuary. These features are rarely, if ever, accessible from dry land and are difficult to reach by boat, so it has been necessary to take to the air to establish their nature and overall scale. Ground survey, funded by English Heritage, was carried out on one of the Collins Creek structures. This demonstrated the difficulties of survey both in terms of accessibility, since work was only possible at the lowest tide, and in obtaining and setting up control points, for which satellite positioning had to be used (Clarke in prep.). Initial radiocarbon dates from two of the features indicate construction during the mid-late Saxon period. More recently continued aerial survey has discovered structures of V-shape form located elsewhere around the Essex coast (Crump and Wallis 1992; Wallis 1993 and Fig. 2.3) which may be anything from medieval to 20th century in date. Several of these structures are confidently interpreted as the remains of timber fish weirs (there is documentary evidence for their late survival off Foulness Island), a particularly fine example of which survives at East Mersea. Other straight alignments may have been retaining revetments or the remains of other, as yet unidentified, features. Support from the RCHME has enabled aerial reconnaissance of the coastal zone to be extended beyond Essex, and as a result similar structures are now known to the north on the Suffolk side of the Stour estuary (Strachan 1996), and also across the Thames estuary in north Kent (unpublished survey information obtained by David Strachan entered onto the county SMR). A recent Essex discovery appeared over the winter of 1995–6 near Bradwell power station. This followed the movement of sand by storms and again emphasises the vulnerable nature of these intertidal structures.

Boats in the intertidal zone

"Thames barge, that's the only way to see Essex!" (to quote an elderly resident) gives emphasis, despite recent decline, to the important role of maritime traffic to the county. This has a long history as the discovery of a wooden paddle made from split oak found during the Hullbridge Survey demonstrates (Wilkinson and Murphy 1995, 155–7 and Fig. 99). This is an important and rare find (now in the National Maritime Museum), recovered from a middle Bronze Age level in the Crouch estuary muds interpreted as a tide-line location. Clearly movement by water was established at this time and anticipates widespread use of the sea which persisted up until the early part of the 20th century. Wrecks of working vessels and sailing craft are abundant on the Essex coast (Finch 1976), but the identification and recording of maritime wreck sites is one aspect of SMR enhancement that is only now starting to be addressed. Many intertidal hulk sites have recently been recorded and mapped as part of the county's aerial survey project, including a large barge 'cemetery' in the Blackwater estuary, and there is potential for a systematic SMR enhancement survey. This is seen to be a preliminary to more detailed surveys of individual hulks comparable to the work being carried out in the Thames by Milne (1995). There is an urgent need to extend this work as many of these sites are being actively eroded.

Location of sea walls and creek systems

There is a long history of sea wall construction in Essex, including notable early Flemish connections on Canvey Island when Dutch engineers were first contracted to reclaim the island (Grieve 1959). Early RAF photography is proving extremely useful for recording stretches of now abandoned sea walls and the position of former creek systems, many of which do not appear on early maps. Whilst some of these are still extant as cropmarks on later photographs, many are no longer visible from the air. The NMP has provided an opportunity to record these coastal walls at an appropriate scale thereby giving an overview of the sea defences which is available for study in conjunction with further cartographic research.

Survey of industrial sites

Related to the boats themselves are the sites of numerous dock and wharf facilities and, associated with these, industrial activities for which a coastal location was beneficial. These include industries for which there have been recent surveys. That of maltings (Gould 1996) established that while quite a number of the buildings survive they have now been reused or stand derelict awaiting conversion. Kilns producing lime for agricultural purposes have fared less well, there being only one extant example in the county (Gibson 1996). This is at Beaumont Quay where not only is the kiln intact, there is also a surviving brick storehouse, stone built quay and the foundations of other associated buildings. The quay was built in 1832 for the Governors of Guys Hospital who owned the estate, reputedly with stone from old London Bridge. Fortunately the site is now in County Council ownership and, following transfer of responsibility to the Planning Department, was surveyed by the RCHME as a preliminary to conservation works and improved site presentation. The resulting plan (Figs 2.4 and 2.5) illustrates the surviving features related to the creek system, sea walls and also the site of *'The Rose'*, one of the many hulks abandoned in the Essex creeks. Other coastal industrial features include tide mills, such as that at Thorrington on a tributary of the River Colne in north-east Essex. This is also in the care of Essex County Council and was recently restored to full working order by the County Council millwright.

Some marsh areas have extensive oyster pits which represent the remains of what was in the past a major industry, but one for which until recently evidence was poorly represented on the SMR. Many oyster pits, shallow depressions in which oyster spat were grown, have now been recorded, largely through the Essex Mapping Project. There are several different types which are believed to reflect their varying date, ranging potentially from the Roman period to 20th century. The height of production was the 19th century and dense concentrations of pits cut into the salt marsh are recorded at some localities, for example, in Paglesham Reach on the River Roach and near Brightlingsea on the River Colne (Fig. 2.6). Many of the sites plotted from RAF photography of the 1940s and 1950s have subsequently been lost through erosion of the salt marsh. The present plotting of surviving sites provides a basis for the organisation of field survey in advance of new development, for example in advance of beach renourishment and groyne construction such as is currently proposed by the Environment Agency at Jaywick, near Clacton.

Fowling was also of significance in the later post medieval period and duck decoy ponds were once numerous along the Essex coast; being particularly densely located along the north side of the Blackwater estuary. Again the National Mapping Project has systematically recorded most, if not all, of these former decoy pond sites (Fig. 2.7), many of which do not appear

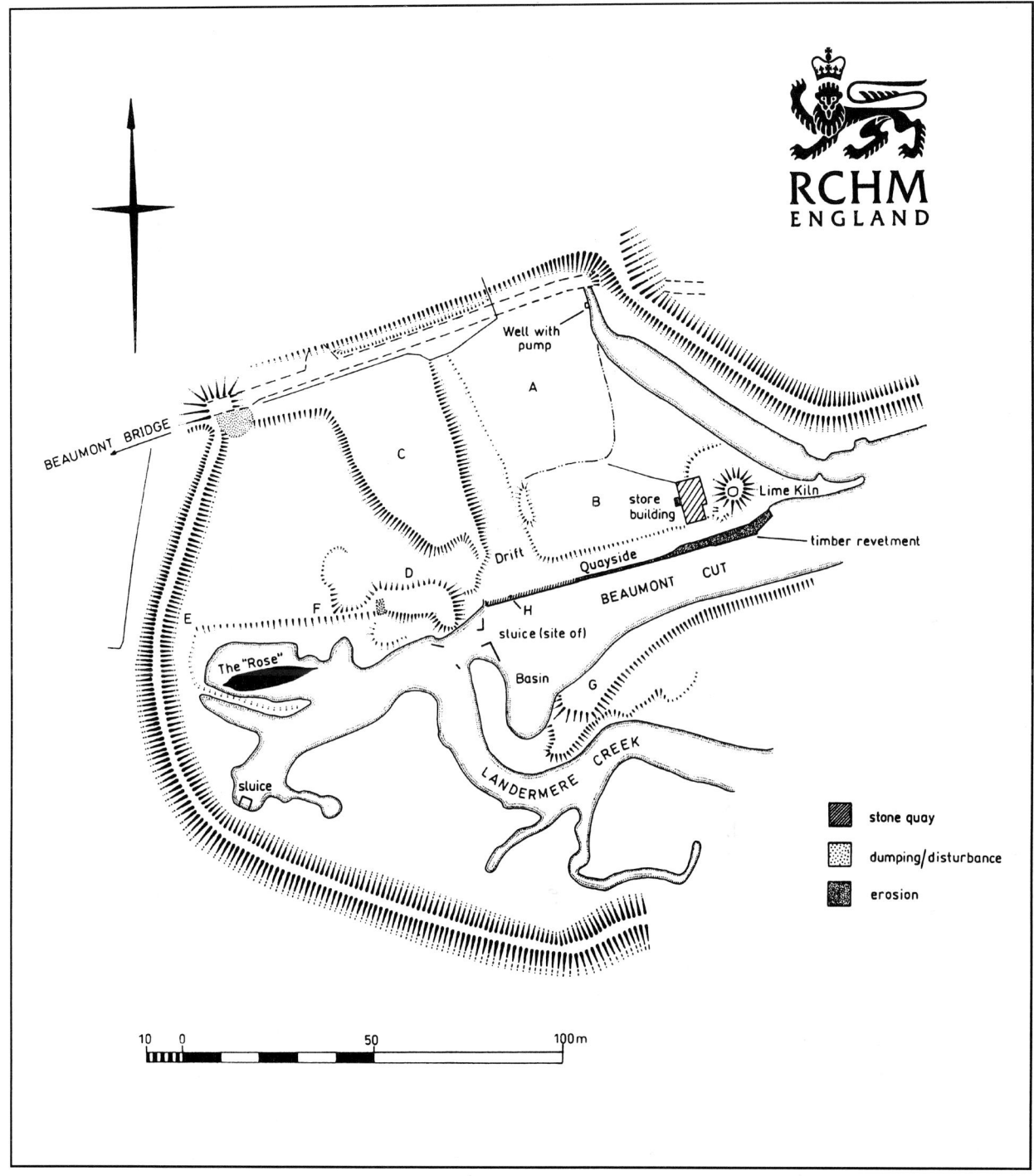

Figure 2.4 Plan of Beaumont Quay, surveyed at 1:1000. (Copyright RCHME).

on the Ordnance Survey or other early maps of the county. Many are now filled in (deliberately or otherwise) although they may still be visible as cropmarks when cultivated, as with one example at Bradwell on Sea (Fig. 2.7 no. 5). A few do remain, such as two examples on Old Hall Marshes (Fig. 2.7 nos 16, 17) and there are some instances where the central pond survives although the arms have silted up (Fig. 2.7 nos 11, 12, 15, 21, 23).

Comprehensive surveys such as this provide a basis for a reassessment of site status, in this instance only one site, Marshhouse Decoy pond near Tillingham, is currently a Scheduled Ancient Monument (Fig. 2.7 no. 4).

Perhaps one of the most important and extensive industries in the county during the Roman and medieval periods was that of salt production. Evidence for this survives in the form of numerous mounds or spreads of

12   *David Buckley*

Figure 2.5 Beaumont Quay aerial view (Photo: ECC).

Figure 2.6 Aerial view of oyster pits cut into the salt marsh at Brightlingsea (Photo: ECC).

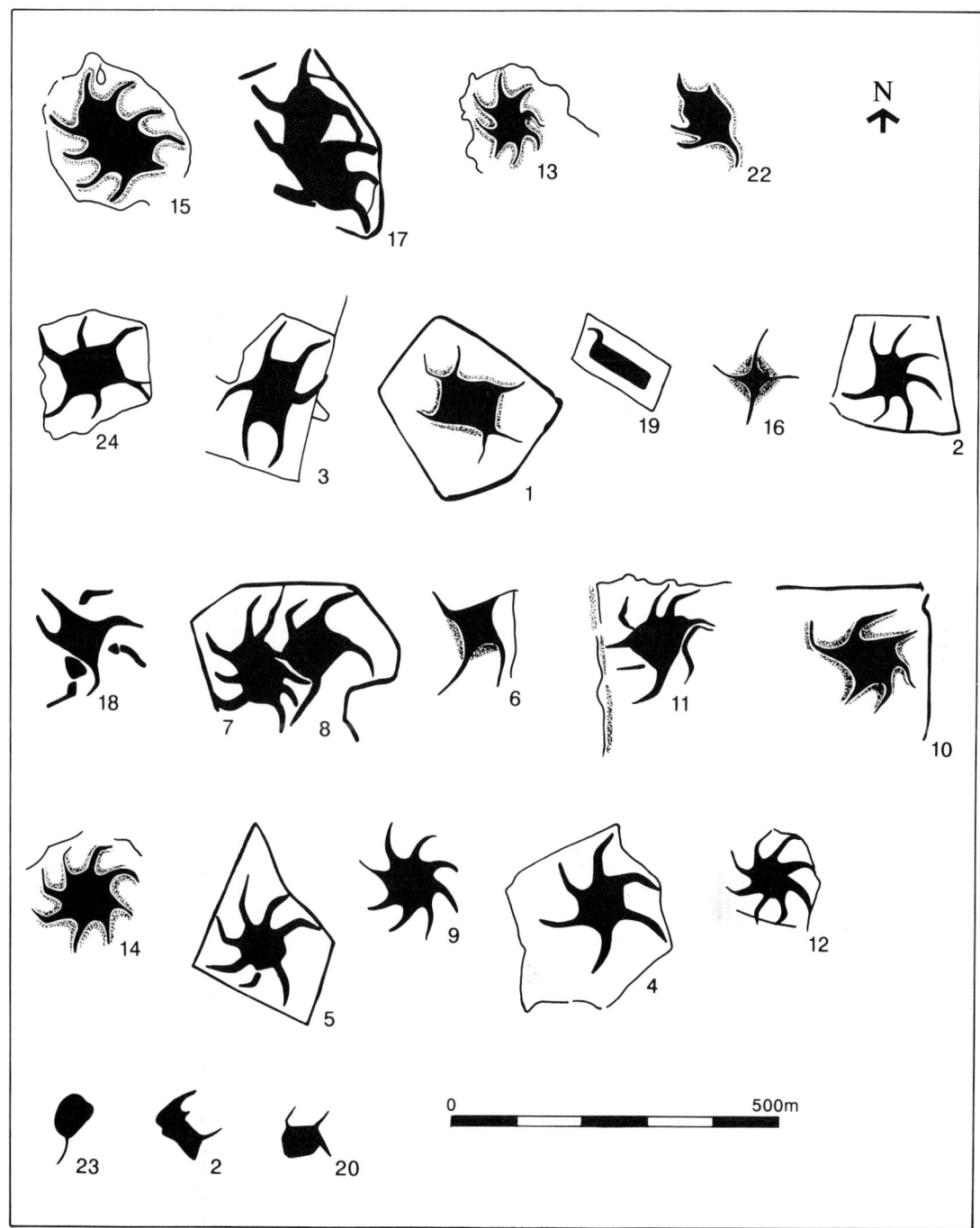

Figure 2.7 Comparative plans of duck decoy ponds in Essex; these twenty four sites were mapped as part of the Essex Mapping Project.

red soil commonly referred to as red hills (Fig. 2.9). The Hullbridge survey found the earliest salt working site in the county, in the Crouch valley, dated to the middle Bronze Age (Wilkinson and Murphy 1995, 157–65). Many of these sites are being actively eroded by the sea, for example at Rolls Farm, Goldhanger, and Leigh Beck, a significant site at the eastern tip of Canvey Island which was investigated by the local archaeological society in 1978 (Eddy 1979, 110). Much research into red hills has taken place over many years (Fawn *et al.* 1990), but the recent aerial survey has continued to increase the list of known sites. In 1995 thirty five new sites were added to the distribution in the area of the Dengie peninsula area alone (Strachan 1996). The location of many sites can be clearly seen to relate to the former coastline as demonstrated by a plot of red hills, old and new, in the Peldon area south of Colchester (Fig. 2.8).

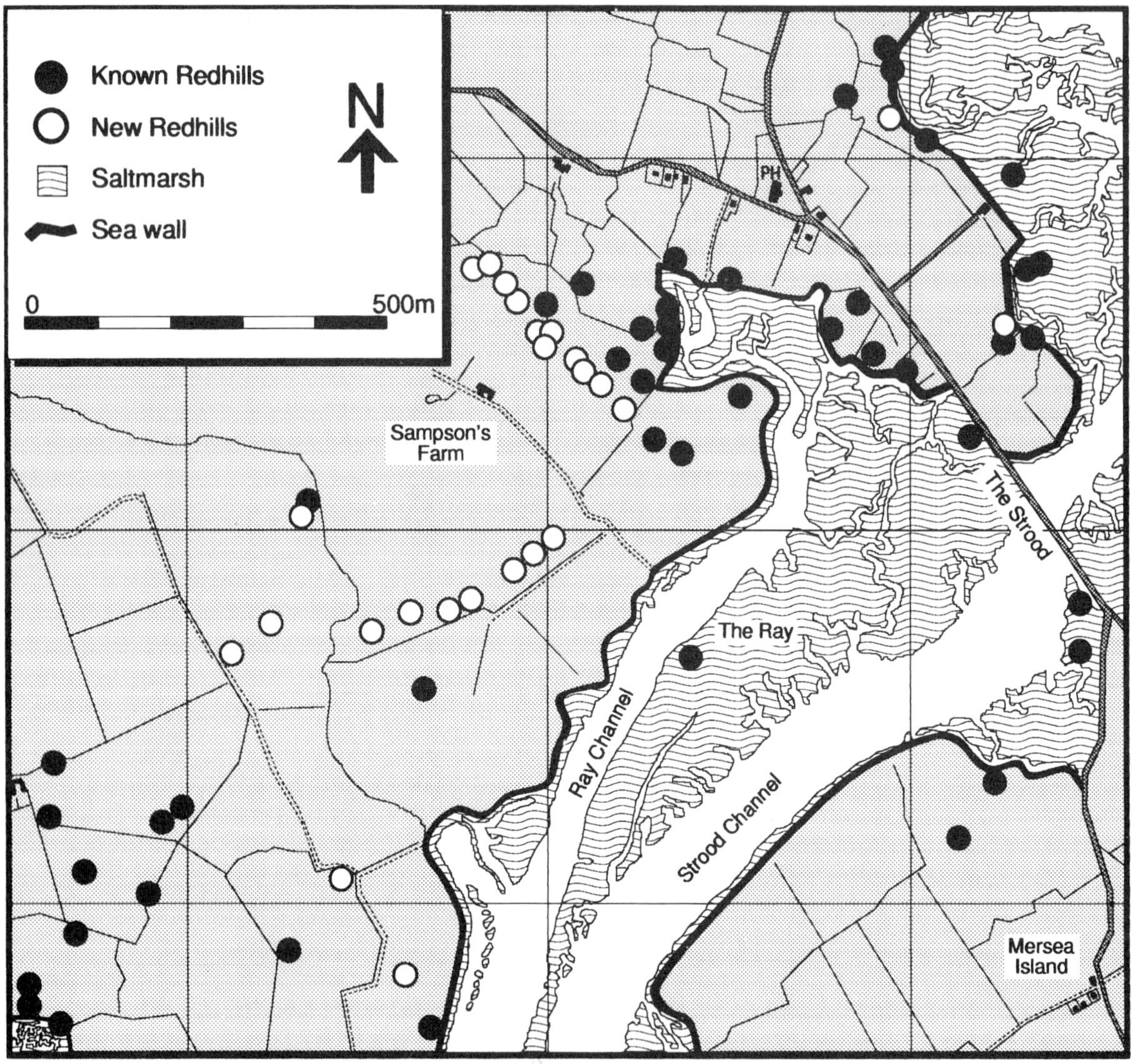

Figure 2.8 Red hill distribution in the Peldon area, Colchester.

Figure 2.9 Red soil from an eroding red hill on the Blackwater estuary, Tollesbury parish (Photo: ECC).

Figure 2.10 Second World War double ended pillbox in the sea wall at Bradwell-on-Sea, offering protection from attack from both land and sea (Photo: ECC).

Defences survey

There has been a long history of defences along the Essex coast starting with the Saxon Shore Fort at Bradwell. The Thames defences include the medieval castle at Hadleigh and Tilbury Fort, which is Tudor in origin with later rebuilds, and makes an impressive site which reflects the importance of the Thames as the main approach to London. These and other sites on both sides of the Thames defended the capital successively against the Spanish (16th century), the Dutch (17th century), the French (18th/19th century) and the Germans (20th century). Elsewhere defences served to protect coastal towns, notably at Harwich, whose medieval town walls were successively replaced by an impressive Napoleonic redoubt and a late Victorian fort at Beacon Hill, both to the south of the town.

Most numerous are the defences of the 20th century which again had a strong coastal emphasis. A survey of WWII defences commenced in 1994 to record pillboxes and related structures throughout the county, including features along the coast. In the coastal areas surveyed up to March 1996 fifty three previously unrecorded sites were identified and added to the SMR. In total the survey has recorded 273 sites in these coastal areas of which eighty four are extant. Whilst many have been deliberately demolished others have been lost to natural erosion, as is the case with two gun battery sites in the County Council Country Park at East Mersea which were lost through the collapse of the cliff on which they once stood. Despite their recent origin many of the surviving sites are now accepted and appreciated features of the coastal landscape as illustrated by pillboxes at Bradwell-on-Sea (Figure 2.10). However, the losses highlight the need for more detailed surveys and the identification of special types of site for protection, as such a rare form of WWII minefield control tower near Burnham on Crouch.

Protection

This paper gives some indication of the quality of evidence for historic sites which exists around the Essex coast and of the efforts which are being made to record it. The importance of the Essex coast and need for appropriate survey, recording and management has been recognised at the national level (English Heritage 1996; Fulford *et al.* 1997) and locally in the Essex Coastal Strategy (ECC 1994). This includes policies for archaeology which will hopefully provide a basis for both future protection and further investigation of the archaeology of the Essex coastal zone. Much of the coast is already designated for nature conservation as Ramsar sites, Sites of Special Scientific Interest, Environmentally Sensitive Areas, and both national and local Nature Reserves. Liaison is being developed to ensure that archaeology is considered appropriately in these areas through an integrated approach (Gilman *et al.* 1995). In addition, management plans have been, or are being, prepared for the Thames, Blackwater and other Essex estuaries. There has been a significant archaeological input to each of these, which it is hoped will help to provide for the future protection of historic sites within their wider landscape.

Acknowledgements

Acknowledgement is made to David Strachan for information relating to aerial survey, to Caroline Ingle for much assistance in the production of this paper and to both for their contributions arising from their involvement in the Essex based part of the RCHME/EH National Mapping Programme. The RCHME/EH is also thanked for agreeing permission to use the survey of Beaumont Quay produced by Paul Pattison of the Cambridge Office. Also thanks are given to the Rt Rev J Went for permission to reproduce his father's photograph of Wallasea Island.

References

Atkinson, M. 1995: "Elms Farm, Heybridge" *Current Archaeol.* 144, 452–458.

Bedwin, O. 1996: *The Archaeology of Essex: Proceedings of the Writtle Conference* (Essex County Council).

Buckley, D.G. 1995: "Thames Gateway: Archaeological and Geographical Context" in *Thames Gateway: Recording Historic Buildings and Landscapes on the Thames Estuary.* RCHME, 3–22 (Proceedings of a one-day conference held at the Society of Antiquaries, London, on 24 March 1995).

Crump, R. and Wallis, S. 1992: 'Kiddles and the Foulness Fishing Industry' *Essex Journal* 27 (2), 38–42.

Eddy, M. (ed) 1979: 'Excavations in Essex, 1978' *Essex Archaeol. Hist.* 11, 101–110.

English Heritage 1996: *England's Coastal Heritage: A statement on the management of coastal archaeology.*

English Nature 1992: *Erosion and vegetation change on the salt marshes of Essex and North kent between 1973 and 1988.*

English Nature and Countryside Commission 1997: *Character of England map.*

Essex County Council and Coastal Districts 1994: *The Essex Coastal Strategy* (Essex County Council).

Fawn, A.J., Evans, K.A., McMaster, I. and Davies, G.M.R. 1990: *The Red Hills of Essex; Salt-making in Antiquity* (Colchester Archaeology Group).

Finch, R. 1976: *Sailing Craft of the British Isles* (Collins).

Fulford, M., Champion, T. and Long, A. (eds) 1997: *England's coastal heritage: A survey for English Heritage and the Royal Commission* (English Heritage).

Gibson, S. 1997: *Comparative survey of Modern Industrial Sites and Monuments No 3: The Essex Lime Industry* (Essex County Council Limited Circulation Document).

Gilman, P.J. 1996: "Archaeological Research and the Essex Sites and Monuments Record" in Bedwin, O. (ed) *The Archaeology of Essex: Proceedings of the Writtle Conference*, 181–191.

Gilman, P.J., Buckley, D.G. and Wallis, S. 1995: "Salt Marsh Loss to Managed Retreat in Essex: An integrated approach to the Archaeological Management of a Changing Coastline", in *Managing Ancient Landscapes: An Integrated Approach,* Berry, A.Q. and Brown, I.W. (eds) 143–154 (Clywd Archaeology Service with ACAO).

Gould, S. 1996: The Essex Malt Industry: History, Technology and Architecture. Comparative Survey No. 1: The Essex Malt Industry (Essex County Council Limited Circulation Document).

Grieve, H. 1959: *The Great Tide.*

Ingle, C. and Strachan, D. 1994: "National Mapping Project 1993" in Bennett, A. (ed) 'Work of the E.C.C. Archaeology Section, 1993' *Essex Archaeol. Hist.* 25, 233–237

Milne, G. 1995: 'Foreshore Archaeology' in *Thames Gateway: Recording Historic Buildings and Landscapes on the Thames Estuary*, RCHME, 23–27 (Proceedings of a one-day conference held at the Society of Antiquaries, London, on 24 March 1995).

Murphy, P. and Brown, N.R. Forthcoming 'Archaeology of the Essex Coastal Landscape' in Green, S. (ed) *The Essex Landscape: in search of its history.* Essex County Council.

Strachan, D. 1996: 'Aerial Survey 1995' in Bennett, A. (ed) 'Work of the Essex County Council Archaeology Section, 1995' *Essex Archaeol. Hist.* 27, 250–253.

Strachan, D. and Ingle, C. 1996: "Essex Mapping Project 1995" in Bennett, A. (ed) 'Work of the Essex County Council Archaeology Section, 1995' *Essex Archaeol. Hist.* 27, 253–255.

Trueman, A.E. 1971: *Geology and Scenery in England and Wales* (Pelican: revised by J.B. White and J.R. Hardy).

Wallis, S. 1993: 'Aerial Survey of the Essex Coast' in Bennett, A. (ed) 'Work of the E.C.C. Archaeology Section, 1992' *Essex Archaeol. Hist.* 24, 193–194.

Wallis, S. and Waughman,. M. 1998: 'Archaeology and the Landscape in the Lower Blackwater Valley', *East Anglian Archaeol.* 82.

Warren, S.H., Clark, J.G.D., Burkett, M.C. and Godwin H. and M.E. 1936: "Archaeology of the submerged land surface of the Essex Coast" *Proc. Prehist. Soc.* 2, 178–210.

Wentworth Day, J. 1943: *Farming Adventure; a thousand miles through England on a horse.*

Wilkinson, T.J. and Murphy, P. 1995: 'The Archaeology of the Essex Coast, Vol. I: The Hullbridge Survey' *East Anglian Archaeol.* 71.

Wilkinson, T.J. and Murphy, P. forthcoming: 'The Archaeology of the Essex Coast, Vol. II: The Stumble' *East Anglian Archaeol.*

Wymer, J.J. and Brown, N.R. 1995: Excavations at North Shoebury: Settlement and economy in South-east Essex 1500 BC–AD 1500. *East Anglian Archaeol.* 75.

3. Archaeology on the North Sea Coast of Lower Saxony: Recent Research

Erwin Strahl

This paper presents the first results an an interdisciplinary project on the coloisation of the clay district along the southern North Sea coast in Lower Saxony (Germany) and on the history of the three-aisled longhouse. A well-preserved longhouse was excavated near Wilhelmshaven, which is to date the only known example from the high Middle Ages. It suggests that the development of the three-aisled longhouse in the clay district was unbroken from the Pre-Roman Iron Age to modern times.

This paper presents the first results of a recent interdisciplinary project carried out from 1990 to 1997 by the Niedersächsisches Institut für historische Küstenforschung (Lower Saxony Institute for Historical Coastal Research), Wilhelmshaven. The excavations took place in the Wangerland area, which is part of the clay district directly north of Wilhelmshaven (Fig. 3.1). This area was dominated, almost until late medieval times, by the Crildum bay. Using evidence from archaeology, botany, geology and geography, the project aimed to investigate the development of the clayland environment during the Middle Ages, and the ways in which this affected the use made of the area by the resident Frisian population. The results presented here are also important for our understanding of the colonization of the clay district, and of the development of a certain type of farmhouse, the three-aisled longhouse, which was built in this area from at least the Pre-Roman Iron Age (Haarnagel 1984).

The clay district, which extends along the southern North Sea coast from the Netherlands up to Esbjerg in Denmark was formed in the Holocene as marine sediments were laid down during a period of rising sea level following the end of the last glaciation. Human colonisation of this district was inevitably largely dependent on marine transgression and regression (Behre *et al.* 1979). Prior to the building of dykes in this coastal area, the slightly elevated levees along the rivers and creeks running into the North Sea could be settled only as long as the mean high water and storm tides did not seriously threaten the settlers. But a gradual rising in the storm tide level, or even just a single violent storm flood, could result in the loss of this colonised land to the sea. Faced with the prospect of having to abandon the district, one solution was to build artificial dwelling mounds to protect the settlers and their animals against the rising water. Such mounds are called *wurten* in German and *terpen* or *wierden* in Dutch. On the German coast *wurten* were built for the first time towards the beginning of the Roman Iron Age.

In the Netherlands the most ancient settlements in the coastal wetlands date to the Neolithic period (Louwe Kooijmans 1987). But if there are any settlements of this date on the German North Sea coast, they remain hidden deep beneath the holocene sediments. Similarly, the raising of mounds to defend settlements against sea water occurs earlier in the Netherlands than in Germany. This is exemplified by the *wurt* of Ezinge in the province of Groningen which dates to the Pre-Roman Iron Age (Waterbolk 1991).

The most ancient settlements known on the Lower Saxony coast are from the Pre-Roman Iron Age, which started after 800 cal BC (Haarnagel 1965). One example is the settlement of Hatzum-Boomborg (6th–3rd century BC), which is situated west of the river Ems a few miles south of the town of Emden. As the North Sea was in a regressive phase at the beginning of the Pre-Roman Iron Age, the houses of the settlement were built on the flat ground of the western levee along the river Ems without being elevated with a *wurt*. The three-aisled longhouses with a byre found at Hatzum-Boomborg are the oldest known so far in the German North Sea coast clay district. Two rows of posts dug in the ground supported the roofs of buildings up to 6.5 m wide and 21m long whose walls were made of wattle and daub. The houses were divided into two parts: at one end was a byre, comprising two rows of boxes along the sides of the houses where the cattle stood with their heads to the wall, while at the other end there was a working and living area with a fireplace. These longhouses do not appear to have been used for the storage of crops, which were instead kept in granaries

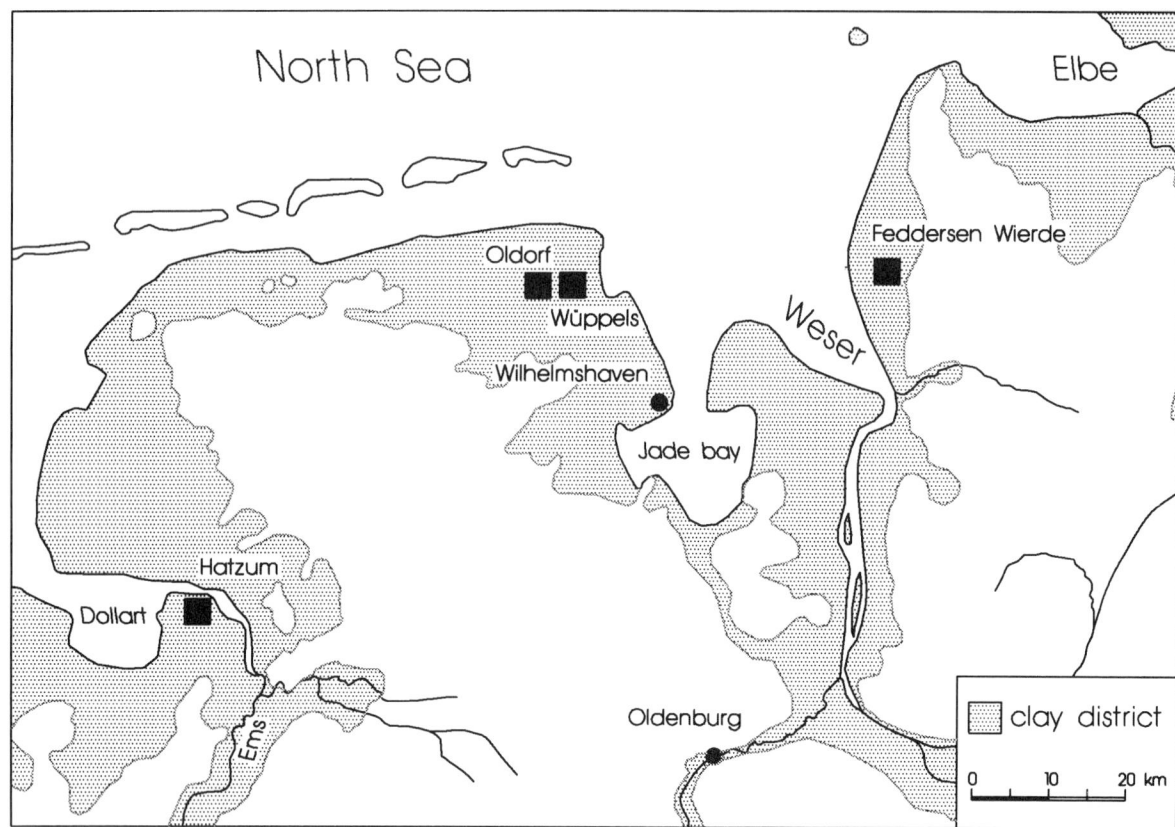

Figure 3.1 Map of northern Lower Saxony (Germany) showing the clay district and places of settlements named in the paper.

next to the house. Occupation at sites along the river Ems such as Hatzum-Boomborg, was threatened during the third century BC by rising storm tide levels, which also began to make farming increasingly impracticable. Without the protection of *wurten*, the district was abandoned to the sea before the end of the century. (In January 1997 a three-aisled longhouse of later Bronze Age date was found at Rodenkirchen *c*. 45km east of Wilhelmshaven on the western levee of the river Weser.)

In the first century BC a regression of the North Sea set in again, and the clay district was colonised anew by the Germanic tribe known as the Chauki. The storm tide level started to rise once more in the 1st century AD, but in contrast to the retreat three centuries earlier, this time settlements were defended by *wurten*, allowing occupation of the area to continue. As the storm tide level continued to rise the *wurten* had to be raised repeatedly, bringing them up to a maximum height of 5m above present sea level. One of the best known examples of a Roman Iron Age *wurt*-settlement is Feddersen Wierde in the clay district north of Bremerhaven. As before, three-aisled longhouses, here up to 7m wide and 29m long, were the most common house type (Haarnagel 1979).

During the Migration period, from the middle of the 5th to the early 7th century AD, the region seems to have been more or less abandoned by the settlers now called Saxons. When the Frisians recolonised the region in the early Middle Ages, three-aisled longhouses were built once again, as at Oldorf, excavated as part of the Wangerland research project (Schmid 1994). As with all *wurten* of the Roman Iron Age and the early Middle Ages, the lower part of the *wurt* at Oldorf was made up of dung and rotten organic material of various kinds, which preserved the structural timbers extremely well. From the 9th century onwards however, clay was used to additionally heighten the *wurten*. Due to its permeability to air, wood is much less well preserved in these clay layers. In the excavation trench at Oldorf, part of the byre of a three-aisled longhouse with cattle-boxes was found in occupation layer 2 (Fig. 3.2). A remarkable feature is an open drain which took the dung out of the byre. A similar feature was excavated on the west coast of Schleswig-Holstein at Elisenhof, but was built more than 100 years after the example at Oldorf (Bantelmann 1975). The building of the three-aisled longhouse at Oldorf was dated by dendrochronology to 650 AD. This is the first reliable date for the Frisian colonisation of the clay district of Lower Saxony following the Migration period.

Up to 1993 little was known about the development of the three-aisled longhouse in the clay district after the early Middle Ages, mainly because of the poor preservation of wood in clay-*wurten*. Since the modern suc-

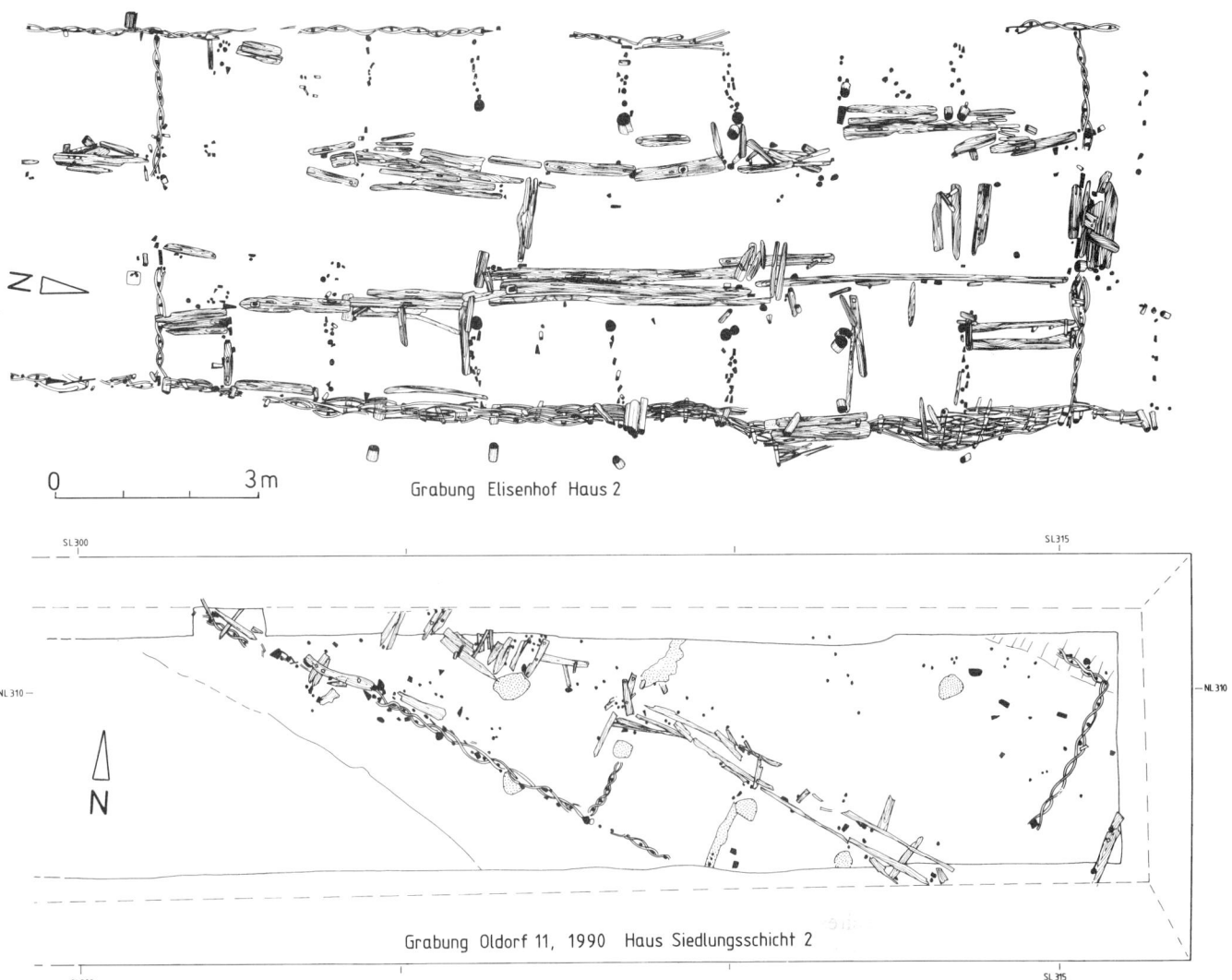

Figure 3.2 Above: Elisenhof, Ldkr. Nordfriesland (Schleswig-Holstein). Byre of a three-aisled longhouse, 8/9th century AD. – Beneath: Oldorf, Ldkr. Friesland (Lower Saxony). Byre of a three-aisled longhouse, c. 650 AD (after Schmid 1994).

cessors of the prehistoric and medieval longhouses cannot be traced back further than the end of the 15th century (Bedal 1993, 110 f.) there remained a dark age of around 500 years. It was known only that on the sandy soils of the pleistocene area, the so-called *geest*, the medieval house developed from a three-aisled longhouse to a single-aisled longhouse and then back again to a three-aisled longhouse as later extensions were added (Zimmermann 1995).

One unexpected achievement of the Wangerland research project was the discovery of a well-preserved house of the high Middle Ages in the clay-*wurt* of Wüppels. Here, a three-aisled longhouse dated by dendrochronology to around 1120 showed some remarkable features (Fig. 3.3). The house, orientated northeast-southwest, was 9 m wide (around 2–3 m greater than the prehistoric longhouses) and more than 21m long. It burned down at least twice but was rebuilt each time. Throughout,

the roof supporting posts continued to be dug in the ground and not placed on a padstone or sill as was done in modern times to prevent the wood rotting. The walls were made of vertical planks covered by clay and the house measured 21m in length by 9m wide, making it around 2-3m wider than prehistoric long houses.

Some elements of the groundplan of the Wüppels house point to types of farmhouse built in the coastal area since early modern times. For instance, a byre with at least five cattle-boxes along the northern wall only was situated in the eastern part of the house. Also, in the first phase the working and living area at the west end was narrower than the byre end. Furthermore, the house had two chambers at the westernmost end – a feature not known from prehistoric and early medieval longhouses, but familiar in farmhouses from early modern times. And last, but by no means least, there is evidence to suggest that grain was stored on a second floor loft of the house. A

Figure 3.3 Wüppels, Ldkr. Friesland (Lower Saxony). Three-aisled longhouse, c. 1120 AD (row of roof supporting posts and row of cattle-boxes on the right).

thick layer of charred grain was found towards the centre of the house, and it seems likely that this fell down when the house was destroyed by fire. The use of the house for storage is one of the most characteristic features of the modern farmhouse, whereas in prehistoric times grain seems usually to have been kept in a separate granary (although there are a few known instances of grain storage within Roman Iron Age longhouses (Zimmermann 1992, 137 f.)). In general, however, storage in a second floor loft is a characteristic of a modern type of farmhouse in our region known as the Low German longhouse. There is no second floor in the other type of modern farmhouse, the huge Frisian *gulfhaus*, where grain is stored on the ground floor (Ellenberg 1990, 120 ff.; Bedal 1993, 105–111).

The three-aisled longhouse of Wüppels is a long-lost link which now throws some light on the development of the prehistoric and medieval longhouse into the modern farmhouses in the clay district of the southern North Sea coast of present day Lower Saxony. And it suggests that the development here has been unbroken from the Pre-Roman Iron Age to modern times – in contrast to the development of farmhouses on the pleistocene sandy soils of the *geest*. The reason for the much larger size of the modern farmhouses in the clay district compared to the prehistoric and medieval three-aisled longhouses lies in economic change: whilst in prehistoric and medieval times stock-rearing predominated over arable cultivation, this changed in early modern times, when large-scale grain cultivation was made possible by the dykes, first built in the 11th century AD, which defended the fertile calcaric soil against the salt seawater.

Acknowledgements

I am grateful to Carenza Lewis for editing the English version of this paper.

References

Bantelmann, A. 1975: Die frühgeschichtliche Marschensiedlung beim Elisenhof in Eiderstedt. Landschaftsgeschichte und Baubefunde. Elisenhof 1. (Bern, Frankfurt/M).

Bedal, K. 1993: Historische Hausforschung. Eine Einführung in Arbeitsweise, Begriffe und Literatur. (Bad Windsheim).

Behre, K.-E., Menke, B., and Streif, H. 1979: The Quarternary Geological Development of the German Part of the North Sea. In: E. Oele et al. (eds): The Quarternary History of the North Sea, 85–113. Acta Universitatis Upsaliensis, Symposia Universitatis Upsaliensis Annum Quingentesimum Celebrantis 2. (Uppsala).

Ellenberg, H. 1990: Bauernhaus und Landschaft in ökologischer und historischer Sicht. (Stuttgart).

Haarnagel, W. 1965: Die Untersuchung einer spätbronze-ältereisenzeitlichen Siedlung in Boomborg/Hatzum, Kreis Leer, in den Jahren 1963 und 1964 und ihr vorläufiges Ergebnis. Neue Ausgrabungen und Forschungen in Niedersachsen 2, 132–164. (Hildesheim)

Haarnagel, W. 1979: Die Grabung Feddersen Wierde. Methode, Hausbau, Siedlung- und Wirtschaftsformen sowie Sozialstruktur. Feddersen Wierde 2. (Wiesbaden).

Haarnagel, W. 1984: Hausbau. In: G. Kossack, K.-E. Behre, P. Schmid (eds): Archäologische und naturwissenschaftliche Untersuchungen an ländlichen und frühstädtischen Siedlungen im deutschen Küstengebiet vom 5. Jahrhundert v. Chr. bis zum 11. Jahrhundert n. Chr. Volume 1: Ländliche Siedlungen, 167–193. (Weinheim).

Louwe Kooijmans, L.P. 1987: Neolithic Settlement and

Subsistence in the Wetlands of the Rhine/Meuse Delta of the Netherlands. In: J.M. Coles, A.J. Lawson (eds): European Wetlands in Prehistory, 227–251. (Oxford).

Schmid, P. 1994: Oldorf – eine frühmittelalterliche friesische Wurtsiedlung. Germania 72, 231–267. (Mainz am Rhein).

Waterbolk, H.T. 1991: Ezinge. In: Reallexikon der Germanischen Altertumskunde 8, 60–76. 2nd Edition. (Berlin, New York).

Zimmermann, W.H. 1992: Die Siedlungen des 1. bis 6. Jahrhunderts nach Christus von Flögeln-Eekhöltjen, Niedersachsen: Die Bauformen und ihre Funktionen. Probleme der Küstenforschung im südlichen Nordseegebiet 19. (Hildesheim).

Zimmermann, W.H. 1995: Haus, Hof und Siedlungsstruktur auf der Geest vom Neolithikum bis in das Mittelalter. In: H.-E. Dannenberg, H.-J. Schulze (eds): Geschichte des Landes zwischen Elbe und Weser. Volume 1: Vor- und Frühgeschichte, 251–288. (Stade).

4. The Archaeology of Coastal Landscapes: The Cleveland Experience

Robin Daniels

This paper outlines recent work which has begun to address the maritime archaeology of the Cleveland area, where the limited availability of resources has concentrated work on the coast, carried out in collaboration with the Royal Commission on the Historical Monuments of England (now English Heritage) and the Nautical Archaeology Society.

Introduction

The starting point for investigation of the coastline of Cleveland was support from the Royal Commission on Historic Monuments of England (RCHME) in commissioning a Maritime Database Project. While work on the peat beds (see below) would have taken place regardless, the existence of this database provides a sound framework from which to build and to argue for further resources.

The continuing enthusiasm for and development of our knowledge of the maritime resource is due in no small part to the enthusiasm of new local members of the Nautical Archaeology Society (NAS). Accordingly, it is desirable that the development of this resource should be a key element in the future management of the maritime archaeology resource.

Maritime Archaeology Database Project

In 1994 a joint project was established between RCHME and Cleveland County Archaeology Section (now Tees Archaeology), with the support of Durham County Council, North Yorkshire County Council and the North Yorks Moors National Park. The aims of this project were two-fold; to research and produce a database of the Maritime Archaeology of the North-East English coast and territorial waters, from Whitby, North Yorkshire to Seaham, County Durham (Fig. 4.1) and secondly to raise awareness of the importance of the Maritime Archaeology of the area (Buglass 1994). This project was led with great success by John Buglass: more than 194 individuals and organisations were contacted to seek information and over 2,243 sites were placed on the database, over 75% of which had not previously been recorded. The entries cover many different types of site (see Fig. 4.2).

While the project has been very successful in creating a database of maritime archaeological sites, it is acknowledged that there is little qualitative information. The entries are drawn largely from reported ship losses and charts and from fishermens' reports of snagged nets. The latter may not be archaeological sites at all. In many cases therefore the identity and date of the site is not known, nor is its degree of archaeological survival. One of the greatest challenges facing maritime archaeology is the verification and field enhancement of this data. This is a huge task that is well beyond the resources of local government – it is in this area that the Nautical Archaeology Society (NAS) and its trained divers can make major contributions.

This has made this awareness raising exercise of crucial importance. Prior to this project there were no NAS trained divers in the Cleveland area and no capacity to carry out 'wet' maritime archaeology. As a result of the high public profile of the Maritime Database Project it became possible to arrange a number of NAS diver training courses and we have subsequently launched a Rapid Response Register in conjunction with the NAS. This provides a list of divers who have at the very least attended NAS Part 1 courses and who are willing to make themselves available at short notice to carry out emergency recording projects. This scheme has already been used very successfully.

Topography

This paper will only deal with that part of the coast which was formerly in the county of Cleveland. This coast has three distinct characters. The southern section from Staithes to Saltburn is characterised by high sandstone cliffs, extensively worked for ironstone, alum and jet, with a few steep and treacherous bays. The section from Saltburn to Seaton Carew is an area of broad, low sand

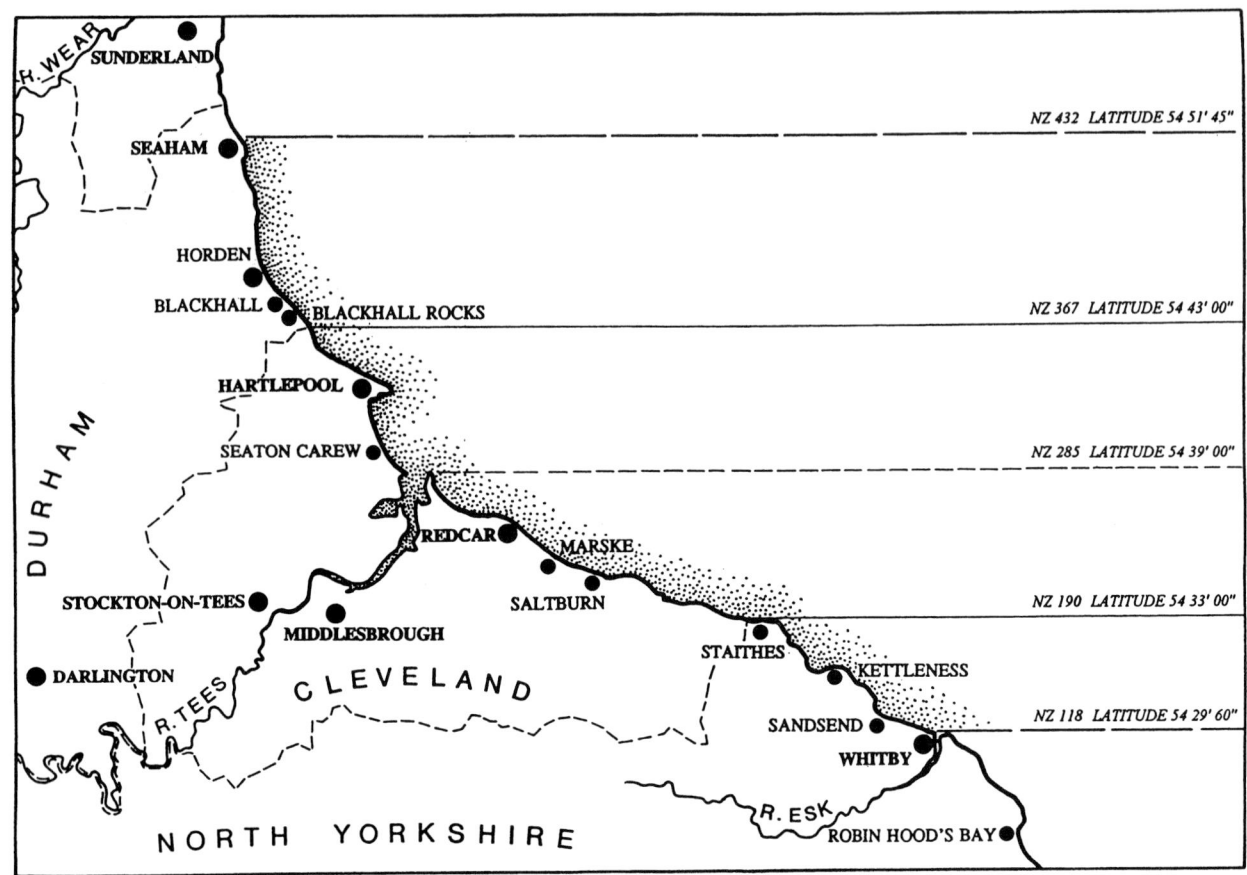

Figure 4.1 Area of Maritime Archaeology Database Project.

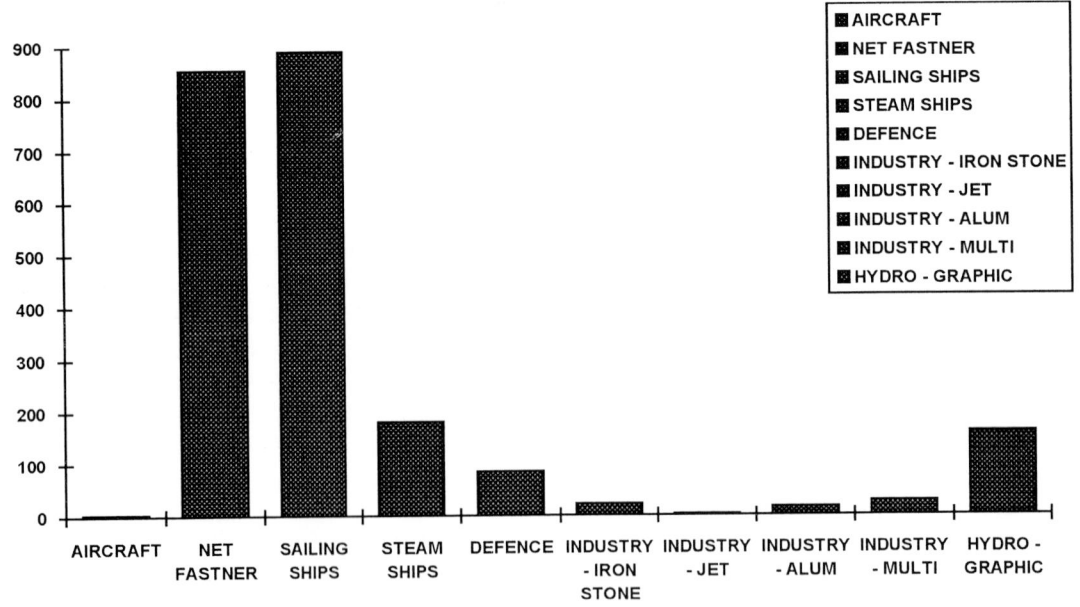

Figure 4.2 Total number of sites by type (in text).

Table 4.1 Documented wrecks in the area between Whitby, North Yorkshire and Seaham, Co. Durham.

YEAR	1200–1299	1300–1399	1400–1499	1500–1599	1600–1699	1700–1749	1750–1799	1800–1849	1850–1899	1900–1945
Wreck Totals	2	2	0	2	1	1	13	291	316	125

dunes with the mouth of the River Tees in its centre. Prior to the 19th century, the Tees was a sluggish meandering river with extensive estuarine saltmarshes. Industrial development has resulted in the straightening of the river, the reclamation of much of the saltmarsh and very recently the construction of a Barrage. From Seaton Carew to Crimdon, the coast begins to feel the effect of the limestone of the Durham Plateau, which has a particular impact in the creation of the peninsula upon which the Anglo-Saxon monastery and medieval town of Hartlepool sits.

Three major types of archaeological sites are present along this coast, these comprise submerged landscapes, wrecks (of all types including ships and aircraft – and probably a few cars in the docks!) and industrial harbours.

Submerged Landscapes

There are outcrops of peat on the coast at Redcar and more extensive deposits between Seaton Carew and Hartlepool. The peat at Seaton Carew has been the most extensively studied and is generally known as Hartlepool Submerged Forest. The area was first studied by C.T. Trechmann in the 1930's (Trechmann 1936) and a range of stray finds have been reported from it ever since, the most significant of which has been a Neolithic skeleton excavated in 1972 (Tooley 1978). In addition to these stray finds, Professor M.Tooley, now of St. Andrews University but formerly at Durham, has carried out extensive analysis of the coastal change data contained in the peats and has worked with Tees Archaeology on two major projects in recent years.

Both projects were part of a major sea defence programme, which involved digging out a large trench along the beach, lining it with geotextile and building a rock armour sea defence on top. In 1990 the first archaeological excavation provided evidence of horizons of human activity from the Mesolithic to the Romano-British period. The results of the limited work in 1990 were built into a project which began in 1995 in conjunction with a second phase of sea defence works. The whole length of the beach was evaluated by Mags Waughman in an effort to define archaeologically significant deposits and to obtain a better picture of the underlying topography (Waughman et al, forthcoming).

There was particular interest in the topography of the beach following the discovery in 1994 of a 3.4m × 1m wattle panel (Plate 4.1), subsequently dated to 4890± (GU-5435 & GU-5436) which was probably part of a fish trap. This proved to be lying in a palaeo-channel where subsequent investigation revealed stakes at the edge of the channel of similar size to those in the wattle panel, which have been radiocarbon dated to the same period. Other finds included a red deer with a wooden point among its ribs.

The full coastal and environmental history of the site is still being analysed but it is particularly interesting to note that while we seem to be dealing with an area of stream channels and wetlands with no clear occupation sites, there is evidence of human activity from all periods dispersed across the whole area.

Wrecks

While both ship and aircraft wrecks are noted on the maritime database, attention has focused on the shipwrecks and we are continuing to enhance the data on these by consulting new sources. There is an inevitable bias in the data towards the better documented losses of the 19th century onwards (see Table 4.1). The inference from these figures must be that there may be large numbers of unrecorded pre-1800 shipwrecks, which we have yet to locate and identify. The archaeological potential of this is huge, as are the resource implications, even if investigation and recording were carried out largely voluntarily.

Tees Archaeology in conjunction with the NAS has carried out a number of recording projects on the remains of vessels which have been discovered on the foreshore. The most notable of these is the substantially intact hull of a late 18th century collier some 80 feet long × 22 feet wide with a nine foot depth of hull surviving (Fig. 4.3 & Plate 4.2). As much of this as possible has been exposed has been recorded through the joint Tees Archaeology / NAS Rapid Response Register, by Gary Green and Peter Pritchard respectively. This type of vessel was the workhorse of the coal trade in north-east England and was successfully adapted by Captain Cook for his voyages of discovery. To the best of our knowledge these are the most substantial surviving remains of this type of vessel, and its study over time should provide valuable information about the vessel and the deposition and erosion

26 *Robin Daniels*

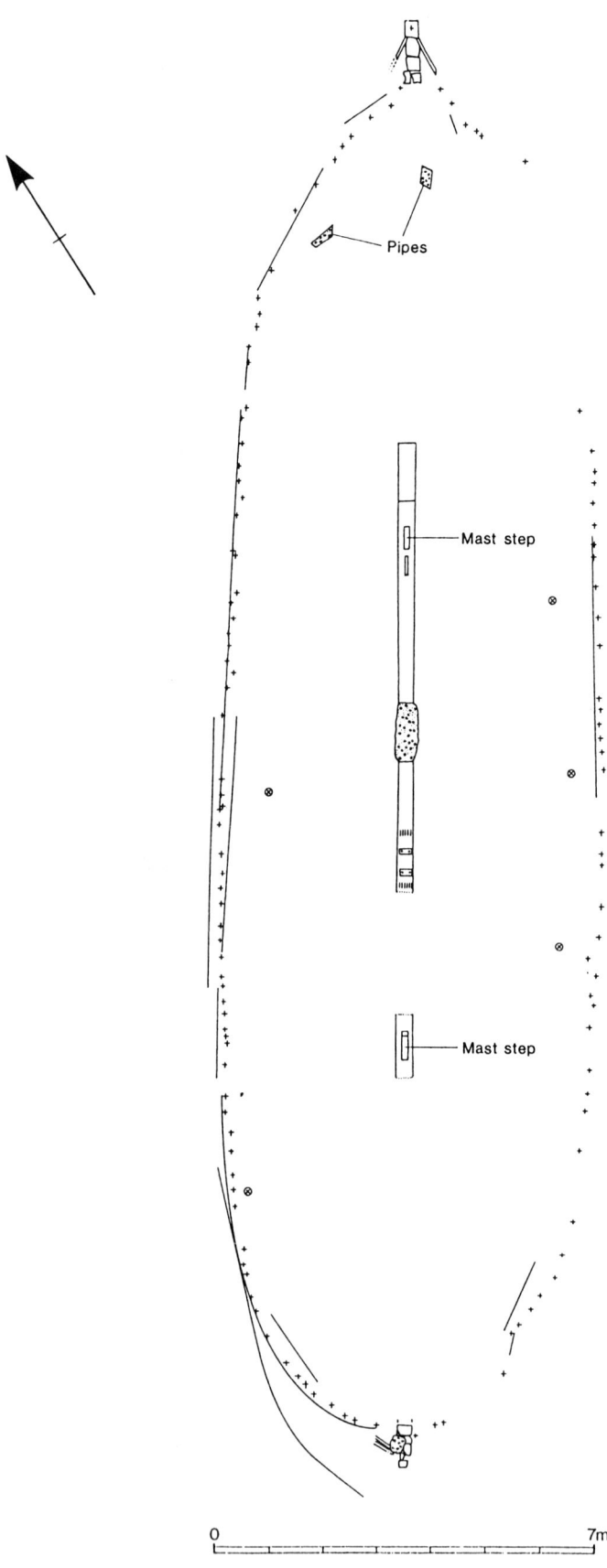

Figure 4.3 Plan of the Seaton Carew collier wreck.

Plate 4.1. Wattle Panel from Hartlepool Submerged Forest.

Plate 4.2 Seaton Carew collier brig wreck.

Plate 4.3 Rock cut harbour at Staithes.

Plate 4.4 Rutways.

regimes present on such a site. The vessel is in the process of being designated an Historic Wreck under the Protection of Wrecks Act 1973.

Work on the collier was preceded by the recording and recovery of an Admiralty whaler of 1944 from Middlesbrough Docks. The latter had been recognised during a site visit to inspect the area prior to substantial alteration and construction work. This wreck generated a huge amount of interest and SLP Engineering, an offshore construction company, enthusiastically provided lifting equipment and expertise to recover the vessel, accompanied by extensive media coverage. This exercise was a dramatic demonstration of the public enthusiasm for shipwrecks far outweighing their archaeological significance; it did however provide excellent experience in the problems and potential of recovering a small vessel and has provided excellent contacts with SLP Engineering which may be useful in the future. The vessel and the partial remains of another are now sited at the Tees Archaeology Service offices and it is intended to build up a maritime archaeology resource in Hartlepool in conjunction with the Museum Service and the NAS. This will provide both an information base and a teaching resource to continue the development of maritime archaeology in the area.

Industrial Harbours

The recognition of industrial foreshore harbours as a severely threatened site type was perhaps the greatest achievement of the database project.

The coastline from Saltburn to Scarborough comprises high sandstone cliffs containing important deposits of alum and ironstone. These were worked from the 17th century onwards and prior to the development of the railway system the only means of transport was by sea. There were, however, no easily accessible harbours in the vicinity of these workings and consequently facilities were constructed on the foreshore. In order to gain access to this foreshore the alum industry, which used a quarrying approach to mineral extraction, constructed steep roadways. In contrast, the ironstone mining industry tended to cut drifts from the foreshore to link up with shafts sunk below the mineral deposits to get the ore out and supplies in. Docks were then cut out of the rocky foreshore and stone and timber quays built (Plate 4.3). In order to get materials to and from the vessels, rut-ways were cut, along which the wagons could run (Plate 4.4) (Owen 1994). Virtually all materials had to come in and out by sea and this must at times have been an extremely dangerous operation.

At least sixteen of these harbour complexes are known but none have been recorded, as the foreshore lay beyond the remit of the Ordnance Survey and the scale of operations never justified proper plan making. Since the abandonment of these facilities, which occurred by the end of the 19th century, they have been heavily damaged by the sea and the need to record them before they are totally obliterated is a pressing one.

While we have little information about the harbour facilities, we have less about the vessels which were used in these operations. There are undoubtedly the wrecked remains of some of these vessels lying just off the harbours and a survey of these facilities and their immediate offshore area is seen as a priority if funding can be obtained.

Conclusion

The establishment of the Cleveland Maritime Archaeology Database has generated a huge amount of interest in and enthusiasm for the maritime archaeology of the area. The harnessing of local NAS trained volunteers alongside Tees Archaeology Service staff has allowed real progress to be made in understanding and recording the potential of the maritime archaeology of the area. It is however, difficult to see how substantial progress can be made in the task of identifying and verifying deep sea sites without access to more resources. But there is certainly a need to begin to define the research priorities of maritime archaeology, given its huge potential and enormous cost.

One of the underlying aims of the project was to put dots on the map of designated wreck sites in order to begin to fill the huge gap in the distribution of such sites along the north east coast. The first dot is now on that map and will hopefully continue to be followed by many others.

References

Buglass, J. 1994: *Lost at Sea, Maritime Archaeology of the North East of England*, (unpub. Tees Archaeology).

Owen, J.S. 1986: Rutways before Railways on the Yorkshire Coast, with details of twelve sites between Saltburn and Scarborough. *Cleveland Industrial Archaeologist* 18, 23–32.

Tooley, M.J. 1978: The History of Hartlepool Bay, *International Journal of Nautical Archaeology* 7.1, 71–74.

Trechmannn, C.T. 1936: Mesolithic Flints from the Submerged Forest at West Hartlepool, *Proceedings of the Prehistoric Society 1936*, 161–168.

Waughman, M. *et al* forthcoming *Hartlepool Submerged Forest*.

5. Maritime Fife: An Integrated Study of the Maritime Archaeological and Historical Resource of Fife

Ian Oxley

Maritime Fife is an inter-disciplinary research project (supported by national heritage organisations and the local authority) which aims to survey, record and protect the maritime archaeological resource preserved in the coastal, foreshore and seabed zones of Fife. The origin of the project lies in the realisation that the full potential of the maritime heritage, which is particularly rich in Fife, has not been fully appreciated to date. This situation is unfortunate in a coastal zone that is subject to harbour, waterfront and coastal engineering works and other possible impacts. Evidence of coastal activities of the recent past are rapidly disappearing through development and we are currently witnessing a sharp decline in the inshore and river fishing industries.

Introduction

Based in the University of St Andrews, Maritime Fife is supported by Fife Council, Historic Scotland, the Royal Commission for the Ancient and Historical Monuments of Scotland (RCAHMS) and Fife Enterprise. The project includes the establishment of an inventory of maritime archaeological sites compatible with Fife region Sites and Monuments Record and the National Monuments Record of Scotland – Maritime (NMRS). Field survey and historical research is carried out to complement the desk-based information gathering stages and evaluations of the deposition environment of the sites (whether terrestrial or marine) to further the study of site stabilisation and management.

Above all, Maritime Fife aims to promote an approach to the maritime heritage which is not restricted by any artificial boundaries whether environmental, such as the Low Water Mark, or historically-derived local authority limits of responsibility.

Fife, a local authority region of Scotland, is a peninsular situated between two major estuaries (the Firths of Forth and Tay) which mean that maritime influences have spread far inland. The coastline varies from dynamic dune systems to eroding sea cliffs; from heavily industrialised seaports and defence establishments to local nature reserves (Fig. 5.1).

Maritime Fife's nominal area of interest is bounded in the south by a line midway across the Firth of Forth, a further line midway across the Firth of Tay in the north, and extending to the territorial limit 12 nautical miles offshore (Fig. 5.2).

Maritime history and museum resources

Fife has a rich maritime history and the aim of the Maritime Fife project is to assess, exploit and enhance the existing maritime historical resources of Fife. The latter may be found in academic institutions, local archives or in the memories of local people whose experiences involved the sea in any form. Documentary sources include Admiralty Court Records, Burgh Records, private muniments and early cartographic records. There is also great value to be found in maritime-related collections in national and local museums (Gale 1992). Clearly, information regarding the maritime history of the region is of great importance in underpinning the usefulness of the Maritime Fife sites and monuments database as a research, amenity and planning tool (see below).

Coastal and maritime archaeology

The sea around Fife has not only shaped Fife in a physical sense but it has also shaped the cultural and economic development of the region. Evidence for the maritime history and archaeology of Fife can be traced from prehistory through the physical remains left by mankind's close involvement with the sea. The evidence ranges from:

1. Shipwrecks, including warships, fishing vessels and merchant ships, from the steam and sailing eras;
2. Submerged landscape sites offshore;
3. Mesolithic hunter-gatherer sites now inland (Coles 1971);
4. Fish traps, jetties, slipways and breakwaters and coastal

30   Ian Oxley

Figure 5.1 World War II coastal defences at Tentsmuir showing the dynamic nature of the coast edge. Sand remaining on top of the concrete blocks and the dune edge in the background illustrate significant changes in the recent past. (Maritime Fife and Historic Scotland).

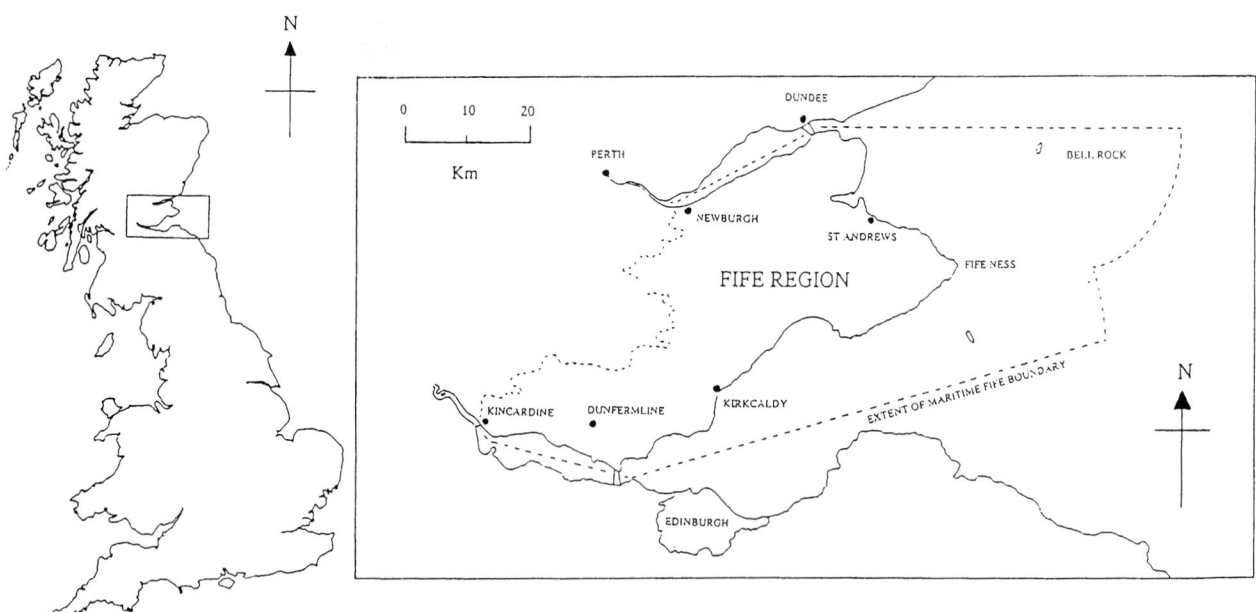

Figure 5.2 Location map showing the approximate extent of Maritime Fife's subject area out to Scotland's Territorial Limit.

middens in the inter-tidal zone and on the coast edge;
5. Historic towns and harbours of the 16th and 17th centuries up to early modern times (Graham 1968);
6. Coastal industrial installations e.g. ship- and boat-building, linoleum manufacture, coal mining, saltworks and tide mills.

There is a great potential for discovering further archaeological evidence from coastal and maritime contexts and this will greatly enhance what is already known about Fife (Fife Regional Council 1989). An area of great interest is likely to be the submerged zones formed by post-glacial flooding of the North Sea which covered large tracts of the prehistoric landscape, and along with it possible evidence of Mesolithic, Neolithic and even Early Bronze Age activity.

Integrated approach

The underlying philosophical approach to Maritime Fife is that it is essential to consider the relationships of all types of evidence of the past in a seamless way. Boundaries or distinctions, such as inland, coastal, foreshore, inter-tidal, and marine, are all artificial devices that do not necessarily have any relevance to the extent of archaeological or historical sources of information. In addition, the existing limits to the responsibilities of national, regional and local authorities (e.g. the Low Water Mark) are of historic legislative origin and have little to do with actual limits of the archaeological resource.

The diversity and interrelation of archaeological evidence must be recognised as existing as a whole, and any strategy of approach must be applied to the land and seabed in its entirety. For example, anchorages and frequently-travelled sea lanes which can provide a valuable insight into the development of sea traffic and trade over time may be marked simply by a spread of debris on the seabed corresponding to a scatter of artefacts on land indicating past occupation in some form. All evidence of the archaeological environment – terrestrial and marine; from whatever period and irrespective of present day administrative boundaries – must be considered in an integrated way before they are considered as independent components (see Martin, this volume).

Involvement of local people

From the outset Maritime Fife has tried to include the interests of local people and visitors to Fife, not just as users of products or information generated by the project but as participants in the data gathering. The latter activity may be in the form of organised events occurring on an intermittent basis (e.g. shorewalks and day schools) or the systematic monitoring of stretches of the coast edge to identify erosion or unexpected archaeological discoveries (e.g. Maritime Fife Watch see below). Local people are also the subject of research through oral testimony.

Maritime Fife talks are delivered to a variety of organisations in Fife such as diving clubs, local historical and archaeological societies, charitable organisations and church groups. Finally, a leaflet with an application form for the recipient to register their interest in particular aspects of Maritime Fife's work (e.g. local boat-building or fishing) was widely distributed and the response was very satisfactory.

It is believed that generally maritime and coastal archaeology has a very poor record in terms of public relations and the ability to raise local awareness. Local people are an important resource often with considerable reserves of enthusiasm, local knowledge, time and commitment. Including them in any project, together with visitors to the area, can prove very rewarding and it is clearly an objective attractive to any local authority offering sponsorship.

Local museum displays

Museum display boards have been produced describing the Maritime Fife project and its aims. The two boards in each set are designed to accompany additional displays that concentrate on a particular aspect of local maritime interest. Three sets of the Maritime Fife boards were produced; one each for the three area museum services of Fife (West, Central and North). The concept of a flexible display system has represented a significant step in raising awareness about the project – the North Fife set of display boards alone were displayed at five local events and exhibitions during a twelve-month period.

Maritime Fife also co-operated with the North Fife museum service in developing the "Maritime Newburgh" exhibition held at the Laing Museum in Newburgh. The exhibition about the maritime history of the locality has generated a great deal of local interest. In particular, the display concentrates on the salmon fishing industry on the River Tay, an industry that has a history over many centuries but which is presently in decline due mainly to economic factors.

Recreational diving clubs

Maritime archaeological projects can enhance the enjoyment of the sport of recreational diving, increase involvement in (and raise awareness of) the maritime heritage, and at the same time recover valuable information about the archaeological heritage. Maritime Fife is working towards achieving these benefits in the following ways. Firstly, encouragement is given to promoting the integration between recreational diver training initiatives and heritage education opportunities (e.g. postgraduate opportunities in the University of St Andrews and the amateur-based, Nautical Archaeology Society Training Programme).

Maritime Fife has a programme of presentations to local diving clubs together with displays and lectures at national diving conferences. The project has also played a significant part in the development of an artificial, marine archaeological training site in a former sea-bathing pool at Cellardyke. Iron guns have been re-located in the pool (which forms a relatively sheltered environment for diver training) and laid out to form a mock wreck site.

Lastly, students and amateur archaeological divers also have the opportunity to participate in fieldwork including pre-disturbance surveys of local wreck sites and site management experiments such as monitoring, stabilisation and *in situ* conservation treatments.

Development of the project

The history of Maritime Fife is closely linked to the archaeological section of Fife Council Planning Service and the project would not have been possible without the support and encouragement of Fife's Archaeological Officer, Peter Yeoman. Coinciding with the re-organisation of local government in Scotland, where Fife's three District Councils (Dunfermline, Kirkcaldy and North-East Fife) were transformed into Areas, a three year plan was proposed in the summer of 1995 (Oxley 1995), with the following broad objectives:

1. to assess the current state of knowledge of coast edge, inter-tidal and submerged archaeological sites in Fife,
2. to establish and maintain an inventory of archaeological sites, supported by databases of bibliographic sources and additional historical information,
3. to enhance local education, heritage interpretation and tourism through museum displays, publications and public events,
4. to develop strategies for the future management of the maritime cultural resource of Fife Region.

Fife Council agreed to allocate £65,000 to fund Maritime Fife for three years and the project has progressed through the following phases to date:

Phase 1. September 1995 – March 1996

During this initial, six month, period Maritime Fife employed an archaeologist and a maritime historian, part-time, to generate data on maritime sites situated in Fife's coast edge, inter-tidal and submerged zones for the database, and to review the state of the maritime historical sources. Evidence of over 150 wreck sites (of mainly late 19th and 20th century date) was obtained from readily-accessible records such as recreational diver guides, the Hydrographic Office of the Ministry of Defence and RCAHMS. This initial phase produced draft reports for each of the District Councils, based on several hundred new records incorporated into the database, showing the range and numbers of archaeological sites located on their coast edge, inter-tidal zone and seabed.

Phase 2. April 1996 – March 1997

Phase 2 of Maritime Fife involved a number of different initiatives: semi-popular reports (intended for wide dissemination) on the *Shipwreck Heritage of Fife* and *Famous Mariners of Fife*, Historic Scotland sponsored Coastal Surveys, and pre-disturbance surveys of four foreshore sites identified during those surveys.

Historic Scotland Coastal Surveys

During 1996 Historic Scotland grant-aided Maritime Fife to carry out two Coastal Assessment Surveys covering the entire Fife coast according to published procedures (Historic Scotland 1996). Both surveys have been designed to provide information on the location and nature of archaeological sites situated on the coast edge together with an assessment of the risk of coastal erosion. The latter is a subject of particular concern in Scotland as a whole (Ashmore 1994, Barclay & Fojut 1994) and in certain areas of Fife in particular (Milner 1996).

The two Fife surveys were carried out by teams of field-walkers comprising archaeologists, geologists and recorder/photographers, timed to coincide with Low Water windows. All records were plotted on Ordnance Survey 1:25,000 Pathfinder maps, with field positions derived from a hand-held GPS unit to an estimated accuracy of between 30–100 metres depending on signal strength. The survey team achieved almost complete coverage of the foreshore, coast edge and hinterland (up to 100 metres from the coast edge). However, recording of the coast edge adjacent to defence establishments such as RAF Leuchars, Crombie and Rosyth naval bases was limited due to M.O.D. restrictions.

Survey results were arranged as maps and gazetteers relating to the condition of archaeological sites and the risk of erosion. Recommendations were made for each site (survey, monitor) and statistics were produced giving an estimate of the number of sites affected by erosion. General results of the two surveys are as follows:

Kincardine to Fife Ness

The first survey (Robertson 1996) was carried out over a period of twelve days in January 1996 from Kincardine in the west to Fife Ness in the east, a survey section of approximately 107 km in length. The survey identified 724 sites, 179 of which were not listed on the NMRS with the majority of these located on the foreshore. This assessment concluded that further archaeological survey and monitoring is required on a number of sites such as the small harbours of Fife, Kincardine foreshore, the stretch of coastline between East Wemyss and Buckhaven, the nineteenth century Wemyss Gas Works and various coastal middens.

Figure 5.3 New archaeological sites in the making. The foreshore at Newburgh in the Firth of Tay with small boats abandoned in the inter-tidal area (Maritime Fife and Historic Scotland).

Fife Ness to Newburgh

The second survey (Robertson 1997), undertaken over a period of 11 days in October 1996, covered the coastline (approximately 70 km in length) from Fife Ness to the Fife boundary west of Newburgh, encompasses the major estuary of the River Tay and the smaller estuary of the River Eden. The survey identified 317 monuments within the target area, including 205 sites located on the coast edge or foreshore and therefore at some risk of coastal erosion. Of particular regional interest are the series of salmon bothies (lodges) and other structures associated with the Tay Salmon Fisheries Industry. At least nineteen structures were seen during the survey, of which very few have been recorded by RCAHMS. Little is known about the nature of the salmon bothies before the mid-19th Century, but it is likely that, in early times, the only means of shelter were 'excavations' by the side of the river. Other industrial monuments related to the salmon industry include ice houses, landing slips and a boat-building complex at Newburgh. The ongoing decline of the river salmon fishing industry on the Tay makes it all the more urgent to record what remains (Fig. 5.3).

Historic Buildings of the coast

As part of the coastal surveys a study was made of the listed buildings situated within 100 metres of the coast edge of Fife. A report was produced (Fairfax 1996) detailing basic information about the buildings and their RCAHMS, Historic Scotland and local authority planning office designations. The results of the review illustrated the complexities of building recording where records are kept by a number of different organisations to different levels of detail and completeness.

Finally, Maritime Fife is compiling a report that integrates the results of the two coastal surveys. The report will: summarise the legislative and administrative background to the coastal archaeology of Fife; describe the coastal geology and geomorphology; review the archaeological heritage; include the site descriptions from the two coastal surveys.

Foreshore surveys

A series of pre-disturbance surveys have been carried out of foreshore sites identified in the Historic Scotland surveys as being either of special interest archaeologically or at particular risk due to coastal erosion including:

1. An area of foreshore at Kincardine, less than 750 metres in length, containing a complex of abandoned hulks, timber piles, stone banks and structures which may represent fish-traps (Fig. 5.4);
2. At Crombie there is a complex of the remains of stone-built structures on the foreshore possibly relating to boat building or cargo handling;
3. An early nineteenth gasworks at Weymss suffering active erosion by the sea;
4. A collection of wharf structures and a substantial inter-tidal wreck situated on the eastern side of the Tay Rail Bridge thought to have been involved in the repair of the Tay Railway Bridge after its tragic collapse in 1879 (Fig. 5.5).

Figure 5.4 A Nautical Archaeology Society Part II survey practical in progress on the foreshore at Kincardine. The wreck structure (one of thirteen) is part of a complex of inter-tidal archaeological features which include former jetties and fish-traps (Maritime Fife).

Figure 5.5 A substantial wreck (Newport, Firth of Tay) of a vessel believed to have been involved in the reconstruction of the Tay Railway bridge (seen in the background) after its disastrous collapse in 1879 (Maritime Fife and Historic Scotland).

Mariners of Fife

To raise awareness about Fife's rich maritime history a report was compiled in which each area is represented by a mariner who has made a significant contribution to maritime history. The selected individuals, representing a progression from the last days of the Scots Navy to the downfall of Napoleon, are as follows:

1. John Boswell (c. 1649–1707), a resident of Kirkcaldy whose activities range from merchant skipper to privateer and include service in the Scots Navy. Boswell's frigate Providence of Kirkcaldy was hired to protect the trade in the Firth of Forth from French privateers and later he was given command of the *Royal Mary*, one of the last warships of the Scots Navy. Boswell was part of the naval force involved in the siege of the Bass Rock from 1691–1694, being responsible for its final surrender.
2. Samuel Greig (1735–1788) of Inverkeithing. After a brief period in the merchant service Greig joined the Royal Navy, then entered the Russian Naval service (in which he rose to the rank of Grand Admiral) and he is considered by the Russians to be one of the founders of their navy. Whilst in the Royal Navy Greig saw service in two of the major engagements of the Seven Years War, Quiberon Bay and the capture of Havana.
3. Frederick L. Maitland (1777–1839) of Lindores. Apart from a successful naval career Maitland earned his place in history as the man who took Napoleon's surrender. He went to sea first on the Royal yacht *Princess Augusta* and from there progressed to being a successful frigate Captain who was able to buy the estate of Lindores with his prize money and build the house which still overlooks the Lindores Loch.

The Shipwreck Heritage of Fife

This report comprises a description of the shipwreck heritage of Fife following an introductory section on shipwreck archaeology and wreck site formation. The range of wreck sites situated in the inter-tidal and submerged zones of Fife are summarised concentrating on the reasons for the casualties and the nature of past maritime activity. The report then moves on to a section of case studies describing six local shipwreck sites or areas. The selected sites include boat wrecks as well as shipwrecks and inter-tidal hulks as well as completely submerged vessels as follows:

1. The remains of at least three different types of vessel on the foreshore at Kincardine.
2. The wreck of the First World War aircraft carrier HMS *Campania* off Burntisland, a vessel which was originally a record-breaking Cunard liner built in 1893.
3. An overview of the many wrecks found at Fife Ness, from 1800 to the present day.
4. The wreck of the First World War torpedo boat destroyer HMS *Success* which was wrecked near Kingsbarns Harbour in December 1914.
5. The remains of an inter-tidal hulk in St Andrews harbour.
6. The wreck of a large vessel on the foreshore at Newport (referred to above).

Each section contains a brief history of the vessels, descriptions of the how the sites were formed along with relevant photographs and diagrams. A final section considers future management strategies for the sites concentrating on ways in which access and the involvement of the general public can be enhanced. This initiative has been modelled on successful overseas examples (Kenderdine 1996, Department of Urban Affairs and Planning 1995) which counter the often negative influence of conventional recreational diver wreck guides by promoting the shipwreck heritage to a much wider audience than the diving community.

Phase 3. April 1997 – March 1998

The final phase of Fife Council funding concentrates on identifying further archaeological sites or important areas at risk; maintaining and enhancing the database; setting up a network to provide monitoring data along the coast edge and on submerged sites; encouraging public involvement; and developing the Maritime Fife information centre.

Maritime Fife Watch

All of these above objectives are part of a new initiative, which in the tradition of Maritime Fife aims to be as broadly-based as possible, building on voluntary projects which have usually been conservation or natural environment based. Maritime Fife Watch involves the establishment of a network of interested individuals (non-diving and diving) who are willing to provide regular information about coastal, inter-tidal or submerged archaeological sites. Areas of interest include recording the location and condition of new archaeological sites or features together with evidence of coastal erosion or other impacts. Maritime Fife is responsible for recording forms and regular meetings. In addition, special events such as guided shorewalks will be organised throughout Fife in order to involve schools, museums, local historical or archaeological societies, the Fife Young Archaeologists Club, as well as the general public.

Maritime Fife Information Centre and the database

The Maritime Fife project is progressing with the development of an effective information gathering, storage and dissemination system. Clearly this is an initiative that can draw on a wide range of source materials relating to Maritime Fife's areas of interest such as local industries including fishing, boat-building and salt manufacture (as per Groom 1995). An important adjunct to any database is a system for filing additional information and documentation relating to database entries and other themes.

Maritime Sites and Monuments Database

The Maritime Fife database, which currently holds 1869 records (152 are shipwrecks) runs on an IBM compatible PC using Microsoft Windows 95 as the operating system. The PC has 16Mb of RAM, an internal CD-ROM and a 1.6Mb hard disk. The database was developed in Microsoft Access and Visual Basic, and was designed to accomodate a rapidly increasing size as historical background research is added. 35mm slides, black and white photographs and other two dimensional images have also been digitised using flatbed and slide scanners. Maritime Fife has experimented with incorporating digital images using an Apple QuickTake camera and software.

The basis of the Maritime Fife database is the terrestrial sites and monuments record developed by Mike Rains for Fife Regional Council. The system consists of tables containing data that is *Site Specific* plus *Bibliographic* and *Archive* references. The standard information recorded for land sites has been enhanced with fields to hold information about the marine and intertidal environments, together with impacts such as dumping grounds, fishing areas and shipping channels. For shipwreck sites, there is the added capability to store information about the vessel itself and its last voyage.

As the convention for locating sites at sea is the use of Latitude/Longitude co-ordinates, the software contains a click button routine to convert Latitude and Longitude to Ordnance Survey grid references, and vice versa. The system will also generate the 1:10,000 OS map sheet (e.g. NO40SW) automatically and contains fields to record the nautical charts that cover the area of the site.

A long-term objective of Maritime Fife is to maintain the database and Information Centre as a permanent research, educational and planning resource.

The way forward

Maritime Fife clearly has a lot of work to do. There is a requirement for a means to predict the existence and distribution of coastal and submerged sites throughout the territory of Fife Region and particularly offshore. There is also a need for an accepted evaluation system (including suitable criteria) for determining the significance of all types of coastal and marine archaeological sites. Thirdly, there is a requirement for making a determination of potential and/or risk as far in advance of any proposed development as possible, and a need for the implementation of a programme of fieldwork to test the validity of these determinations through surveys and site assessments.

Throughout the short history of the project what has become increasingly obvious is not only the growing number of widely varying factors which contribute to the existence of archaeological sites in the coastal and marine zones of Fife, but the complexity of the inter-relationships between those factors. It is likely that the querying and layering powers of GIS are going to be the most advantageous for managing the varied and extensive data-sets which are involved, as all the data can be geographically referenced. To this end Maritime Fife is co-operating with RCAHMS and other local organisations (e.g. the Forth Estuary Forum) in assessing the feasibility of the computer mapping of maritime databases and the possibilities of developing a maritime archaeological GIS.

Further advances can be made in raising awareness and altering behaviour relating to the treatment of accidental or unexpected finds in the coast edge, intertidal and marine zones. Initiatives which have been successful elsewhere in Scotland, such as the Highland Region leaflet explaining what to do with marine finds (HRC 1994) will be explored, as will the promotion of better communication between the curatorial archaeological community and marine industries developing such initiatives as the Code of Practice for Seabed Developers (JNAPC 1995).

Conclusions

In common with terrestrial environments there will be very little of the seabed or coastal zone which has not been affected by the activities of mankind, particularly in a region as closely linked to the sea as Fife. Therefore there will be numerous ways in which evidence of the past can be gained from the study of coastal and marine environments.

Before the establishment of Maritime Fife through the foresight of Fife Council, the archaeological resource of the study area remained largely unquantified and unexplored. Evidence of the extent, condition or significance of completely submerged marine sites was particularly lacking.

Decision-making which is effective can only be achieved if accurate information is available in a consistent way. This information is required to inform and improve development control procedures for coastal and inshore planning. It is hoped that the successful partnership between Maritime Fife, Fife Council and Scotland's national heritage organisations will result in an effective programme for the protection and management of the region's maritime cultural resources. In addition, the Maritime Fife model has demonstrated that at the same time public involvement and academic research opportunities can also be generated and encouraged.

Acknowledgements

The Maritime Fife project would not have been possible without the foresight and support of Fife Council and in particular the commitment of Peter Yeoman and Sarah Govan. Grateful thanks are also due to Geoff Moy, Mike King, Dallas Mechin and Douglas Cooper. Assistance and encouragement has come from Scotland's heritage organisations and the participation of Patrick Ashmore (Historic Scotland), Diana Murray and David Easton (RCAHMS) is gratefully acknowledged. Many people have given of their time and energy to work on the various phases of the project but a special acknowledgement must be made to past and present Maritime Fife staff including Annabel Wood, Michael Dun, Phil Robertson, Deanna Groom and Neil Dobson.

References

Ashmore, P.J. 1994: *Archaeology and the Coastal Erosion Zone: Towards a Historic Scotland Policy.* (Historic Scotland, Edinburgh).

Barclay, G.J. and Noel Fojut, 1994: *The Management and Conservation of the Built and Maritime Heritage in the Coastal Zone.* (Historic Scotland. Unpublished report).

Coles, J.M. 1971: The Early Settlement of Scotland: Excavations at Morton, Fife. *Proc. Pre. Soc.*, Vol. XXXVII Part II.

Department of Urban Affairs and Planning, 1995: *Shipwreck Atlas of New South Wales.* (Department of Urban Affairs and Planning, Sydney, NSW).

Fairfax, D. 1996: *A compilation of the listed Historic Buildings in the coastal zone of Fife.* (Maritime Fife & Fife Council. Unpublished report).

Fife Regional Council 1989: *Fife's Early Archaeological Heritage – A Guide.* (Fife Regional Council, Glenrothes).

Gale, A. 1992: *Catching the Tide: The Status and Future of Maritime Collections in North East Museums.* (North of England Museum Service, Newcastle).

Graham, A. 1968: Archaeological notes on some Harbours in Eastern Scotland. *Proc. Soc. Antiq. Scot.*, 101: 200–285.

Groom, D. 1995: *Sources and Methodologies for establishing a Maritime Sites and Monuments Record for the Highland Regional Council Archaeology Section.* (Unpublished M.Litt. thesis, Scottish Institute of Maritime Studies, University of St. Andrews).

Historic Scotland 1996: *Coastal Zone Survey.* Archaeology Procedure Paper 4. (Historic Scotland, Edinburgh).

HRC, 1994: *Maritime & Underwater Archaeology in the Highland Region: Archaeological sites and finds – what to do if you find something.* (Highland Regional Council Archaeology Section, Inverness). (leaflet).

INPC, 1995: *Code of Practice for Seabed Developers.* (Joint Nautical Archaeology Committee, National Maritime Museum, London).

Kenerdine, S. 1995: *Shipwrecks 1656–1942: A Guide to historic wreck sites of Perth.* (Western Australian Maritime Museum, Perth).

Milner, A.C. 1996: *Coastal Archaeological Resource Management.* (Heriot-Watt University. Unpublished M.Sc. thesis).

Oxley, I, 1995: *MARITIME FIFE: An Integrated Study and Interpretation of the Maritime Archaeological and Historical Resource of Fife.* (Scottish Institute of Maritime Studies, University of St Andrews, St Andrews, Fife Unpublished report).

Robertson, P. 1996: *Coastal Assessment Survey for Historic Scotland: Kincardine to Fife Ness.* (Maritime Fife, University of St Andrews. Unpublished report).

Robertson, P. 1997: *Coastal Assessment Survey for Historic Scotland: Fife Ness to Newburgh.* (Maritime Fife, University of St Andrews. Unpublished report).

6. A Maritime Landscape in East Fife

Colin J. M. Martin

This paper considers the archaeological potential in maritime terms of the coastal landscape between St Monans and Fife Ness at the south-eastern end of the Fife peninsula in Scotland. Representative sites characteristic of such a landscape are sampled.

Pittenweem harbour is shown to derive from a geological fault which encouraged early settlement of the area, which was subsequently developed by phases of rock cutting and the addition of built features. Archaeological excavation at the interface between the shore and the harbour has yielded structural evidence of a phase of development which took place c1630–40, just before the town's prosperity was halted by the effects of the Civil War. Associated with these features was a closed deposit of pottery, clay pipes and other material which included a wide range of Continental imports dating from c1550 to a period close to that of deposition. The deposit undoubtedly reflects the exent of the burgh's trading contacts from the mid sixteenth century to the earlier part of the seventeenth, and perhaps derives from a collection built up by a single household over that period.

The development of navigation aids is represented by the surviving lower storey of Scotland's oldest lighthouse, erected in 1636 on the Isle of May. An unusual monument to a later lighthouse is provided by the remains of a builders' yard on Fife Ness, associated with efforts to erect a light on the Carr Reef in 1807–11. These comprise a rock-cut jig for pre-assembling the interlocking masonry courses, settings for a tramway, a quay and a crane-base.

Close to Fife Ness lie the remains of a tide-mill, with a masonry dam and rock-cut mill race with seatings for a wheel and other structures. Its origins are unknown, though it was still in use during the late eighteenth century. Between Pittenweem and St Monans, rescue excavation close to a rapidly eroding foreshore has revealed the extensive remains of a salt-pan complex established during the 1770s and active until 1814. Cartographic analysis and cropmark photography has recovered in some detail the wider industrial landscape of coal mines and waggonways of which the salt manufactury was a part, and shown how these various elements were linked with the outlet port at Pittenweem.

Introduction

A landscape is composed of numerous interacting elements, none of which should be studied in isolation. Nor can the landscape itself be understood without reference to its neighbours, by whatever criteria the entities involved are defined – physical, climatic, cultural, or political. Particularly dynamic forms of interaction are likely to be encountered along the boundaries of distinctively different landscapes, where mechanisms of cause, effect, and interdependence may often be observed with unusual clarity. An extreme example of such a boundary is the coastline, which separates the sea and its shifting perils from its essentially static terrestrial hinterland.

This paper stems from an unstructured study, extending over a quarter of a century, of some 15 km of varied coastline in East Fife (Fig. 6.1). Its driving force was the author's sustained physical presence in the locality – living for fifteen years a stone's throw from the quayside of a busy East Neuk fishing harbour, with a back garden containing stratified deposits going back to c. 1300. Recreational walks along the foreshore – that no-man's-land eschewed (at least until recently) by both terrestrial and underwater archaeologists – revealed unexplained rock cuttings which resolved themselves, after much time and investigation, into features relating to a salt-making enterprise, a lighthouse construction-yard, and a tide-mill. As the enquiry gained impetus a programme of aerial survey and documentary search identified a vanished eighteenth-century industrial landscape and traced the line of the horse-drawn waggon way which carried its products to a nearby harbour. The substance of these investigations is presented here in summary form, not as definitive or comprehensive statements but as an indication of the

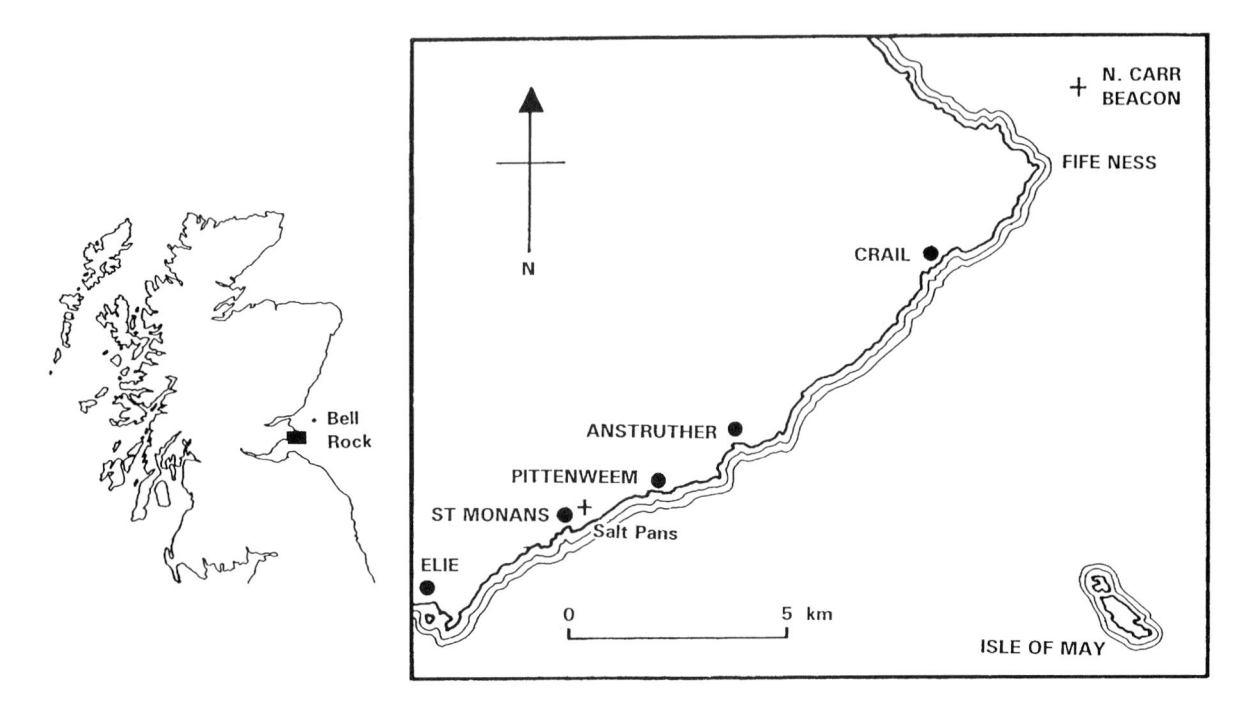

Figure 6.1 Location map, indicating sites mentioned in the text.

Figure 6.2 Pittenweem Harbour from the air, photographed in 1987. Note the ribbon of harbour-front housing which cuts into the foot of the steep slope running down from the burgh centre. The site of the excavation behind 5 Mid Shore and 2 School Wynd is arrowed.

Pittenweem Harbour

Pittenweem (Fig. 6.2) is a small harbour town 11 km SW of the Fife peninsula's eastern extremity. Its name is of Pictish origin. The choice of this location for settlement was conditioned by a narrow fan-shaped creek, with a beach at its head, which has subsequently been enhanced and protected by a succession of built works to create a small but secure harbour on a coastline not otherwise well endowed with natural shelter. It is on record as a seaport in 1228, and was created a Royal Burgh in 1541. A confirmation charter was issued in 1633 (Graham 1969: 263–4). By the sixteenth century the burgh's main activity was continental trade, based on the produce of its agricultural hinterland and of the coal and salt industries which had developed in its vicinity. Because the market potential of its sparsely-populated hinterland was slight, most of the return cargoes of wine and manufactured goods found their way to Edinburgh via its service port of Leith. Pittenweem thus enjoyed dynamic trading links with continental Europe and with its own national capital. Throughout the later sixteenth century and for the first four decades of the seventeenth the town was extremely prosperous.

This prosperity was abruptly curtailed by the effects of the Covenant and the Civil War. In 1639 burgh and harbour were fortified (Cook 1867: 31 and 35). Trade ceased abruptly, and by 1640 the town's merchant fleet lay in the harbour 'wrackit at the full sea' (*ibid*.: 53). Five years later more than fifty Pittenweem men, most of them mariners, were killed at the battle of Kilsyth (*ibid*.: 54–5). Economic decline was exacerbated by outbreaks of plague. By the turn of the century matters were somewhat improved (Sibbald 1710: 299), although the focus of trade had shifted from the continent towards England.

In 1979–80 excavations in the adjacent gardens of 5 Mid Shore and 2 School Wynd revealed a previously unsuspected paved road, or wynd, leading down the steep slope from the High Street to the shore (Fig. 6.3). Ceramic evidence immediately beneath the paving suggested that this road had been laid down around the middle of the sixteenth century, and it is tempting to suggest a link between this development and activity following the granting of the burgh's first charter in 1541.

The wynd terminates abruptly in a 2 m drop occasioned by a terrace cut into the slope, evidently to provide level footings for the row of houses along Mid Shore, fronting the harbour's edge. This suggests that it was the building of these houses (or, more precisely, their predecessors) that rendered the wynd redundant. Close to the point at which the wynd now terminates its sides had been revetted with masonry (a technique still visible in surviving wynds

Figure 6.3 The excavation in the garden of 5 Mid Shore, looking south towards the harbour. The surface of the paved wynd is visible in the foreground. In the centre the tail end of the sealed ash pit deposit may be seen. Beyond the fence the ground level drops 2 m to the terrace upon which the harbour-front houses are built.

nearby), and the cutting thus formed had subsequently been partially blocked by the construction of a reducing wall which butted onto the western side of the wynd and extended about half way across it. When the wynd was cut through and rendered obsolete this feature became a convenient receptacle for a mass of rubbish which included ash, shells, fish and animal bones, pottery, and clay pipes. The material had evidently been thrown in through the gap in the reducing wall over a relatively short period, since no humus was observed within the clearly defined tip lines. The gap was subsequently sealed with loose rubble, and the rubbish pit in due course became covered by a humic build-up some 1 m deep.

The rubbish pit thus represents a closed and undisturbed archaeological deposition of some magnitude. It was particularly rich in imported ceramics of the sixteenth and early seventeenth centuries. Types identified include Hispano-Moresque lusterware, Spanish olive-jar, Portuguese tin-glazed ware, Saintonge polychrome, Loire ware, central French chafing-dishes, Normandy stoneware, salt-glazed Rhenish stoneware, Delftware, and considerable quantities of Dutch and north German cooking wares. Fragments of a Werra-ware slip-trailed dish carried the digits '1 8', indicating a date of 1618 (Hurst *et al.* 1986, 242–250). Very little English or Scottish pottery was noted. The quality, character, and wide date range of the deposit suggests that it derives from a collection built up over the better part of a century, and that it came from a household (or perhaps a hostelry) whose inhabitants had enjoyed extensive and direct trading links with the continent. It is not unreasonable to suppose that its sudden deposition resulted from a major clear-out, perhaps connected with the development of housing along the shore which the circumstances of the wynd's abandonment implies. Three Charles I second issue turners securely stratified just above the wynd's surface give the deposit a *terminus post quem* of 1632 (Stewart 1955, 157 and Plate XVIII).

A *terminus ante quem* is best arrived at by a consideration of the substantial collection of clay pipes associated with the ash pit deposit and the levels above it (Martin, 1987). With one exception the eighteen pipe bowls found within the ash-pit are Dutch. The exception is a bowl of early Scottish form carrying the initials 'W B'. This mark is that of William Banks, who is known to have been active in Edinburgh as early as 1622 (RPCS, XIV: 589). In contrast the deposits above the ash pit contained a large number of Scottish pipe bowls, dating typologically from *c.* 1640 to *c.* 1720. This group included only three early Dutch bowls, two of which were found in the disturbed level just above the ash-pit deposit and may well be strays from it. The third was a surface find. The contents of the ash-pit are therefore likely to pre-date the general cessation of Dutch pipe exports to central Scotland, and the emergence of a domestic industry which was flourishing in Edinburgh by the early 1640s (Gallagher 1987).

Cargoes of pipes from Holland were still coming into the Firth of Forth as late as 1635, when a Dundee barque freighting goods bought in Holland was wrecked near Dunbar. Among the goods plundered by local people were 'one thousand pound weight of tobacco and seven barrell pypes' (RPCS VI, 240–1). During the same decade, however, there is evidence of a growing domestic industry, manifested by a challenge to the Banks monopoly which reached its climax in 1642 (RPCS VII, 324–5). Dutch imports are unlikely to have continued far into the 1640s, when economic and political pressures must finally have killed them off. This is clearly reflected by the almost total dominance of Scottish pipes in the upper levels of the Pittenweem deposit, and by the poor standard of manufacture and finish which most of them demonstrate. They are hardly the products of a competitive market.

The evidence therefore suggests a date for the ash-pit deposit somewhere towards the close of the decade 1630–1640. That the deposition was related to major structural developments along the harbour front seems beyond question, and it is tempting to suggest that the burgh's confirmation charter of 1633 may have provided an impetus for these changes.

The humic build-up above the ash-pit was much disturbed, and probably results from regular rubbish dumping interspersed with deep garden cultivation until the beginning of the eighteenth century. Stratigraphy was nowhere clearly apparent, although high concentrations of bone, pottery, and clay pipes were encountered throughout. Most of the pottery was of a dark well-fired fabric with external green glaze characteristic of the products of the kiln site at Throsk near Alloa (Caldwell and Dean 1992), with which close parallels of form and decoration were noted. Such pottery is common in Scottish domestic contexts until well into the eighteenth century, and it may have been connected with the distribution of French wine imported through Leith – a mainstay of the trading dynamic by which harbour towns like Pittenweem flourished.

The topsoil contained numerous mussel shells associated with mid-nineteenth to early-twentieth century pottery, indicative of the mussel-baited long-line fishing which characterised the economy of the burgh during that period.

This small excavation, focused at the interface between a harbour frontage and its urban hinterland, thus clarifies the relationship between the burgh and its harbour area during important periods of their symbiotic evolution. The contents of the closed ash-pit deposit, moreover, demonstrate the pan-European nature of Pittenweem's maritime contacts during the sixteenth and early seventeenth centuries. Customs records for the same period indicate a similar spread of trading activity for Scotland as a whole (McNeil and Nicholson 1975, maps 116 and 117). It is encouraging to find that, on occasion at least, the investigation of documentary sources and archaeological evidence can lead to similar conclusions.

Shipping and naviagtion aids

A revealing complement to closed deposits of maritime significance such as those found in the Pittenweem ash-pit might be provided by appropriate shipwrecks, each one of which would represent a discrete episode of mercantile endeavour frozen in transit. Though none has yet been discovered in this vicinity, the level of maritime disasters in more recent periods associated with the Fife peninsula suggests that such sites will exist, and a number of tangible clues have already emerged. Off the Isle of May, fishing operations have yielded a seventeenth century Spanish olive jar and a fourteenth century Langerwehe flagon (Fig. 6.4; see Hurst *et al.* 1986, 184–190). Both are now in the Scottish Fisheries Museum at Anstruther. The discovery in 1914 in a cave close to Fife Ness of substantial quantities of second century amphora fragments of southern Spanish origin – at least five vessels

Figure 6.4 Fourteenth century Langerwehe flagon recovered off the Isle of May.

Figure 6.5 The surviving lower storey of the first Isle of May lighthouse, built in 1636.

appear to have been represented – are most likely to come from a Roman wreck on the adjacent and hazardous Carr Rocks (Wace and Jehu, 1915: 237–41; Martin, 1992: 22–23). This whole area is ripe for systematic underwater investigation.

Fife's nodal position on the shipping routes of eastern Scotland is emphasised by early attempts to mark navigational dangers. The first purpose-built lighthouse in the kingdom was erected on the Isle of May in 1636 (Eggeling 1960, 33). It was described by Sibbald in 1710 as "a tower forty feet high, vaulted at the top end and covered with flagstones, whereon all the year over there burned in the night-time a fire of coals for a light". When it was replaced by the present lighthouse in 1816 the intention had been to demolish the earlier tower to prevent it obscuring a sector of the new light. However the Commissioners of the Northern Lighthouse Board, when they visited the island in 1814, were accompanied by Sir Walter Scott. On hearing of the proposal to demolish the old light he "recommended 'ruining' it *a la picturesque*, i.e. demolishing it partially". It was therefore reduced to a single-storey building about twenty feet high, and later modified further by the addition of a romantic crenellation to its roof (Fig. 6.5).

An average of one ton of coal was burned each night in the light's open brazier, and considerably more during storms. The ash deposits which grew up around the base of the tower were, from time to time, thrown down the slope, but in 1791 a tragedy occurred when the lighthouse keeper and his family were suffocated by fumes from the part-burnt ashes (OSA Anstruther Wester, 37). The resultant coal-ash midden is readily identifiable today to the north-east of the lighthouse and, in spite of major disturbance by rabbits, probably incorporates deep and well-preserved stratigraphy relating to the beacon's 180 years of operation between 1636 and 1816.

The replacement light on the May was constructed by Robert Stevenson (1772–1850), whose greatest achievement had been to build, between 1807 and 1811, a lighthouse on the Bell Rock, an isolated reef some twelve miles east of the entrance to the Tay (Stevenson 1824). Less well known is his attempt to erect a warning structure on the Carr Rock, a tiny platform submerged except at the lowest tides (*ibid.*, 53–59). This rock lies at the seaward end of a reef complex which extends 2 km beyond the headland of Fife Ness. Work there began in 1812, but from the outset the project encountered difficulties. To cut seatings into the rock for the first layer of masonry

*Figure 6.6 Aerial view of the complex of industrial monuments at Fife Ness. The letters indicate: **A**, the location of Stevenson's work-yard; **B**, the quay associated with the beacon project; **C**, a probable lime kiln; **D**, the rock-cut tide mill; **E** and **F**, segments of the dam associated with the mill.*

required the construction of a cofferdam which had to be pumped out between each tide, and it was not until 1815 that two courses of interlocking masonry, and part of a third, had been laid.

In September the whole construction and its supporting apparatus was demolished by a storm. Undeterred, Stevenson persisted with the enterprise, and by late 1816 the foundations had been raised above the level of spring-tides. Since the space available on the rock was not sufficient for a full lighthouse the intention was to mount a large warning bell in a cupola, using the rise and fall of the tidal water to drive the mechanism. However, in November 1817 the greater part of the edifice was again knocked down by heavy seas. The original plan was therefore abandoned, and the surviving foundation used as the base for a beacon of iron pillars on which a hollow warning-ball was erected. This construction still stands.

The work-yard which supported these endeavours has recently been identified at Fife Ness, the nearest land adjacent to the proposed beacon (Fig. 6.6). It consists of a masonry quay at the edge of a natural creek on record as 'a haven or harbour' from at least 1632 (Graham, 1968: 241). The structure includes the degraded remnants of a U-shaped or circular footing, 4.3 m in diameter, which has been interpreted as the base of a crane. Some 15 m back from the quay is a setting of concentric and eccentric rock-cuttings. These are almost certainly the seatings for another crane, and for a platform for dressing and jigging the interlocking sandstone blocks of which the beacon was to be constructed (Fig. 6.7). Between the quay and these features is a series of slots which can be identified as settings for a narrow-gauge tramway of the kind used by Stevenson on the Bell Rock for handling the masonry blocks during construction (Stevenson 1824, 507 and Pl. X). The rock platform on which these features stand appears to have been artificially levelled. These arrangements are paralleled by those of the work-yard established at Arbroath to support the construction of the Bell Rock light, which Stevenson has described in some detail (*ibid.*, 181). A putative lime kiln close to the Fife

A Maritime Landscape in East Fife

Figure 6.7 Robert Stevenson's work-yard at Fife Ness, established for the construction of the Carr Rock beacon, 1812–1817. The rock-cut features in the foreground are probably associated with a crane base and the jigging of interlocking masonry.

Ness site (Graham 1968, 241) is also probably to be associated with Stevenson's activities, as at Arbroath.

Amongst the tumble of masonry from the collapsed pier two sandstone blocks of dovetailed configuration characteristic of lighthouse construction have been identified. These are presumably rejects or wasters from the work-yard.

Tide mill

A short distance to the north west of Stevenson's work-yard are the remains of a tide mill (Fig. 6.6 D, E and F). Little is known of its history except that it appears still to have been in use in 1790 (OSA, Crail, 174). The surviving features consist of two segments of a dam, much collapsed, which link a rocky islet with the shore to form an irregular reservoir extending approximately 100 m in either direction. At the southern edge of the islet a dog-legged channel has been cut to form an inlet passage by which the rising tide would fill the reservoir. Once filled, the water was allowed to flow back under the control of a sluice to turn a water-wheel (presumably one which could be raised and lowered), of which various rock-cuts slots designed to accommodate its machinery have survived (Fig. 6.8). Other rock-cut features in the vicinity probably relate to associated structures.

Figure 6.8 The rock-cut channel of the tide mill at Fife Ness, showing slots associated with its machinery. Beyond, footings of the dam can be seen.

Figure 6.9 The late eighteenth century salt-works at St Monans, from the air. To the left is the windmill which drove the pump machinery. Nine pan buildings (now partially excavated) lie immediately behind the eroding cliff-edge. Rock cuttings in the foreshore indicate the location of a settling tank, and the inlet and outlet channels associated with it.

Figure 6.10 The inlet cut at the St Monans salt-works, looking seawards. In the foreground are slots for a sluice gate.

An industrial hinterland

The OSA (St Monans, 739) records that the salt works to the east of St Monans were 'one of the neatest and best contrived' in the area, and goes on to note that 'the coal and salt, besides what is sold to the country, are exported at Pittenweem'. These enterprises reflect the initiatives of a local improving landowner, Sir John Anstruther, who in the 1770s applied modern technology (including a steam pump) to mine the rich coal deposits which lay between Pittenweem and St Monans. The coal was transported from the main pithead to Pittenweem harbour by means of a horse-drawn waggonway. The adjacent salt-pans were set up to exploit the lowest-grade coal, which was not marketable, so deriving profit from an otherwise worthless commodity. A branch line of the waggonway conveyed the so-called 'pan' coal to the works (Martin 1991; Whatley 1984).

Recent work has identified much of the archaeology of this abandoned eighteenth century industrial enterprise in a landscape which has now reverted to agriculture. The only upstanding structure to have survived is a windmill tower, now restored as a visitor centre, on the raised beach east of St Monans. This provided the power by which brine was pumped up to a complex of nine panhouses, built by Sir John Anstruther between 1772 and 1774 (Whatley 1984, 37). These buildings are recorded in the first edition of the O.S. 6" map (surveyed in 1852). In 1985 the seaward wall of the easternmost pan building

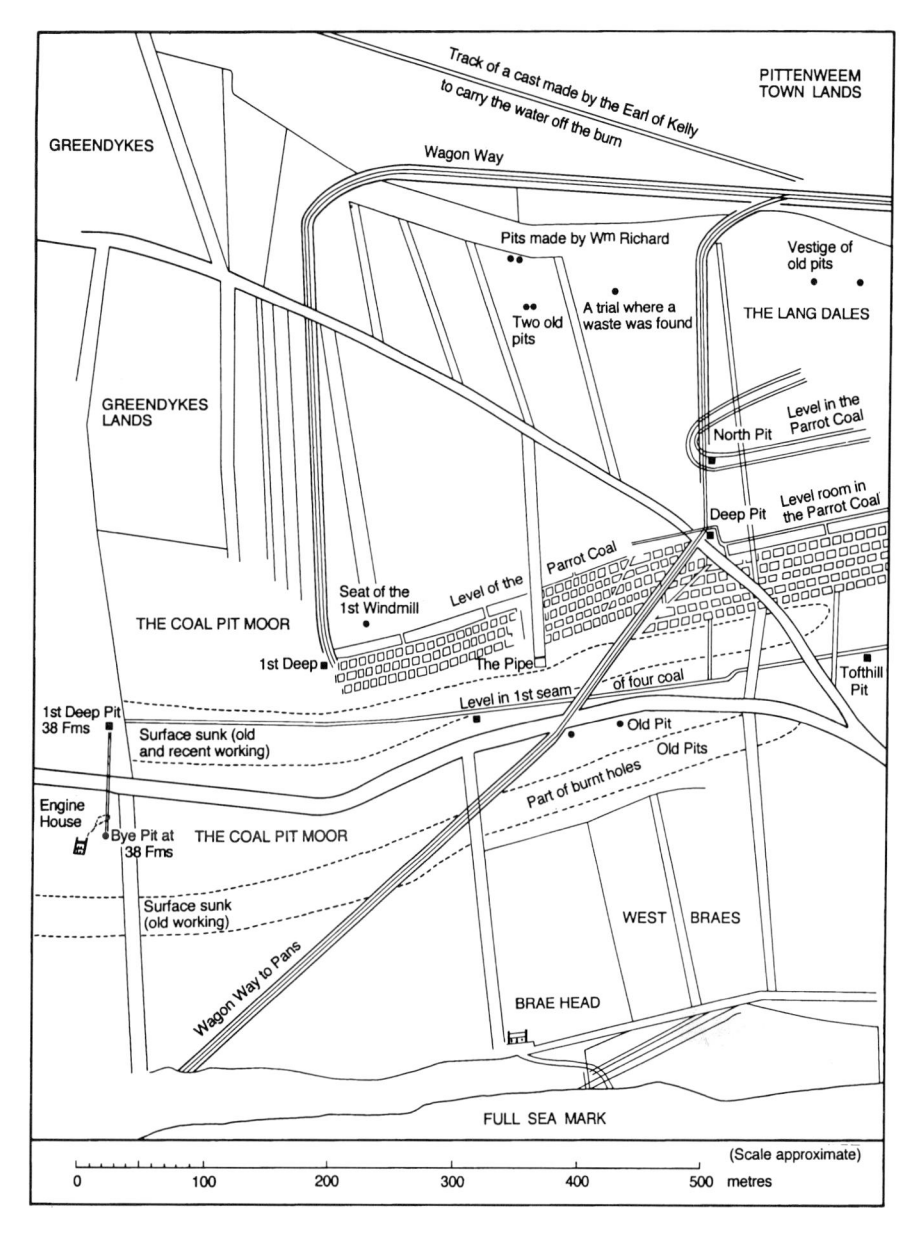

Figure 6.11 Gavin Hogg's survey of the Pittenweem coalfield in 1789 (RHP 22), redrawn for clarity and with simplified captioning.

was revealed by coastal erosion, and a rescue excavation of the structure was conducted by Scotia Archaeology on behalf of Historic Scotland (Lewis 1989). Subsequent work, co-ordinated by Fife's Regional Archaeologist, Peter Yeoman, has uncovered and consolidated the upper structural elements of the remaining eight panhouses. In their immediate hinterland other features have been identified, including coal chutes by which the waggonloads of coal were distributed to the panhouses and housings for the reciprocating arms and transmission machinery by which power from the windmill was transmitted to a seawater pump. In the eroding cliff-face elements of what appear to be a horizontal pump-barrel have been recorded.

Various rock-cut features on the foreshore can be identified as a seawater inlet channel and sluice, the footings of a rectangular settling-tank, and the route of a wooden pipe by which water was drawn up from the settling tank to the pans (Figs. 6.9 and 6.10). A deep channel close to the present shoreline has preserved, within its shingle infill, two jointed sections of the elm water-pipe *in situ*.

A well-engineered incline leading from the raised beach to the level of the panhouses has been identified as the final part of the waggonway which brought fuel to the saltworks from the coal mine in the hinterland. A reconstruction of that hinterland during its late eighteenth century industrial phase has been facilitated by the

Figure 6.12 Aerial photograph of part of the St Monans-Pittenweem industrial hinterland, taken in July 1984 (NGR NO 532028). Crop-marks in ripening barley pick out a palimpsest of successive landscapes. The linear feature on the left, associated with two power cable posts, derives from a railway demolished in 1965. The dark line running diagonally across the picture is a boundary ditch, identifiable in Hogg's map of 1789. It is apparently associated with the rig-and-furrow cultivation which abuts on it. The curved double line indicates the side ditches of the eighteenth century colliery waggonway, also surveyed by Hogg. Towards the top right features of probable prehistoric date may be discerned.

existence of a survey conducted by Gavin Hogg, Sir John Anstruther's factor, in 1789 (RHP 22 1789; Fig. 6.11). This shows in considerable detail not only the various pitheads, underground workings, and waggonway routes, but also indications of earlier industrial activity and field boundaries which relate to the pre-enclosure landscape. The good natural drainage provided by the gravel geology of this landscape is enhanced by the abandoned coal galleries, rendering the arable fields above particularly responsive to crop-mark formation (Fig. 6.12). Aerial reconnaissance conducted since 1984 has yielded extensive crop-mark data, much of which can be interpreted by comparing it with the Hogg survey (Fig. 6.13).

Conclusion

These examples, though perhaps of interest and some relevance in themselves, are no more than arbitrary snapshots within the space/time continuum of an ever-changing maritime landscape. A more systematic study is currently being undertaken under the aegis of Maritime Fife (Oxley, this volume), which when complete will provide a database which will allow the coastal archaeological resource of this region to be better understood, quanitified, and – one hopes – more sensitively managed. Even on the limited scale of the present investigation, however, the dynamics of change are frequently evident. Recent developments at Pittenweem Harbour have buried and perhaps destroyed evidence of earlier structural phases, while coastal erosion at the St Monans saltworks has been progressing at the rate of about a metre per decade for at least a century and a half. The long-term future of this unique industrial monument requires decisive action now. Archaeologists involved in the management of coastal landscapes such as this one have key roles to play in helping to understand and record these changes, and in seeking to mitigate their more damaging effects.

Unpublished primary source

RHP 22. 1789: Ms. map in the Scottish Record Office, RHP 22, "Sketch of the surface of the Pittenweem lands ... and the lands adjoining thereto ... " Drawn by Gavin Hogg.

Published primary sources

RPCS. 1889–1908: *Register of the Privy Council of Scotland*, Second Series, vols. I–VIII. Edinburgh.

OSA. 1791–1799: *The* [Old] *Statistical Account of Scotland*, edited by Sir John Sinclair. Vol. X. Fife. Facsimile edition, Edinburgh 1978.

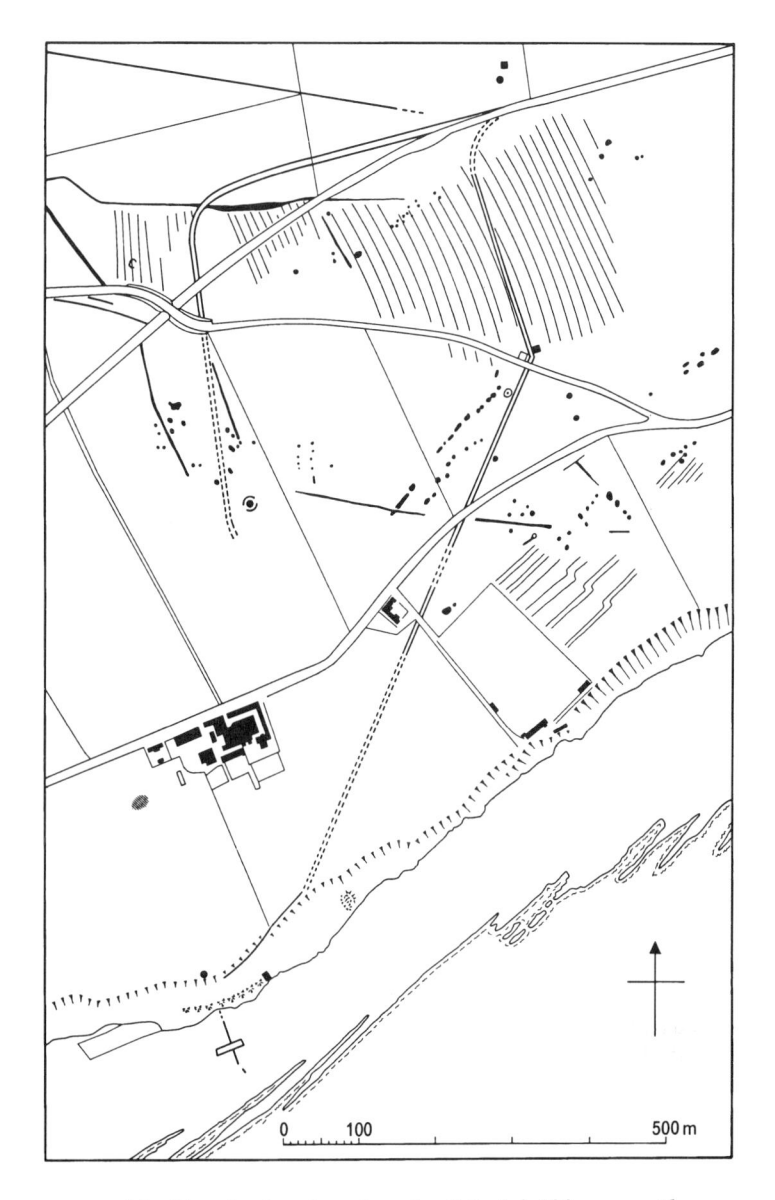

Figure 6.13 The area covered by Hogg's plan, based on the O.S. 1:2,500 map, with crop-mark features added.

References

Caldwell, D.H. and Dean, V.E. 1992: The pottery industry at Throsk, Stirlingshire, in the 17th and 18th centuries, *Post-Medieval Archaeolol.*, 26: 1–46.

Cook, D. 1867: *Annals of Pittenweem.* Anstruther.

Eggeling, W.J. 1960: *The Isle of May.* Edinburgh.

Gallagher, D.B. 1987: The 17th century: the documentary evidence [for Edinburgh pipemakers], in P. Davey (ed.), *The Archaeology of the Clay Tobacco Pipe. X. Scotland.* Oxford, BAR British Series 178, 3–13.

Graham, A. 1968: Archaeological Notes on some Harbours in Eastern Scotland, *Proc. Soc. Antiq. Scot.*, 101: 200–285.

Hurst, J.G., Neal, D.S., and van Beuningen, H.J.E. 1986: *Pottery produced and traded in north-west Europe, 1350–1650.* Rotterdam.

Lewis, J. 1989: The excavation of an 18th century salt-pan at St Monance, Fife, *Proc. Soc. Antiq. Scot.*, 119: 361–370.

Lewis, J., Martin, C.J.M., Martin, P.F., and Murdoch, R. 1998: *A Lost Industrial Landscape: the coal and salt enterprises at Pittenweem and St Monans, 1771–1814.* Tayside and Fife Archaeological Committee, Monograph 2 (Glenrothes, in press).

Martin, C.J.M. 1987: A group of pipes from Mid Shore, Pittenweem, in Peter Davey (ed) *The Archaeology of the Clay Tobacco Pipe. X. Scotland.* BAR British Series 178 (Oxford).

Martin, C.J.M. 1992: Water transport and the Roman occupations of north Britain, in T.C. Smout (ed) *Scotland and the Sea.* (Edinburgh).

Martin, P. 1991: *Pits, Pans, and People: the social impact of coal mining and salt making in St Monans and Pittenweem, c.1770–1820.* Centre for Tayside and Fife Studies (Dundee), Occasional Paper No. 3.

McNeil, P. and Nicholson, R. (eds) 1975: *An Historical Atlas of Scotland.* (St Andrews).

Sibbald, R. 1710: *The History ... of Fife and Kinross.* (Edinburgh).

Stevenson, R. 1824: *An Account of the Bell Rock Lighthouse.*

Stewart, I.H. 1955: *The Scottish Coinage.* (London).

Wace, A.J.B. and Professor Jehu 1915: Cave excavations in East Fife, *Proc. Soc. Antiq. Scot.*, 49: 233–255.

Whatley, C.A. 1984: *'That Important and Necessary Article': the salt industry and its trade in Fife and Tayside c.1570–1850.* Abertay Historical Society Publication (Dundee), No. 22.

7. The Archaeological Potential of the Scottish Intertidal Zone: Some Examples and an Assessment

Alex Hale

This paper aims to assess the archaeological potential of the Scottish intertidal zone, to review the history of the few investigations in that zone and to propose a model for the detection of further monuments. An example of an intertidal site will be used to illustrate the potential value of further research, and the paper will conclude with a proposal for future investigations of these invaluable monuments.

Introduction

Scotland possesses approximately 70% of the British coastline and this inevitably means that it has, potentially, a large number of intertidal archaeological monuments. Until recently, estuaries and their intertidal zones were recognised primarily as natural habitats, especially as breeding grounds for both sea and bird-life. Because the predominant view of the intertidal zone in the past saw it as a natural habitat, man's primary contact with it was to take advantage of the numerous resources it could provide. This naturalistic view of the margin between the land and sea has stimulated a great deal of research, much of which can be useful to archaeologists.

Intertidal archaeology in England has been practised, using what could be considered modern archaeological techniques, since Hazzeldine Warren investigated a series of structures on the Essex coast in 1936. However, earlier investigations have been documented in Scotland and these will be referred to below. In the 1980s, one project was to signal the revival of intertidal archaeology in England. The Hullbridge Basin Survey on the Essex coast applied research-based objectives with a management assessment project and resulted in a comprehensive project (Wilkinson & Murphy 1986). Later, the Severn Estuary Levels Research Committee was established and both the English and Welsh intertidal zones of the River Severn became the subject of extensive research (Allen & Fulford 1986, Bell 1993). This project combined research strategies with planning implications, primarily coping with the transport network of the area. Both projects illustrated the different means by which intertidal archaeology can be researched, funded and integrated into archaeology as a whole.

In Scotland, however, little intertidal research has been carried out. The English and Welsh work clearly illustrated the potential of this kind of research and this paper aims to begin to redress the balance for the Scottish intertidal zone. This will be achieved by reviewing the previous investigations and illustrating the potential of one such site. The intertidal zone is the area between the lowest and the highest astronomical tides and it consists of varying biogenic and minerogenic zones. Although it has been researched by the geological, geomorphological and biological disciplines, it remains ill-defined in archaeological terms. It is hoped that this paper will help to define the Scottish intertidal zone.

Previous work on intertidal sites in Scotland

Two main groups of intertidal sites were the foci of investigations during the early part of this century in Scotland. The first group consisted of as many as eight sites in the Firth of Clyde and the second of five sites in the Beauly Firth. A single outlying site was also investigated near the Isle of Eriska (Fig. 7.1).

The Firth of Clyde

The group of sites in the inner Firth of Clyde drew the attention of archaeologists, scholars and amateurs whose investigations resulted in a number of publications between 1889 and 1908. The group numbers up to eight sites within as many kilometres between Erskine bridge and Langbank (RCAHMS). The first site investigated, Dumbuck (Bruce 1900) on the northern shore of the Clyde, was excavated by a local amateur archaeologist, Mr. John Bruce with help from a local artist, Mr. William Donnelly and Dr. Robert Munro, who is considered the pioneer of crannog research.

The Dumbuck investigations involved excavations during consecutive low tides, similar to Hazzeldine Warren's 'snatch and grab' technique (Hazzeldine

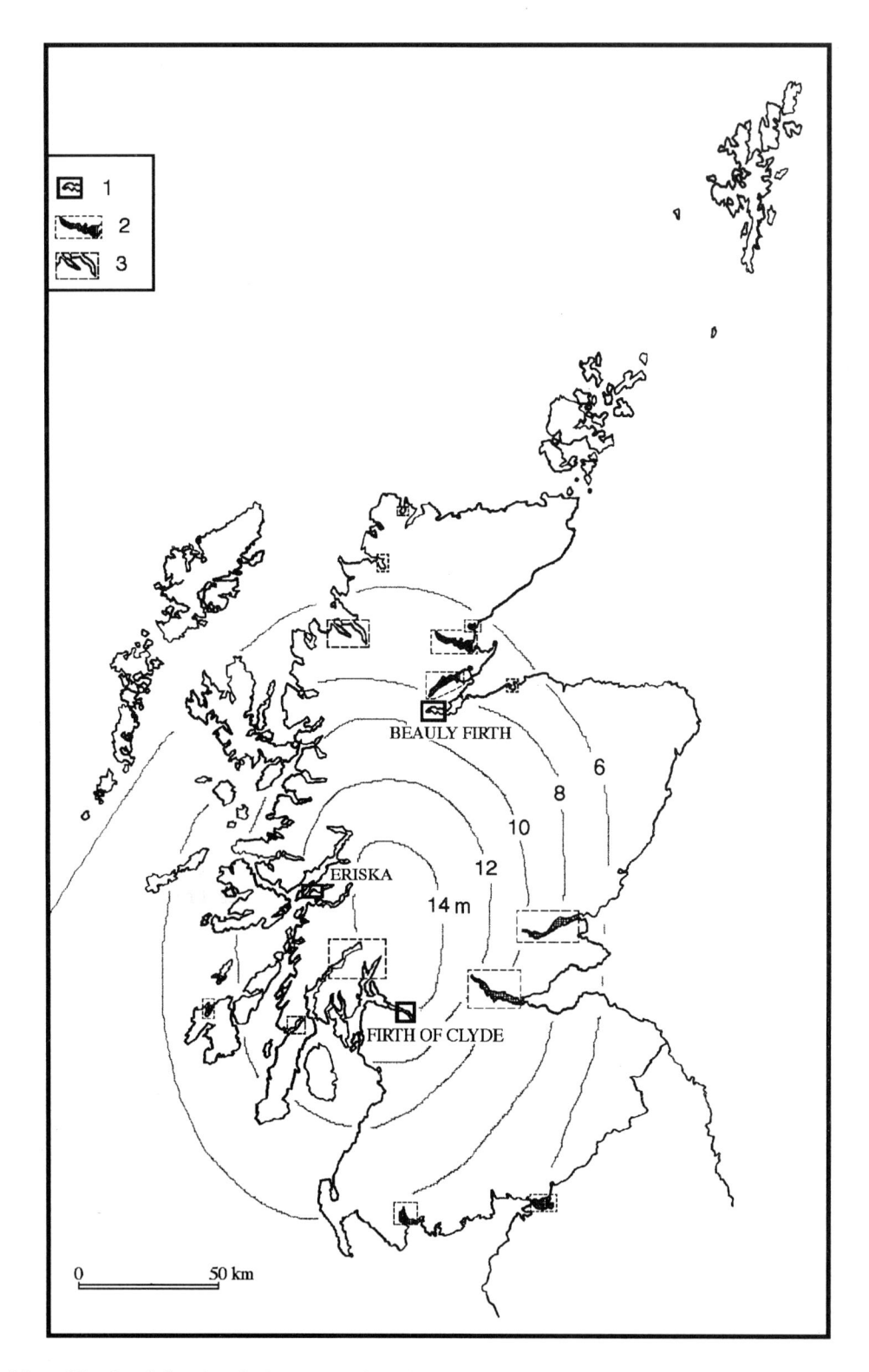

Figure 7.1 Map of Scotland showing the Main Postglacial Isobases (after Sissons 1976) and the areas with known intertidal sites (1), areas with sites probably present (2) and areas with sites possibly present (3).

Warren, *et al* 1936). The results of the excavation indicated that the organic components of the site were very well preserved. The site consisted of three horizontal oval timber platforms laid one on top of the other (Bruce 1900). Surrounding the platform were a number of retaining piles and the centre of the site consisted of a stone surrounded wattle-lined pit (ibid. p. 438). Associated with the site was a stone causeway running from the site to the shore, a surrounding stone 'breakwater' and a wooden log-boat which was found in a dock structure (ibid. p. 439).

The small finds included animal bones (ibid. p. 440–41) and Munro's notorious 'queer things of the Clyde' (Munro 1905). These stones, consisting of pieces of slate carved with abstract and semi-figurative markings, produced a lengthy discussion between a number of academics, including Munro. These discussions ultimately have affected our knowledge of the site and its archaeological importance, as they have diverted our attention away from the structural components of one of the first excavated intertidal sites in Scotland. This diversion during the early period of these investigations may have contributed to our present problem of classifying these sites (Barber & Crone 1993).

Bruce also investigated a second site near the village of Langbank, on the southern shore (Bruce 1908). These excavations revealed a roughly circular ring of piles, which surrounded a few horizontal timbers, possibly the remains of a platform (ibid. p. 44). To the east of the piles was a large midden deposit and the site was surrounded by a stone scatter (ibid. p. 45). The animal bones found on the Langbank site were similar species to those that had been found on Dumbuck, some of which showed signs of cut-marks and could possibly have been used as tools (ibid. p. 49–51). Langbank also yielded the first dating evidence from a Scottish intertidal site, which came from an engraved bone comb and a La Tène pennanular brooch from the Langbank site (Stevenson 1966). Carved stone objects, similar to those at Dumbuck, were found on this site. Their authenticity was subject to some discussion between a number of antiquarians, most notably Robert Munro who called the objects 'grotesque "idols"' (Munro 1905 p. 149).

Excavation on another of the Clyde sites, Erskine Ferry, during the early part of this century indicated a structure with very substantial mortised piles surrounding a mass of worked horizontal timbers. Unfortunately the exact date of the excavation is unclear because it was never published. However, the Royal Commission on the Ancient and Historical Monuments of Scotland holds a number of excellent photographs of the investigation. A reference to the site also appears in the Proceedings of the Society of Antiquaries of Scotland remarking on a number of the organic remains discovered (Callander 1910–11).

Since these early investigations no further work was carried out on these sites, until in the early 1980s W S Hanson of Glasgow University investigated the site known as Erskine crannog, on the Clyde's southern shore (Hanson 1985). The site was planned, after some of the surface stones had been removed and the exposed timbers cleaned, with the aid of photogrammetry. The plan indicated a horizontal platform of radially placed timbers, surrounded by a ring of vertical piles. Some of the timbers indicated jointing and showed signs of half-checks. A quern stone was found on the surface of the site and a number of the timbers were sampled for radiocarbon assay (Hanson pers. comm.) (see Table 7.1).

No further research has been carried out on the Clyde sites and they remain a group of sites classified as crannogs, although little is known of their topographical situation at the time of construction and, possibly more importantly, their purpose.

Table 7.1 The calibrated radiocarbon dates from the Erskine intertidal site (Crone 1993, Hanson pers.comm.).

SURRC reference	Age BP uncalibrated	Calibrated date BC (68%)	(95%)
GU-2186	2210±50	320BC-200 BC	400 BC-160 BC
GU-2187	1970±60	60 BC-AD 90	120 BC-AD 190
GU-2328	1950±50	10 BC-AD 120	100 BC-AD 150
GU-2383	2170±60	260 BC-160 BC	390 BC-100 BC

Eriska

A site adjacent to the southern shore of the Isle of Eriska in Argyll was investigated by Munro in the summer of 1884. He excavated a trench across the site and found a horizontal platform laid directly onto the clay sub-surface. There is no record of any piles surrounding the site, although his notes regarding the wood-working techniques and small finds are useful (Munro 1885). Like most Scottish intertidal sites it remains unclassified since this brief investigation.

The Beauly Firth

Documentary evidence for the second group of intertidal sites, in the Beauly Firth, can be traced to 1699. James Fraser, Minister for Kirkhill recorded the sites in a letter to Mr. J. Wallace of Edinburgh: '*Here are three great Heaps of Stones in this Lake, at considerable distance one from the other, these we call Cairns in the Irish. One of a huge bigness [sic], (in the middle of the Frith [sic]) at low water, is accessible; and we find it has been a Burial place by the Urns which are some times discovered. As the Sea encroaches and wears the Banks upwards, there are long oaken Beams of 20 or 30 Foot long found; some of these 8, some 12 or 14 feet under Ground. I see one of them 14 feet long, that carried the mark of the Ax [sic] on it, and had several Wimble bores in it.*' (Philosophical Transactions volume XXI, page 231)

Christian Maclagan visited one of the Beauly sites, although she confused the name of the site and its position with another site in the same Firth. She described the intertidal zone and the number of sites present, including the problems of access to the sites. The description also included the removal of timbers from the site known as

Figure 7.2 Aerial photograph of Redcastle intertidal site (taken by G.D.B. Jones).

'Black Cairn': *'Our boatmen declared they had often drawn out of it beams 9 or 10 feet long and 3 feet broad, fresh and fit for use. They had great difficulty in pulling them out, which they did by fixing their anchors in a log or pile.'* (Maclagan 1875 p. 89) Maclagan also mentioned the presence of urns on one of the sites, however, this has not been substantiated.

The other renowned early crannog investigator was Odo Blundell who visited the Beauly Firth in the summer of 1909, (Blundell 1909–10). He intended to visit one of the sites and use diving equipment borrowed from the Clyde Navigation Trust (Ibid. p. 12). On arrival at the shore he discovered the site, Black Cairn (Carn Dubh in Gaelic) was fully exposed. He documented the size of the site and the presence of a number of timbers on its surface and amongst the sub-surface sediments. One of the timbers he photographed has been re-discovered during recent fieldwork in its original position (Hale 1994).

In 1936, Carn Dubh was visited by members of the Inverness Field Club and Scientific Society who found a number of sub-surface timbers, a possible whetstone and a well-preserved, vertical pile between 2½ and 3 feet below the surface, showing cut-marks. The letter describing the investigation and photographs of the site and pile are held in Inverness Museum (INVMG correspondence file 1.8.12).

Since these two brief periods of investigation into the Beauly sites no further work had taken place. In 1991, Professor Barri Jones of Manchester University took a series of aerial photographs of the group and this led the author to reconsider these sites (Fig. 7.2).

The Redcastle intertidal site

In 1991 Redcastle, one of the sites in the Beauly Firth, was surveyed. The site is situated in an area of extensive mudflats and well-developed drainage channels. The surface of the site is covered with large Old Red Sandstone stones, covering a layer of pebbles and sandy gravel. Small-scale excavations have revealed some of the types of well preserved organic remains, surface and underlying, found on an intertidal site. In the sandy gravel were found the upper surfaces of a number of substantial, horizontal timbers (Fig. 7.3). These timbers showed signs of working; cut-marks, mortise holes, a cross-piece of two timbers and vertical piles to retain the horizontals. Two of these were sampled for radiocarbon assay (see Table 7.2).

Table 7.2 (Hale 1995).

Sample number	SURRC reference	Age BP Uncalibrated	Calibrated date BC (68%)	(95%)
RDC'94. P3 (quercus)	GU-4542	2570±50	805–769	825–540
RDC'94. T5 (alnus)	GU-4543	2550±50	801–607	814–530

The position of the horizontal timbers suggested a period of lower tide-level than today when, at high tide,

Figure 7.3 Timbers excavated on Redcastle intertidal site (taken by A. Hale).

the site is covered to a depth of between 30cm and 85cm. The timbers were levelled to Ordnance Datum and the depth to which they were covered was 1.2m.

Firth & Haggart's paper 'Loch Lomond stadial and Flandrian shorelines in the inner Moray Firth area, Scotland' (1991), indicated a sea level lower than today's. Since the timbers on the Redcastle site were felled the sea level has risen and the site has become inundated. The period between the laying of the timbers and the inundation is unclear, very little fine-grained sediments, such as those deposited by a flood, overlie the timbers. Coarser grained sands and gravel cover them and may indicate a high energy, low-frequency event, such as a storm. The condition of the timbers indicates that the site was inundated relatively quickly. The upper surfaces of the timbers had deformed heartwood and the lower sections showed no distortion. This suggested that the upper surfaces were partially exposed, although not enough to completely destroy the timbers, whilst the lower sections were buried in the fine-grained sands and silt. The timbers may have been laid upon an unconsolidated surface such as a tidal flat or a salt marsh at or above high water mark. The excavations on the Redcastle site have illustrated the potential of one intertidal site and it is hoped that a more substantial research project will be based on the site in the future

Factors affecting the preservation and detection of sites in the intertidal zone

The reasons why these sites have for so long been the focus of so little research may be due to their position within a very dynamic environment. The diurnal changes in sea level restrict access and limit the amount of time that can be spent on site. More recently the misconception that wetland, underwater or marine research was costly and time-consuming may have contributed to the marginalisation of these sites. However, a number of wetland and intertidal research projects both in this country and elsewhere have indicated the considerable potential these environments can contribute to archaeology (Coles & Lawson 1987).

The trends by which Scottish freshwater crannog sites and subsequently intertidal sites have once again become the focus of further research, will briefly be reviewed. Morrisson documented the history and problems associated with and the initial results of freshwater crannog research (1985). The extensive work on the freshwater crannog at Oakbank in Loch Tay, Perthshire by Dixon has illustrated the approaches necessary to research such a site and the wealth of data available (Dixon 1981, pers. comms.). Other works have indicated the ways in which crannog studies have diversified (Sands 1994).

The known intertidal sites mentioned above have appeared within the overall class 'crannog' (Crone 1993). The problem of classification of crannogs is the lack of comprehensive excavation data. The data would allow structural and artefactual interpretation, leading to various characteristics being identified and incorporated into a classification system. The same is even more apparent when studying the intertidal sites. Only two sites from the Clyde have been excavated, neither of which used modern techniques. The classification question is therefore one that cannot be resolved at present due to the paucity of excavated sites. The term 'crannog' has been used in Scottish archaeology to describe all sites (occasionally non-sites) that appear as mounds of stone within watery environments. This has produced a huge number of sites, of which less than 10% have been investigated and none completely. Part of this paper aims to investigate the possibility of defining a sub-group and identifying the topography common to that group. By identifying the dynamics of the intertidal zone and its effects on the preservation and detection of archaeological sites the possibility of a sub-group will be examined below.

Local topography and sedimentary regimes

The known Scottish intertidal sites are located within sheltered firths. These environments have relatively short fetches, reducing wave height and energy. This reduction of energy is significant in the detection and also the survival of an intertidal monument. Lower wind speeds within sheltered firths also help to prevent wave action damaging sites. The erosive/depositional affects that have occurred to a site are essential when interpreting intertidal remains and it is vital to monitor the sites as a management consideration.

The sedimentary regime within a firth can affect the intertidal sites. High energy environments may erode or accrete around an intertidal site, with the obvious effect of the site's disappearance. Variations of sediment, both laterally, vertically and over time will all alter a site's appearance. The depositional and erosional forces within the intertidal zone can expose, bury and destroy monuments. Research into estuarine dynamics is extensive and illustrates the changes that occur in the intertidal environment (Dyer 1972, Buller & McManus 1974/75). For example, salt and freshwater mixing will have the effect of defining two major channels in well-developed estuaries, one for the inflow of salt water and the other for the freshwater outflow (Dyer 1979, 6). This may cause more damage to sites adjacent to these channels.

The amount of sediment within a firth is dependent on the incoming riverine load, the incoming marine load from longshore drift and the outgoing marine regime. Within both the Moray and the Clyde firths, the intertidal sites are situated in the innermost protected areas near the mouths of the incoming rivers. Situated in the sheltered part of these firths, the intertidal sites are affected by weaker wave energy, reduced by the extensive inter and subtidal zones (Reineck & Singh 1980).

Sea level changes

Sea level changes with varying frequency: tides occur diurnally, storms occasionally, and isostatic changes over much longer periods of time. But all of these are important topographical changes that affect both site detection and survival. Diurnal changes are most apparent when investigating intertidal sites, since they can disrupt fieldwork schedules and affect survey projects. The height of both the water and the site is a critical factor when locating sites of this nature. At neap tides if the water level is not sufficiently low a site may be submerged. The presence of sites within the subtidal zone cannot be disregarded, as they may have suffered post-depositional submergence following a change in sea level. Storm damage, even within sheltered firths, can be highly destructive to delicate organic remains preserved in the fine-grained, highly mobile intertidal sediments. Isostatic and eustatic changes are vital to the interpretation of the post-abandonment history of intertidal sites.

The Scottish landmass was affected by the last ice-sheet retreat and this has led to a number of glacio-isostatic recovery studies (Smith & Dawson 1983). The Rannoch Basin was identified as the centre of glacio-isostatic recovery and the west coast has been recorded as recovering at a rate greater than the east. Various studies have identified the rates of uplift and the position of the postglacial shorelines during the ice-sheet retreat (Sissons 1976) (Fig. 7.1). As a result of this sites on the west coast may have been lifted out of the intertidal zone and may consequently be prone to terrestrial erosion. However, the Outer Hebrides have been subsiding and sites here may have been submerged.

Estuarine environments, especially in Scotland, often possess geological records of the isostatic recovery and these, combined with knowledge of the position of structural remains from intertidal sites, can be used to identify the sea-level position at the date when the site was constructed (Haggart, Hale & Firth forthcoming). Compared with the Beauly Firth, much less research has been carried out into the sea level of the Clyde. However, it is hoped that future archaeological intertidal research will contribute to this.

The gradients of the topography of the intertidal and the supratidal zones are also factors to be considered. A low-gradient environment will be affected over an extensive area by even a small marine transgression. The resultant flood may inundate shore-side sites, salt and freshwater marsh sites and other remains within the extended intertidal zone. Equally a regression in sea level will expose a greater area to colonisation by the surrounding inhabitants, both natural and human. This is an example of the transgressive/regressive changes that influence the physical structure of sites, due to erosion, deposition and burial but which can also affect the nomenclature of a site. A site found today in the intertidal zone was not necessarily constructed or used in that environment, and vice-versa. It is therefore essential to understand the environmental context of a site when it was built and the sea-level changes that have occurred subsequently to its abandonment.

Regional sea-level studies in Scotland have varied from area to area and over the past 15 years research in the Moray and Beauly Firths has increased substantially (Haggart 1982, 1986, 1987). As previously discussed, this research has led to detailed sea-level movements being identified and a refined curve being proposed using the combination of stratigraphic, pollen and diatom analysis and radiocarbon assay. These studies are invaluable to the interpretation of the position of the intertidal sites in the Beauly Firth, relative to mean high water springs (MHWS).

Work by Haggart has indicated a higher sea-level position prior to c. 6000 B.P., thereafter it fell, from approximately 9m above Ordnance Datum (O.D.) to a position similar to today, when local datum is -2.25m O.D. During the period of higher sea level, the present intertidal zone would have been a subtidal environment. The subsequent fall in sea level would expose the subtidal zone and its associated features would become the intertidal zone (Reineck & Singh 1980). Continental research has indicated changes in settlement patterns according to topographical variations within the intertidal and marine environments. The construction of settlements upon raised sand and peat mounds is well known from the Dutch intertidal zone (Waterbolk 1981).

The present Beauly Firth shoreline is bordered by intertidal and supratidal salt marshes. Some of these deposits have formed small cliff features at MHWS. The salt marsh cliff supports the sequence of events proposed by Firth and Haggart (1989): a higher sea-level, followed by a regression, during which time the salt marsh encroached onto the mudflats, followed by a small rise in sea-level to its present position. This suggests a period during which time the sea level was slightly lower (0.5m-1m), possibly the time when the supratidal zone was more extensive and the Redcastle site was constructed. The rise in sea level would potentially cut back the salt marsh and leave the site surrounded by intertidal mudflats. Consequently, the need to locate the sea-level position when these sites were constructed and used is vital to their interpretation.

Potential threats to the archaeology of the intertidal zone

Other factors affecting the intertidal archaeological record include modern disturbances caused by land reclamation for agricultural and other purposes. Around the upper reaches of the Clyde, reclamation has taken place on both the southern and northern shorelines. This can effect the sea-level position and alter the sedimentary and run-off regimes. Land at the head of the Beauly Firth has been protected by the construction of levees and sea walls, which has canalised the river mouth altering the discharge velocity.

The construction of modern training walls, harbour installations, pipeline laying, off-shore dredging or channel dredging and land reclamation for development are all modern-day activities which, unless monitored by archaeologists, can be detrimental to the intertidal record. For example, an intertidal site was lost in Scotland when a breakwater was constructed at the mouth of the River Ness in the Beauly Firth, prior to 1868. This caused the destruction of the site known as Cairn Airc (Ordnance Survey 1st edition, Inverness and Bona sheet, 25 inch to 1 mile series).

Dredging poses another serious threat to some sites. The upper Firth of Clyde was heavily dredged between 1758 and the early part of this century. This has affected the water level and the sedimentary regimes considerably. In 1758 the high water depth at Erskine (mid-channel) was 13 feet, while by 1965 it was over 40 feet deep (Riddell 1979).

Land reclamation by developers and farmers can dramatically alter the topography of an intertidal site. The effects of marshland 'recovery' can alter the pH of the geology, lower the water table and introduce chemical nutrients into the environment. The initial effects of reclamation may appear to maintain the integrity of a site. However, closer research has shown the detrimental effects of this form of development (Barber & Crone 1993; Leech 1994).

The potential for the identification of environments in which intertidal sites survive will now be assessed. The Clyde and the Beauly Firths have been used to create criteria that can be applied to the Scottish intertidal zone, with the aim of locating further possible sites.

An assessment of the Scottish intertidal archaeological sites

An initial model of the Scottish coastline has been formulated for identifying the possible location of further intertidal sites. The model is based on the two groups of sites in the Beauly and Clyde intertidal zones and the topographic and geomorphic attributes associated with those sites. The model incorporates the topography and preservation criteria that identify emergent, shallow, sediment-rich environments, often firths, with low-lying and extensive sheltered intertidal zones. These criteria are based on the situations of the known intertidal archaeological sites.

On the basis of those criteria an assessment of the potential archaeological resource of coastal Scotland has been made. Three categories of actual and potential site presence have been used:

(1) areas with known intertidal archaeological sites.
(2) areas with a high probability of archaeological sites being present because all the criteria were met.

(3) areas with potential for intertidal archaeological sites being present because some of the criteria were met. (Fig. 7.2).

This preliminary model aims to highlight areas that compare with the identified topographical criteria. It should be regarded as finite and only as a preliminary approach to be used to suggest some location parameters for further intertidal sites. The model can be tested at a local level by aerial photographic and field walking, in order to verify any possible sites. Historic Scotland has instigated a series of coastal assessment surveys, which could be used to examine the model proposed in this paper (Ashmore 1994).

Conclusions

Archaeologically, the intertidal zone has been conceived and acknowledged as a resource zone for populations inhabiting the surrounding dry land and as a communication route between the dry-land populations (Maltby 1986). It has bee suggested that the Scottish freshwater crannog sites were habitation units (Morrison 1985, Dixon 1994). Whether the intertidal sites are habitation units similar to freshwater crannogs remains unclear.

The notion that settlement sites could be constructed within an intertidal zone has developed from research in the Netherlands. The Dutch sites suggest quite different attitudes to the intertidal environment, during the late Iron Age (1st century BC) than today (Louwe Kooijmans 1974, Brandt, van der Leeuw & van Wijngaarden-Bakker 1984). The archaeological interpretation of a site and the occupants' perception of a wet environment are quite different phenomena (Louwe Kooijmans 1991). The first is a material interpretation of environment, site and small finds. The second is all of those combined with the assumption that the inhabitants of the late Iron Age structures, in intertidal zones, had similar requirements to ours today. Dutch and British research has shown that today's need to live high and dry is not reflected in prehistoric settlement patterns (Abbink 1986, Housley 1988, Coles & Coles 1996). Other sites on the German coastline, found in sheltered estuarine (previously intertidal) zones have also been classed as habitation sites and dated to a similar period, c.100 bc (Schmid 1978). The possibility of archaeological sites in Scotland's intertidal zone is therefore an intriguing question which, given the development pressures identified above, needs to be urgently addressed.

The model proposed has identified a number of possible locations that fulfilled the criteria indicating that they are likely to posses further intertidal sites. The testing of the model is the first step in the location of these sites. Site surveys and the excavation of a site would help define whether the Scottish intertidal sites are a sub-group of the crannogs. The presence of a group of sites in the Scottish intertidal zone that may be quite distinct from freshwater crannogs, is an exciting and challenging research project, which should not be overlooked. The identification and interpretation of the Scottish intertidal sites can also help the reconstruction of the environment and changing sea-level of the prehistoric North Sea basin.

Acknowledgements

I would like to thank Drs. Geraint Coles, Anya Clayworth and Nick Dixon for their help and useful suggestions with the drafts of this paper. Thanks also to Dr. Hanson of Glasgow University for allowing me to use the radiocarbon dates from the Erskine site and to Professor Barri Jones of Manchester University for his encouragement and aerial photographs.

The intertidal fieldwork was carried out with grants from Historic Scotland, the Society of Antiquaries of Scotland and the Abercromby Travel Fund, Department of Archaeology, University of Edinburgh. The research of the Redcastle intertidal site was carried out whilst the author was a recipient of a Wingate Scholarship.

References

Abbink, A.A. 1986: 'Structured allocation and cultural strategies'. In Brandt, R.W, van der Leeuw, S.E. and Kooijman, M.J.A.N. (eds), *Gedacht over Assendelft Working Paper* 6, 23–32.

Allen, J.R.L. & Fulford, M.G. 1986: 'The Wentlooge Level: A Romano-British saltmarsh reclamation in Southeast Wales', *Britannia* 17, 91–117.

Ashmore, P.J. 1994: *Archaeology and the Coastal Erosion Zone: Towards a Historic Scotland Policy*, (Historic Scotland, Edinburgh).

Barber, J.W. and Crone B.A. 1993: 'Crannogs; a diminishing resource? A survey of the crannogs of southwest Scotland and excavations at Buiston Crannog', *Antiquity* 67, 520–33.

Bell, M. 1993: 'Intertidal archaeology at Goldcliff in the Severn Estuary'. In Coles, J., Fenwick, V. and Hutchinson, G. (eds) *A Spirit of Enquiry: Essays for Ted Wright*. 9–13, (Exeter: Warp).

Blundell, O. 1909–10: 'On further examination of artificial islands in the Beauly Firth, Loch Bruiach, Loch Moy, Loch Gary, Loch Lundy, Loch Oich, Loch Lochy and Loch Treig'. *Proceedings of the Society of Antiquaries of Scotland* 44, 12–33.

Brandt, R.W., van der Leeuw, S.E. & van Wijngaarden-Bakker,, L.H. 1984: 'Transformations in a Dutch estuary: research in a wet landscape', *World Archaeology* 16 (1), 1–17.

Bruce, J. 1900–01: 'Notes on the discovery and exploration of a pile structure on the north bank of the river Clyde east from Dumbarton rock', *Proceedings of the Society of Antiquaries of Scotland* 34, 437–62.

Bruce, J. 1908: 'Report and investigations upon the Langbank pile dwelling', *Transactions of the Glasgow Archaeological Society* 5, 43–53.

Buller, A.T. & McManus, J. 1974/75: 'Sediments of the Tay Estuary. I. Bottom sediments of the upper and upper middle reaches', *Proceedings of the Royal Society of Edinburgh*, B. 75, 41–64.

Callander, J.G. 1910: 'Notice of the discovery of two vessels of clay on the Culbin sands, the first containing wheat and the second from a kitchen-midden, with a comparison of the Culbin sands and the Glenluce sands and the relics found on them', *Proceedings of the Society of Antiquaries of Scotland* 45, pp. 164.

Coles, J. & Coles, B. 1996: Enlarging the Past. (*Society of Antiquaries of Scotland Monograph Series, Number 11*).

Coles, J. and Lawson, A.J. (eds) 1989: *European Wetlands in Prehistory*. (Clarendon Press, Oxford).

Crone, B.A. 1993: 'Crannogs and chronologies', *Proceedings of the Society of Antiquaries of Scotland* 123, 245–54.

Dixon, T.N. 1981: 'Preliminary excavation of Oakbank Crannog, Loch Tay: Interim Report', *The International Journal of Nautical Archaeology and Underwater Exploration*, 10, 15–21.

Dixon, T.N. 1994: 'Defining, Classifying and Evaluating the Resource-Archaeology', in Maitland P.S., Boon P.J. and McLusky, D.S. (eds), *The Fresh Waters of Scotland: A National Resource of International Significance*, 261–275. (John Wiley and Sons).

Dyer, K.R. 1972: 'Sedimentation in estuaries', in Barnes, R.S.K. and Green, J. (eds), *The Estuarine Environment*, 10–32. (Applied Science Publications, London).

Dyer, K.R. 1979: 'Estuaries and estuarine sedimentation', in Dyer, K.R. (ed), *Estuarine Hydrography and Sedimentation*, 1–17 (Cambridge University Press).

Firth, C.R. and Haggart, B.A. 1989: 'Loch Lomond Stadial and Flandrian shorelines in the inner Moray Firth area, Scotland', *Journal of Quaternary Science* 4 (1) 37–50.

Fraser, J. 1699: 'Part of a letter wrote [sic] by Mr. James Fraser, Minister of Kirkhill, near Inverness, to J. Wallace at Edinburgh, concerning the Lake Ness', *Philosophical Transactions Volume XXI*, 231.

Hale, A.G.C. 1994: 'Carn Dubh intertidal crannog, Highland region', in *Discovery and Excavation in Scotland*, 33.

Hale, A.G.C. 1995: 'Redcastle intertidal crannog, Highland region', in *Discovery and Excavation in Scotland*, 44.

Haggart, B.A. 1982: 'Flandrian sea-level changes in the Moray Firth area', unpublished PhD thesis University of Durham.

Haggart, B.A. 1986: 'Relative sea-level change in the Beauly Firth, Scotland', *Boreas* 15, 191–207.

Haggart, B.A. 1987: 'Relative sea-level change in the Moray Firth area, Scotland', in Tooley, M.J. and Shennan, I. (eds) *Sea level changes*, IBG Special Publication 20, 67–108.

Haggart, B.A., Hale, A.G.C. and Firth, C.R. Forthcoming: 'A revised Holocene sea-level curve for the Beauly Firth area, North East Scotland'.

Hanson, W.S. 1985: 'Erskine crannog, Strathclyde region', in *Discovery and Excavation in Scotland*, 50.

Housley, R.A. 1988: 'The Environmental Context of the Glastonbury Lake Village'. *Somerset Levels Papers*, 14, 63–82.

Hazzeldine, Warren S., Piggott S., Clark, J.G.D., Burkitt, M.C., Goodwin, H. and Goodwin, M.E. 1936: 'Archaeology of the Submerged Land-Surface of the Essex Coast', *Proceedings of the Prehistoric Society* 9, 178–210.

Leech, T.A. 1994: 'Assessment of the Archaeology of the Essex Coastal Zone', *Essex County Council Planning Department, Archaeological Advisory Group Paper*.

Loowe Kooijmans, L.P. 1974: *The Rhine/Meuse Delta* (Oudheidkundige Medelingen Leiden 53/4).

Loowe Kooijmans, L.P. 1991: 'Wetland exploitation and upland relations of prehistoric communities in the Netherlands', in *East Anglian Archaeology*, 50.

Maclagan, C. 1875: *The Hillforts, Stone Circles and Other Structural remains of Ancient Scotland*. (Edinburgh).

Maltby, E. 1986: *Waterlogged Wealth* (Earthscan).

Morrison, I. 1985: *Landscape with Lake Dwellings: the crannogs of Scotland* (Edinburgh University Press).

Munro, R. 1884–85: 'Notice of an artificial mound or cairn situated 50 yards within the tidal area on the shore of the island of Eriska, Argyllshire', *Proceedings of the Society of Antiquaries of Scotland* 19, 192–202.

Munro, R. 1905: *Archaeology and False Antiquities* (Methuen, London).

RCAHMS. – Royal Commission on the Ancient and Historical Monuments of Scotland, National Monuments Record card index.

Reineck, H-E. and Singh, I.B. 1980: *Depositional Sedimentary Environments*. (Springer-Verlag).

Riddell, J.F. 1979: *Clyde Navigation* (Edinburgh).

Sands, R. 1995: 'The recording and archaeological potential of toolmarks on prehistoric worked wood-with special reference to Oakbank Crannog, Loch Tay, Scotland', (Unpublished PhD thesis University of Edinburgh).

Schmid, P. 1978: 'New archaeological results of settlement structures (Roman Iron Age) in the north-west-German Coastal area', in Cunliffe B. and Rowley T. (eds) *Lowland Iron Age Communities in Europe*, B.A.R. International Series 48, 123–146.

Sissons, J.B. 1976: *The Geomorphology of the British Isles: Scotland*. (Methuen, London).

Smith, D.E. & Dawson, A.G. (eds) 1983: *Shorelines and Isostasy*. (Academic Press)

Stevenson, R. 1966: 'Metalwork and some other objects in Scotland and their cultural affinities' in Rivet A.L. (ed) *The Iron Age in Northern Britain*, 17–44.

Waterbolk, H.T. 1981: 'Archaeology in the Netherlands: delta archaeology', in *World Archaeology* 13 (2), 240–54.

Wilkinson, T. J. and Murphy P. 1986: 'Archaeological Survey of an Intertidal Zone: the Submerged Landscape of the Essex Coast, England', in *Journal of Field Archaeology* 13 (2), 177–94.

8. Intertidal Archaeology in Strangford Lough

Brian Williams

The success of a number of interesting projects in the intertidal zone in various parts of Ireland and Britain clearly demonstrated the need for a greater amount of data to inform a protection programme in Northern Ireland. In response to this requirement, an intertidal archaeological survey of Strangford Lough was carried out over four months in 1995.

Strangford Lough

Strangford Lough is a large (150 km^2) marine inlet lying in the drumlin landscape of eastern County Down. Virtually land-locked, it is separated from the Irish Sea by the Ards Peninsula to the east and is bounded to the south by the Lecale Peninsula. It is connected to the open sea by the Strangford Narrows, an 8 km long channel with a minimum width of 0.5 km. The Lough is 30 km long from head to mouth and up to 8 km wide (OS 1/50,000 sheet 21; Hydrographic Chart 2156). The characteristic landform of the area is the drumlin: these are small, relatively low oval hills, few of which reach heights of more than 50 m. Within the Lough itself, drumlins appear as islands; in sheltered zones, especially in the west, they retain their form, but in more exposed locations they have been eroded. Where this has been most severe, little remains other than rocky reefs, known locally as 'pladdies'. The Lough is renowned for the richness of its flora and fauna and is particularly famed for its wildfowl. It is surrounded by agricultural land, much of it of good productive quality. Since their arrival in Ireland some 9000 years ago, people have been drawn to the mild and fertile shores of Strangford Lough and a rich heritage of sites of archaeological and cultural interest has been left imprinted on this landscape (Jope, 1966).

The survey

Before undertaking fieldwork several months were spent searching high quality 1/5000 scale colour aerial photographs of the intertidal zone, taken at the time of low water. These, combined with a study of cartographic and published sources, produced evidence for several hundred sites on the foreshore. Fieldwork was conducted by a private company, Management for Archaeology Underwater, from June until September 1995. The four archaeologists engaged in the survey were trained in boat-handling, radio operation and mud safety. Close liaison was maintained with Belfast Coastguard at all times. Considerable progress was made in a very detailed search of the Lough encountering a range of features that fall into the broad groups of communications, farming and fishing.

Communications

Boats

The remains of three large sailing ships and a smaller vessel were found. The schooner *Fanny Crossley* which was abandoned and largely broken up at Ringneill Quay in 1939 survived only as a few fragments. Another vessel of similar proportions survived only as a stern fragment close to an old lead mine at Castleward Bay. Better preserved was the coal schooner *Hilda Parnell* which caught fire and was subsequently abandoned at Quoile Quay in 1922 (Gifford 1987, 28–31; Colmer 1988, 45). The building of a tidal flood-control barrage in 1957 has left the vessel on dry land with a well-preserved stem and sternpost, keel and floors. A smaller vessel, almost certainly not of great age, lies in Castleward Bay with vertical frames protruding from the mud defining a double-ended boat. The remains of the brig *Nimble* and several other vessels of 19th and 20th-century date lie on the sea-bed at Ballyhenry Bay where there was a breakers yard.

Landing stages

A wide variety of slipways, piers and jetties was encountered. The simplest form was the cleared slipway which was created by clearing boulders off a rocky beach to create a safe approach for small boats. Some could be dated by their association with old buildings but many were unassociated and difficult to date. Boulder-built farm quays were commonly found and according to local tradition were used until relatively recently for the transport of animals, potatoes or grain and other farming activities. Causeways linking islands to the mainland were also noted. At Ringhaddy the stone footings of a jetty and an adjacent cleared slipway were found in association with a late medieval castle. Pottery and musket balls were found in deep water off the end of the jetty. A similar arrangement of jetty and cleared slipway was found at the 16th century Mahee Castle. A drystone built pier, known as The Seneschal's Quay, was found adjacent to the Anglo-Norman motte and medieval tower house at Ardkeen, the headquarters of the Savage family, Seneschals of Ulster. Large, well-built stone quays were recorded at Strangford, Castleward, Audley's Castle and Killyleagh and while they are shown on early maps the date of their original construction is not known.

Harbour

The early monastic site of Nendrum on Mahee Island is known to have had facilities for visiting vessels (Reeves 1847). Stone structures close to the monastery on the shore in Ballydorn Sound are thought to constitute an early harbour and the discovery of 13th century green-glazed pottery indicate its possible use into the medieval period.

Farming

The modern field system in Ireland was laid out in the 18th and early 19th centuries. Field boundaries extend in many instances down to low water as a mark of ownership and more practically to prevent animals straying. Examples were recorded where the field boundary extension did not have a corresponding boundary on land and no record of an enclosure on any of the Ordnance Survey maps. In all probability the remains in the intertidal zone reflect earlier field boundaries long since swept away elsewhere in land reorganization.

Farm quays were simple stone structures for the loading and unloading of farm produce and materials and are remembered in local tradition as having had this function. On Dunsey Island a long abandoned sheep dip was found located close to a farm quay. These simple structures were all recorded in this trial season of fieldwork but as our understanding of the structures of the intertidal zone increases relatively modern structures such as these will receive less detailed attention.

The harvesting and processing of seaweed was an important activity for Irish coastal communities. Historically, brown seaweed (wrack and oarweed) was gathered by those with rights to do so to be used as an organic fertilizer, or to be burned to provide 'kelp', rich in salts and used in glass making. Seaweed grows well on the stony shores of Strangford Lough and walls were encountered in these weed-rich areas unassociated with the adjacent fields which may represent wrack ownership boundaries. Kelp kilns were recorded in a number of cases and a group on Chapel Island is of particular interest. These survive as boulder-built round 'cairns'. On muddy shores where seaweed is less common, boulders were laid out in wrack grids to provide a root attachment for the plants. At Greyabbey Bay there is evidence that a stone fishtrap was dismantled and reused as a wrack grid. Documentary sources for the 18th and 19th centuries indicate that kelp production was a major part of the economy of the region (Buchanan 1958).

Fishing

Fishing from boats was a major activity in the past and Strangford Lough was considered the best fishery on the east coast of Ireland in the 18th century (Harris 1744). Fishing fleets were maintained at Kircubbin, Portaferry and Strangford but there is little evidence for this activity surviving in the inter-tidal zone.

Fish traps

A variety of types of fish traps have been recorded in the first season of fieldwork. While it is not possible to ascertain the date of the stone-built traps, there is an association with ecclesiastical sites. On the foreshore on the north side of Mahee Island beside Nendrum monastery is a simple stone-built fish trap. A 'V'– shaped natural bay is formed into a triangular-shaped trap by the addition of a straight wall. The early monastic site on Dunsey Island, associated with a 6th century saint, now has no visible remains but it is thought to lie on the south end of the island. Between the southern shore of Dunsey Island and the nearby northern shore of Island More two curving arms of a stone-built trap enclose an area almost circular in shape. Memories of the use of fish traps survived into the late seventeenth century and were documented by William Montgomery in his Description of Ardes Barony written in 1683: *'the same waters or brooks (as turned the horizontal mills, called Danish or ladle mills) being enclosed in Walls of loose Stones on the strand of the Lough Coyn in little bays made wares or fish yards, which walls did suffer the tides to come insensibly through them till four hours' flood which (for the last two hours) flowed over the wall; then did the sea run strong, and the fishes followed the stream, and finding food brought down thithe by the fresh water brook, and yet the bay was calme; the fish remained there til the first ebb left the wall to appear, and then shuch through, as it came in insensibly, so that the fish not getting back through the wall, were taken; but since fish days were neglected, those yards decayd'* (Hill 1869).

The main evidence for fish traps was found in Greyabbey Bay on the eastern shore of Strangford Lough. The area is best known for its late 12th century Cistercian abbey but there is also a well-preserved rath, a defended farmstead of the Early Christian period, close to the shore of the bay. Submerged ancient tree stumps in the intertidal zone of the bay indicate that this was dry land in the early years of human settlement. Radiocarbon dates demonstrate that the trees were growing in the Mesolithic period: GrN-21909 gave a result of 7940 BP±30 (6996 cal BC-6958 cal BC) and GrN-21911 the earlier date of 8360 BP±30 (7482 cal BC-7458 cal BC). (All calibrated dates are quoted at 68.3% (1 sigma) confidence levels). Careful searching of the tidal channels in the bay found evidence of three wooden fish traps. All three were V-shaped in construction, each built across small tidal channels. A small trap with arms some 36m in length was located at the south-west edge of the bay at the Ragheries in Ballyurnanellan townland. A radiocarbon sample from one of its component stakes provided a date of 880 BP±20 (1167 cal AD-1211 cal AD). A large V-shaped wooden trap in Bootown townland with arms some 300m long was found to have wattle interwoven at the base of its oak stakes. A radiocarbon date for one of the stakes provided a date of 900 BP±20 (1053 cal AD-1083 cal AD). A similar V-shaped trap stratified below a stone fish trap near South Island in Ballyurnanellan townland showed signs of having been maintained and refurbished over a period of time. Two radiocarbon samples were taken from different parts of the trap to try and establish if the trap had sustained a long period of use. Sample GrN-21906 provided a date of 940 BP±20 (1037 cal AD-1054 cal AD) while sample GrN-21907 gave a date of 760 BP±15 (1275 cal AD-1285 cal AD). These results indicate that the fishtrap was indeed used for a period of some 230 years, from the latter years of the Early Christian period into the medieval period.

Stone fish traps were located around the bay and by their large size and careful positioning must have provided a formidable obstacle to any fish if they were all in use at the same time! While it is not possible to date the traps without excavation, mention has already been made of the stratigraphical relationship where a stone trap overlies a wooden example near South Island. Four of the stone traps are V-shaped in form, while a fifth is crescent-shaped. Three are set close to the modern centre of tidal channels and the fact that they are positioned off-centre may indicate that the channels have moved since the traps were constructed. The remains of a linear structure close to the east shore of South Island seems to represent a dismantled trap from which the stones have been reused in laying out wrack grids. Evidence from aerial photographs indicates that there are other fish traps in the area, particularly to the north of Greyabbey Bay, but these await recording in a further field season. (This area was subsequently surveyed in 1996 with very interesting results).

Shellfish must have contributed to the diet of people of all periods around Strangford Lough. A cockle bed on Dunsey Island was found to have Mesolithic flint blades lying in it and presumably this means that the (still living) shellfish community has been there for some 8,000 years. Close to South Island in Greyabbey Bay just below Low Water Springs, in a position that never quite dries out, an oyster midden was found together with flint flakes and a fragment of deer antler. There are surprisingly few shell middens recorded in the Northern Ireland Sites and Monuments Record and this current project did not add greatly to the number. A large rectangular stone structure in the inter-tidal zone in Castleward Bay close to the 18th century Castleward Estate has been interpreted as an oyster tank.

A preliminary season has indicated that there is considerable potential for archaeological survey in the intertidal zone in Strangford Lough and as archaeologists become more experienced at working in this environment much more evidence may be discovered.

References

Buchanan, R.H. 1958: *The Barony of Lecale, County Down. A Study of Regional Personality*. (Unpublished Ph thesis, The Queen's University of Belfast).

Colmer, A.W.K. 1988: "The Hilda Parnell" or "The Hilda" over 30 years ago', *Lecale Miscellany*, 6, 45.

Harris, W. 1744: *The Antient and Present State of the County of Down*, (Dublin).

Hill, G. (ed) 1869: *The Montgomery Manuscripts (1603–1706)*, (Belfast).

Gifford, D. 1987: 'The Hilda Parnell', *Lecale Miscellany*, 5, 28–31.

Jope, E.M. (ed) 1966: *An Archaeological Survey of County Down, HMSO*, (Belfast).

Reeves, W. 1847: *Ecclesiastical Antiquities of Down, Connor and Dromore*, (Dublin).

9. Exploitation and Modification: Changing Patterns in the use of Coastal Resources in Southern Britain during the Roman and Medieval periods

Stephen Rippon

Coastal wetlands offer a wide range of natural resources including rich sasonal grazing and the opportunity for salt production.The decision to embank and drain these marshes is an important one, because while it increases their agricultural productivity, it leads to the loss of these valuable natural resources.This paper provids a brief comparative summary of how various areas of marshland around southern and eastern Britain were exploited during the Roman and Medieval periods which will be published more fully elsewhere (Rippon forthcoming).During the Roman period reclamation was restricted to the Severn Estuary, which may be part of a more general trend towards increased investment and surplus agricultural wealth in the region which is also reflected in the abundance of 3rd and 4th century villas.The medieval period saw more widespread reclamation and the intensive use of these marshes for mixed and arable-based agriculture.One exception was the Essex Marshes, where a highly fragmented pattern of landholding, and proximity to London, which provided a major market for fresh dairy produce, meant that many of the marshes saw relatively little investment in embanking and drainage: the profits from sheep farming outweighed the benefits, costs and risks of reclaiming.

Introduction

This is a study in the implications of reclamation. The construction of sea walls to prevent the tidal inundation of coastal saltmarshes, and the digging of a complex drainage system to remove freshwater run-off, represents a major transformation of the landscape. Coastal wetlands offer a wide range of resources – fish, wildfowl, seasonal grazing, the opportunity for salt production, reeds for thatch, and withies for hurdles, fences and building. However, these rich natural resources are lost following drainage as mankind changes from being a landscape exploiter, to a landscape modifier. The costs of reclamation were considerable: the labour and materials used in constructing the flood defence/drainage system, and the loss of the rich natural resources described above. The threat of flooding could also never be removed. However, the benefits of reclamation were a longer growing and grazing season, less disruption due to flooding, and the possibility of permanent settlement (though until the advent of under-drainage it was difficult to keep livestock in the fields over winter due to the waterlogged ground conditions). Overall, reclamation was a high cost, high risk but high return undertaking.

The current perception of an extensive coastal saltmarsh is of an under-developed tract of land which would be better reclaimed and put to some use (eg Williams 1990). This paper will show that in the past such a perspective has not always been taken, and though suitable technology existed, and there were great pressures to create new agricultural land, coastal wetlands were not always reclaimed.

The Severn Estuary: a story dominated by reclamation

This paper has been born out of the *Gwent Levels Historic Landscape Study* funded by Cadw and the Countryside Council for Wales (Rippon 1996a), and research into the Severn Estuary wetlands generally funded by the British Academy (Rippon 1997). Both projects examined the evolution of these low-lying coastal landscapes over the past 2,000 years. The story was one dominated by reclamation, which started on the Welsh side of the Severn Estuary in the early Roman period, and continued on the English side of the Estuary during the late Roman period. Just one area of coastal alluvium around the Severn Estuary appears to have been left as a saltmarsh during the Roman period: the Brue Valley in central Somerset (Rippon 1997). Why should this have been?

The waters of the Severn are very muddy and upstream

Figure 9.1 The long narrow fields that characterise the carefully planned landscape in central Wentlooge (reproduced by kind permission of Michael Fulford).

water salinity levels do decline, but this is probably not the whole story. The Gwent Levels (Wentlooge and Caldicot) appear to have been reclaimed by the legionary authorities based at Caerleon, presumably to provide pasture and meadow to support livestock, including horses (Fulford *et al* 1994). The military establishment would also have required salt, but this could not have been obtained from the nearby Gwent Levels since that area had been reclaimed: an alternative supply was required which appears to have lain on the opposite side of the Estuary. Work by John Allen and Michael Fulford on the production and distribution of BB1 pottery from Dorset, has suggested that shipments were brought from Ilchester to a port on the river Parrett at Crandon Bridge near Bridgwater (Allen and Fulford 1996). The pottery was then carried across the Severn to the military establishment in South East Wales. It may not be a coincidence that the only area of the Severn Estuary Levels that was devoted to salt production (the Brue Valley) lay next to Crandon Bridge and this shipment route.

There is no evidence to suggest whether salt production was under military control, as was the case initially with lead mining nearby on the Mendips (Todd 1993; Whittick 1982). However, it does appear that reclamation of the remaining parts of the Somerset Levels was not a military operation. The Roman landscape on the Wentlooge Level (near Cardiff) was carefully planned on a large scale, with blocks of long narrow fields (Fig. 9.1) between parallel boundaries up to 5 km long (eg Blackwater, Rhosog Fawr/ Sealand, and Broadstreet/Hawse Reens: Fig. 9.2). This is in sharp contrast to the much smaller-scale and more irregular layout of Roman field systems on the North Somerset Levels such as Kenn Moor (Fig. 9.3) and Puxton near Weston-super-Mare (Fig. 9.4) (Rippon 1994; 1995; 1996b; 1997). Whilst the dangers of reading too much into morphology alone must be recognised, it does appear as if a very different approach was taken to reclamation on the two sides of the Severn Estuary. The Gwent Levels saw a highly co-ordinated strategy – a 'grand design' – in contrast to the more piecemeal approach in Somerset. It is tempting to postulate that the Somerset Levels were reclaimed by the numerous villa-estate owners that lived either on the Levels (at Lakehouse Farm and Wemberham) or around the fen-edge.

Most of the Severn Estuary Levels were affected by an episode of post-Roman flooding which in many areas buried the Roman landscape under *c.* 0.7 m of alluvium. In other places the Roman drainage systems were simply abandoned and now only survive as earthworks. Only in the central part of the Wentlooge Level did the Roman drainage system survive to be incorporated into the medieval landscape.

In Somerset recolonization was well underway by the 11th century, illustrated by the numerous settlements, abundant ploughteams and relatively high value recorded in Domesday. Indeed, during the medieval period, the Somerset Levels became some of the most highly valued agricultural lands in the region. The Saxon sea walls protected a huge area that was only gradually enclosed and drained as demand for land increased; this piecemeal process, like that of woodland assarting, led to an irregular landscape with little overall planning (Fig. 9.5). Despite

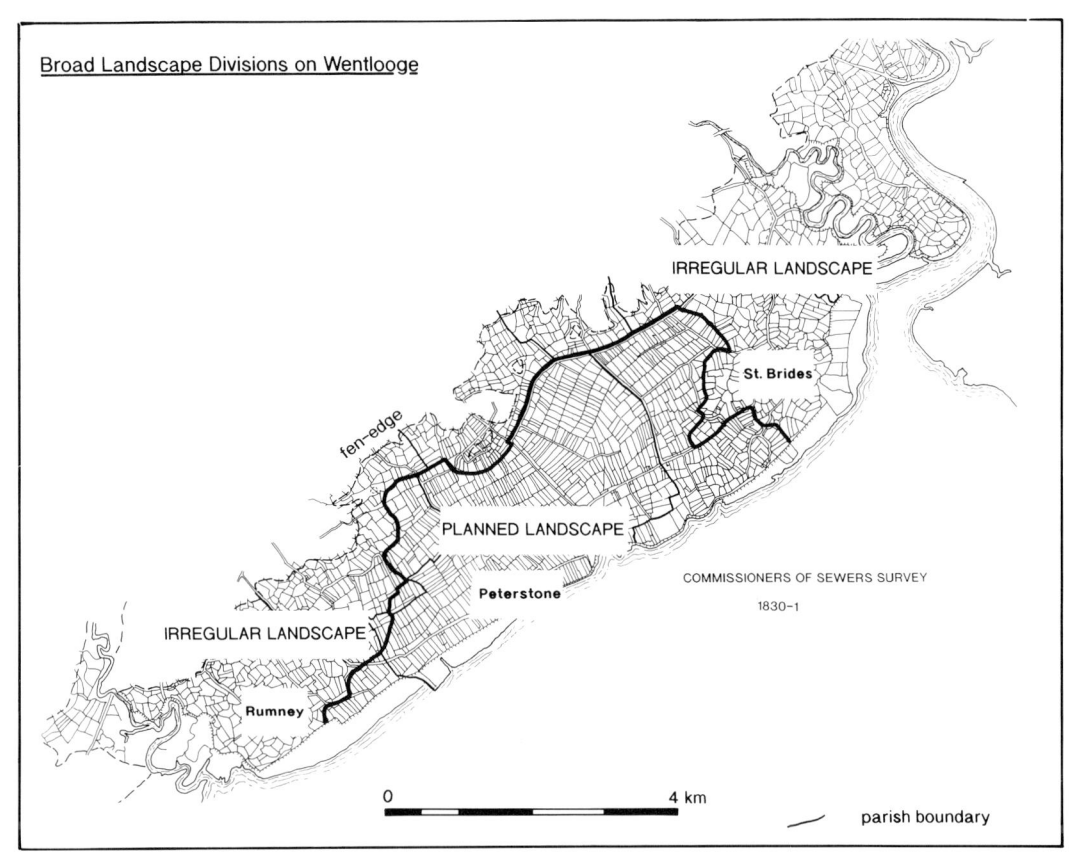

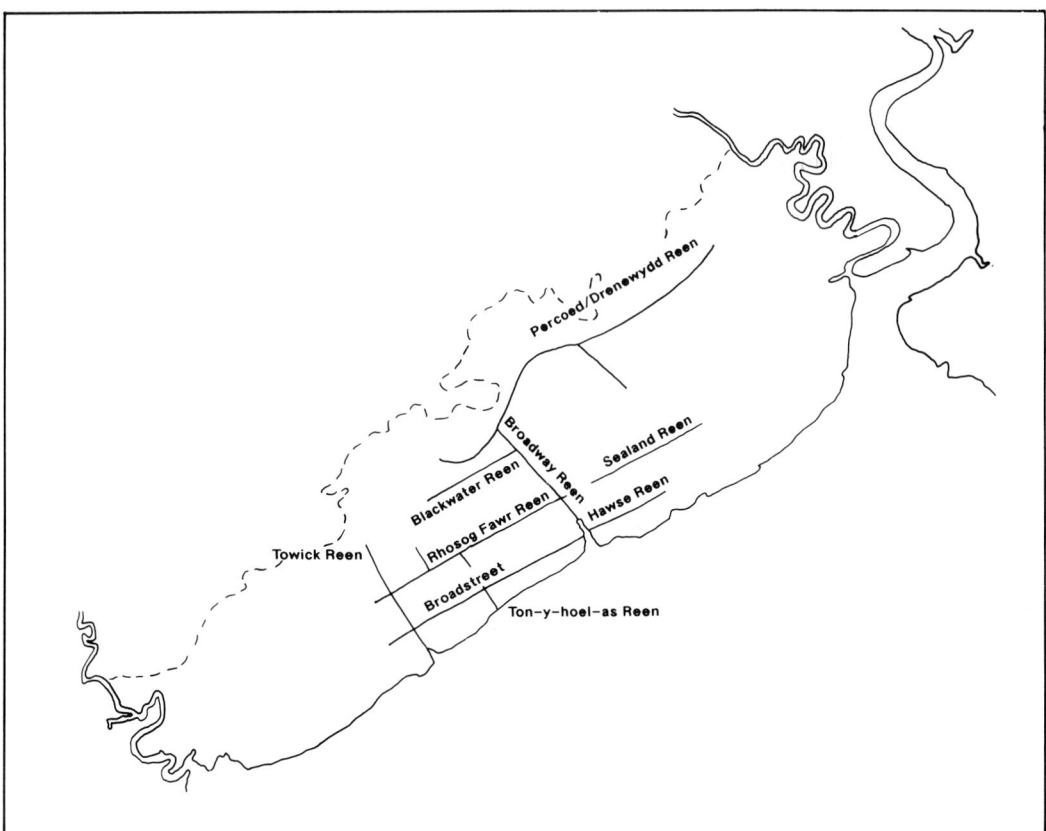

Figure 9.2 A characterisation of the 19th century field boundary pattern on the Wentlooge Level (top) and major elements of the Roman landscape (bottom). The carefully planned Roman landscape, comprising blocks of long narrow fields between parallel boundaries up to 5 km long, only survives in the central part of the Wentlooge Level (around Peterstone). To the south west (around Rumney) and north east (around St Brides), the more irregular landscape dates to the medieval period (see Figure 9.5 for a similar type of landscape).

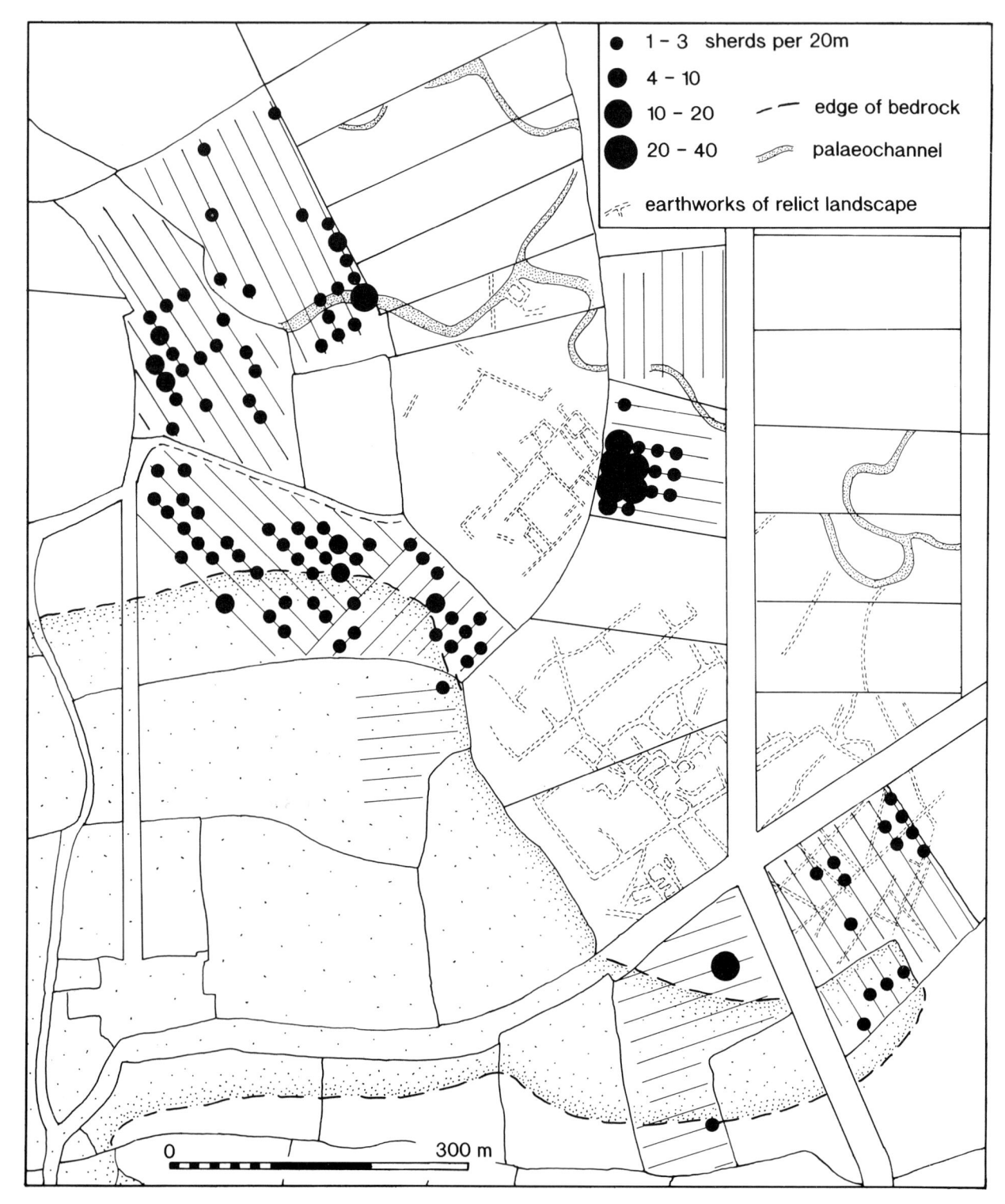

Figure 9.3 The Roman landscape at Kenn Moor, on the North Somerset Levels. This system of small paddocks and fields possess a general coherence, but lack the rigid planning seen on Wentlooge. Fieldwalking has enabled a focus of occupation to be identified (at the centre), with relatively intense manuring evident elsewhere (see Rippon 1995; 1997).

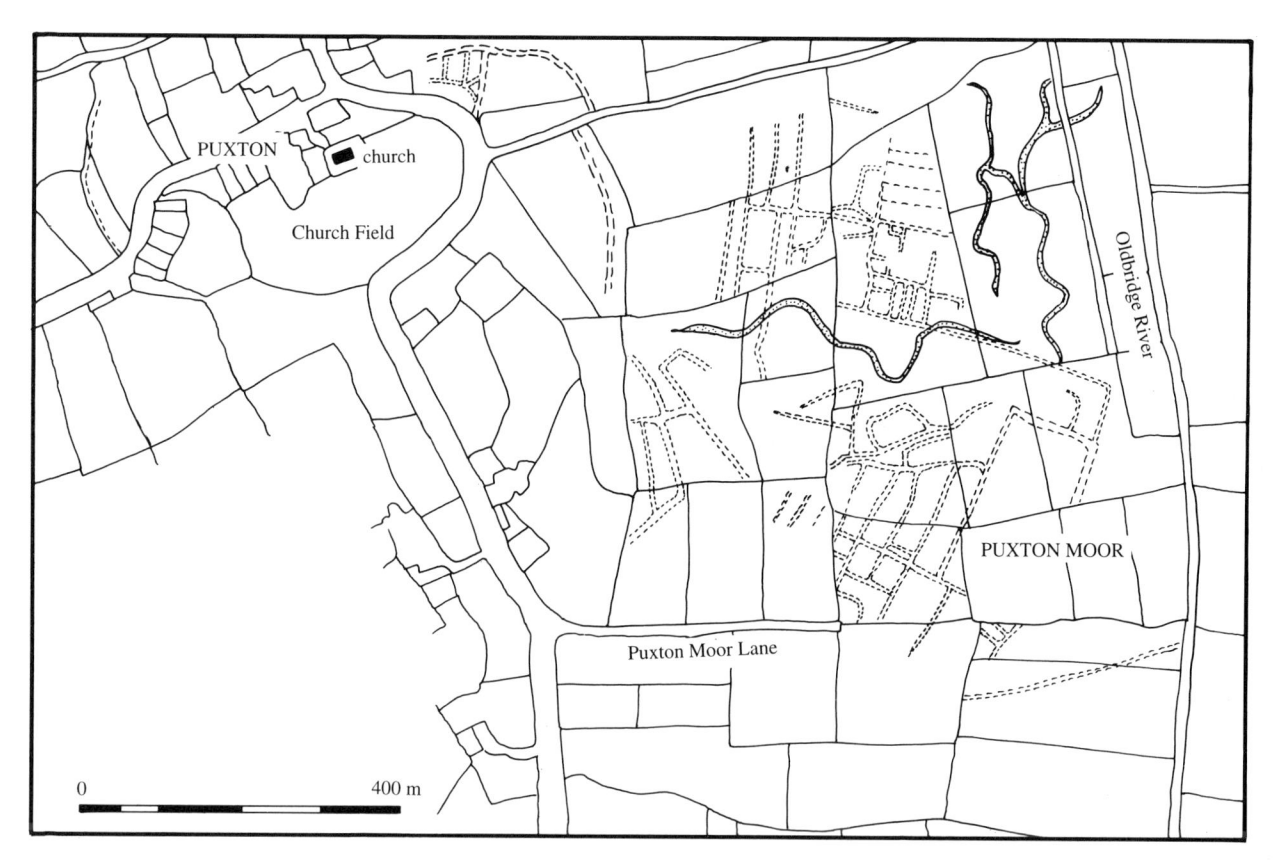

Figure 9.4 The Roman landscape at Puxton, on the North Somerset Levels (shown with dashed lines). As with Kenn Moor, the system of small paddocks and fields possess a general coherence, but lack the rigid planning seen on Wentlooge (see Rippon 1996b).

periods of climatic and population decline, leading to sea walls being moved back in the late medieval period, most of the Levels remained as agricultural lands until the present day. Being close to a series of towns and ports, notably Bristol, demand for the agricultural produce of the Levels was always high, and there is less evidence for settlement desertion than there is on the surrounding uplands. The lowest-lying areas were finally enclosed and drained in the 19th century, completing the task of reclamation begun around 1,000 years earlier.

Overall, the same basic landscape history has been uncovered on each of the Severn Estuary Levels: an Iron Age saltmarsh, Roman reclamation, a brief period of post-Roman abandonment, recolonization in the early medieval period, and continued expansion of the enclosed and drained lands thereafter with just a minor set-back in the late medieval period. This then is the view from South West Britain, dominated by reclamation and the intensive use of coastal wetlands for agriculture.

The Roman exploitation of coastal wetlands elsewhere in Britain

If we now compare the Roman attitude towards wetland exploitation around the Severn Estuary with the rest of Britain, a varied picture emerges. On the coastal marshes of southern England, such as around Poole Harbour (Farrar 1975), Chichester Harbour (Bradley 1975) and Romney Marsh (Cunliffe 1988; Reeves 1995), salt production was widespread during the late Iron Age and early Roman periods.

There is a similar picture in North Kent and Essex, where much of the coast is lined with numerous so-called 'red hills', comprising the structures concerned with procuring salt through boiling sea water, and the associated mounds of burnt clay debris (Evans 1953; Fawn *et al* 1990; Miles 1975; Buckley, this volume). Such sites occur with a remarkable frequency, suggesting that most if not all of the Thameside Marshes were open to tidal waters until at least the 3rd century, when the industry disappears. However, even during the late Roman period, there is little evidence for reclamation of the coastal alluvium.

The extensive Roman drainage systems of Fenland are well known, and this landscape certainly saw considerable investment in the form of canals, ditched drainage systems and the probable fen-edge catchwater known as the Car Dyke (Hall and Coles 1994, 105–21; Hallam 1970; Simmons 1979). However, the field systems in Fenland lack the overall coherence of those on Wentlooge (Figs. 9.1–9.2), and a closer parallel may be the more piecemeal landscapes on the North Somerset Levels (Figs. 9.3 and 9.4; cf Hallam 1970, maps A–J). Indeed, palaeoenviron-

Figure 9.5 The Saxon/medieval landscape at Kingston Seymour, North Somerset Levels. The irregular pattern of fields, created through piecemeal enclosure and drainage is very different to the carefully planned Roman landscape on Wentlooge.

mental research on a number of Roman sites in Fenland has established that saltmarsh conditions were present, and that crops, notably barley, were being grown in such an environment (eg Murphy 1994, 27–8). The distribution of salt production sites, which occur many miles inland from what must have been the contemporary coastline (Hall and Coles 1994, 115–17), supports the hypothesis that there cannot have been a Roman sea wall around the Wash. The lack of villas on Fenland may also be explained by this absence of flood defences, rather than the presence of an imperial estate as has been suggested in the past: the landscape was sufficiently flood-free for its occupation by farmsteads, but was too risky for investment in villas. Thus, Fenland in Roman times was very different to the Severn Estuary Levels.

From this rapid review, it should be clear that there were marked differences in the Roman approach to wetland exploitation and management in Britain. During the first and second centuries, the south and east coasts saw extensive salt production, developing from an industry that was established during the late Iron Age. The Severn Estuary, in contrast, has very little evidence for pre-Roman salt production: just two late Iron Age salterns have been recorded in the Somerset Levels (Leech 1977), though Bronze Age briquetage has been found on a settlement in the Brean Down sandcliff (Bell 1990). It was during the early Roman period that the salt industry took off in the Brue Valley (close to the port at Crandon Bridge) at the same time as the Gwent Levels were reclaimed by the military authorities.

During the 3rd century, the salt industry declined in southern and eastern England, though there was a major expansion of salt production in Somerset at the same time. The date when most of the Somerset wetlands were reclaimed is not entirely clear at present, though the 3rd century was certainly a period of marked settlement expansion with villa construction on and around the Levels (Rippon 1994; 1995; 1997). This later Roman investment in the Levels may form part of a wider trend in the Romano-British countryside. The late Roman period is recognised as one of innovation and investment, for example in the construction of villas, most notably in central-southern and south-west Britain (Jones 1989; Millett 1990, 195; Rippon 1997). It may be in the context of this period of agricultural wealth that many of the Severn wetlands were reclaimed.

Patterns of Medieval Reclamation

During the Middle Ages there were also marked regional variations as to how coastal resources were exploited within southern Britain. It was not just in the South West, around the Severn Estuary, that coastal wetlands were extensively reclaimed and cultivated by the 11th century: the same is seen in Romney Marsh (Brooks 1988; Gardiner 1988; Tatton-Brown 1988) and Fenland (Darby 1940; Hallam 1954; 1965). By contrast the Pevensey Levels do not appear to have been reclaimed until after Domesday, and around the Thames Estuary large areas of coastal wetland were left as tidal saltmarshes, or at least only saw rudimentary flood protection but no large-scale arable cultivation, until at least the late medieval period (Cracknell 1959; Smith 1939; 1943, 184–8; Smith 1970).

The extent of these largely unimproved sheep pastures in the 11th century is demonstrated in both Essex and

Kent by the extensive flocks of sheep recorded in Domesday (Darby 1977, 149–58). By the early 14th century large areas of former saltmarsh in both areas had been protected by sea walls but were still largely used for grazing sheep and cattle (Evans 1953, 120–38; Smith 1943, 184–8; Ward 1987). Other marshes do not appear to have been embanked at all. For example, at Langenhoe in Essex 14th century bailiffs' accounts describe expenditure on bridges, hurdles and raised causeways that were constructed on the saltmarshes to allow sheep to escape at times of exceptionally high tide (Smith 1970, 25). There is little evidence for embankment on Canvey Island before the 15th century (Cracknell 1959) or the neighbouring Hadleigh Marshes until at least the late 16th century (Rippon 1999).

Winter storms meant that such marshes could only have been of use during the summer. It seems curious that even around 1300, when population pressure was at its greatest, so many of the marshes around the Thames Estuary were left as relatively unimproved pasture. The technology to embank and drain these areas certainly existed, illustrated by the work undertaken in the Fenland, Romney Marsh and Somerset (Darby 1940; Rippon 1997; Smith 1939; 1943, 166–88; Williams 1970). Other factors must have been at work. The ability to reclaim the Essex Marshes may have been impaired by the fragmented pattern of landholding. There was a strong monastic interest in southern Essex, with many ecclesiastical estates having parcels of the Thameside Marshes (Fowler 1907; Harvey 1977; Ward 1987, 97–108). Large areas were also in lay hands, such as Sweyn's 11th century barony in South Essex which included extensive areas of coastal marsh. However, most of the marshes were divided into numerous small parcels of land that would have been difficult to drain on their own. By the late 12th century an active land market had developed, with lay and ecclesiastical landlords alike actively acquiring areas of marshland (Harvey 1977, 193, 418; Place 1992, 9; Ward 1987, 98). For example, in 1258/63 Westminster Abbey was granted a marsh called 'Dybershope' on Canvey Island, and by 1315 they had acquired marshes called 'Monkswyk' and 'le Shore' (*WD*, f.605, f.609, f.616). In 1364/5 a further 40 acres of marsh called 'Bartlescote' was purchased (*CPR* 1391–6, 133). It appears from examples such as these that the Island was already divided into relatively small parcels, probably by natural creeks, and that no one landowner was able to control, and so improve, large tracts of land.

One cause of this fragmented pattern of landholding was the tradition of intercommoning by which numerous local communities, many several miles inland, had rights of pasture on the Thameside Marshes. Once the marshes were enclosed, the various parishes whose occupants formerly had rights of common pasture each received a parcel of land. The island of Foulness for example was shared between the parishes of Sutton, Rochford, Shopland, Little Stambridge and Little Wakering (Cracknell 1959, 10), while the three islands of Canvey, Foulness and Wallasea were divided between a total of 18 parishes (Cracknell 1959, 10; Round 1903, 369; Smith 1970, 9).

In the same way, areas of the Thameside marshes became part of medieval manors whose lands were scatted over a wide area, with the coastal lands providing a specialised environment which formed part of the integrated agricultural economy. For example, in 1360/1 the bailiff of Writtle manor (in the centre of Essex) accounted for 110 year-old lambs and 8 'multoni' (male sheep kept for wool, meat and skins) sent to Foulness Island for the summer (Smith 1970, 11). This is part of the complex pattern of fragmented manors in Essex which is also reflected in the ownership of woodland enclaves by distant manors (Rackham 1986; Rippon 1999).

Therefore, the fragmented pattern of landholding may have impaired a landlord's capacity to reclaim land. The construction of a sea wall, and its subsequent maintenance, was an expensive business and became particularly uneconomical for small parcels of marsh where the length of embankment per acre reclaimed was high. Thus, the desire to reclaim the marshes may not have been strong due to the cost. However, another factor was the profits that landlords were able to gain from the marshes without investing large sums in reclamation. A critical factor was clearly the role of London which provided a huge market for agricultural goods, and in particular fresh dairy produce (Thirsk 1967, 49). Landowners in Essex appear to have exploited their geographical location and developed a strong coastal economy. For example, in 1575, a survey was carried out of *'all the Ports, Creeks and Landing Places in England and Wales'*. Essex was recorded as having 135, compared to 29 in Surrey, 18 in Kent, 17 in Suffolk and 12 in Norfolk (Darby *et al* 1979, 257–8). While this partly reflects the heavily indented coastline of Essex, it must to a great extent reflect the emphasis that was placed upon maritime trade with London which is documented from at least the 13th century (Ward 1987, 105). There was also cross-Estuary trade between Essex and Kent (Ward 1987, 104), while agricultural goods (including dairy produce) were even shipped directly from Thameside manors, such as Barking and Fobbing, to the continent. For example, in 1367 John Burgeys of Fobbing obtained a royal licence to ship sixty weys of cheese from Fobbing to Flanders (Ward 1987, 104).

Another reason why so many of the Thameside Marshes may have remained unreclaimed is the demand for salt. Though Roman salterns have received considerable attention (de Brisay and Evans 1975; Fawn *et al* 1990), medieval coastal salt production around the Thames Estuary has seen relatively little research. Domesday records 46 salt pans on the Essex coast, largely in the north east of the county. It is difficult to believe that there were no 11th century salterns on the Thameside marshes, and one suspects that we are witnessing one of the many inconsistencies of the Domesday survey (Darby 1977, 265). In fact, excavations, earthworks and documentary references show that all around the Essex coast salt production continued into the post medieval period (Barford 1988; Christy 1907). This is in contrast to the Severn Estuary where there is almost no evidence for salt production. This is partly accounted for by the widespread reclamation, but also the easy access to salt from inland sources in the West Midlands (Darby 1977, 261–3; Morris 1985). Documents attest to the distribution of Midlands salt via the road network ('saltways': Darby 1977, 263; Morris 1985, 345), though the river system, notably the Severn, was also presumably used.

There are many points of contrast between the Thames and Severnside Marshes during the medieval period. Around the Severn reclamation started well before the Norman Conquest, whereas in Essex some marshes remained unreclaimed until the 17th century. A critical factor was the role of London in providing a major market for dairy produce. The Thameside economy during the medieval period appears to have been geared towards specialised production for the market, in contrast to Somerset where strongly arable-based mixed farming dominated many areas. Crop yields were high and this was presumably the most profitable way to use a marshland landscape in this particular region.

The role of monastic houses appears to have been most significant when they were in sole control of an area. For example, the great Cistercian houses are well known for improving their estates through drainage from the mid 12th century (Donkin 1958), and the documentary record gives the impression that monasteries were at the forefront of reclamation during the Saxon and medieval periods (eg Brooks 1988; Rippon 1997; Williams 1970; 1982). In Somerset and Romney Marsh, many of the ecclesiastical estates represented extensive tracts of land transferred *en bloc* from royal hands to the church as early as the 7th century (Brooks 1988; Rippon 1997). By contrast in Essex and northern Kent the ecclesiastical estates tended to be smaller and more fragmented, and despite active policies of acquisition during the 12th and 13th centuries, they never came to dominate the Thameside marshes in the same way. Thus, for a variety of reasons including fragmented landownership, proximity to markets, and the highly valued natural resources, the seemingly logical decision to reclaim wetlands was not taken.

Conclusions

The preceding discussion has shown how coastal wetlands offer a wide range of resource procurement strategies, and though the modern perspective very much favours reclamation and arable-based agriculture there are alternatives. Around the Severn an emphasis upon reclamation is seen ever since the Roman period, though even then careful decisions were made to reserve one area (the Brue Valley) for its natural resources, notably salt. Elsewhere in Britain, the major investment of resources represented by reclamation does not appear to have occurred until at least the Saxon period. There were, however, exceptions, most notably around the Thames Estuary where extensive areas of marshland were left unreclaimed or little improved until the end of the medieval period. Here, the fragmentary pattern of landholding appears to have been a hindrance to improvement, while the demand for dairy produce on the part of London meant that there was little incentive to reclaim the marshes. Therefore, both in the Roman and medieval periods, careful and conscious decisions had been about how to exploit coastal resources, and in certain instances, the wealth of natural resources were more highly valued than the benefits of reclamation.

Acknowledgements
Aspects of this research have been generously funded by the Britsh Academy, Cadw: Welsh Historic Monuments, and the Countryside Council for Wales. I would like to thank all those individuals and organisations around Britain who have helped with this work, and in particular Michael Fulford who started it all off.

Abbreviations
CPR: Calendar of Patent Rolls.
WD: Westminster Domesday (Westminster Abbey Muniments Room)

References

Allen, J.R.L. and Fulford, M.G. 1996: The Distribution of South-East Dorset Black Burnished Category I Pottery in South-West Britain, *Britannia* XXVII, 223–281.
Bailey, M. 1989: *A marginal economy?: East Anglian Breckland in the later Middle Ages.* (Cambridge University Press).
Barford, P.M. 1988: After the Red Hills: Salt Making in Late Roman, Saxon and Medieval Essex, *Colchester Archaeological Group Annual Bulletin* 31, 3–8.
Bell, M. 1990: *Brean Down: Excavations 1983–87.* English Heritage Archaeological Report 15.
Bradley, R. 1975: Salt and settlement in the Hampshire Sussex Borderland, in de Brisay and Evans (eds) 1975, 20–25.
De Brisay, K. and Evans, K. 1975: *Salt: the study of an ancient industry.* (Colchester Archaeological Group).
Brooks, N. 1988: Romney Marsh in the Early Middle Ages, in Eddison and Green (eds) 1988, 90–104.
Christy, M. 1907: Salt Making, *Victoria County History of Essex* volume II, 445.
Cracknell, B.E. 1959: *Canvey Island: The History of a Marshland Community.* Leicester Department of English Local History Occasional Papers 12.
Cunliffe, B. 1988: Romney Marsh in the Roman Period, in Eddison and Green (eds) 1988, 83–7.
Darby, H.C. 1940: *Medieval Fenland.* (Cambridge University) Press.

Darby, H.C. 1977: *Domesday England*. (Cambridge University Press).

Darby, H.C., Glasscock, R.E., Sheail, J. and Versey, G.R. 1979: The changing geographical distribution of wealth in England: 1086–1334–1525, *Journal of Historical Geography*, 5.iii, 247–62.

Donkin, R.A. 1958: The Marshland Holdings of the English Cistercians Before c.1350, *Citeaux in de Nederlanden* IX, 262–75.

Eddison, J. and Green, C. 1988: *Romney Marsh: Evolution, Occupation, Reclamation*. Oxford University Committee for Archaeology monograph 24.

Evans, J.H. 1953: Archaeological Horizons in the North Kent Marshes, *Archaeologia Cantiana* LXVI, 103–46.

Farrar, R.A.H. 1975: Prehistoric and Roman saltworks in Dorset, in de Brisay and Evans (eds) 1975, 14–20.

Fawn, A.J., Davies, G.M.R., Evans, K.A. and McMaster, I. 1990: *The Red Hills of Essex: Salt Making in Antiquity*. (Colchester Archaeological Group).

Fowler, R.C. 1907: Religious Houses, *Victoria County History of Essex* volume II, 84–203.

Fulford, M.G., Allen, J.R.L. and Rippon, S.J. 1994: The Settlement and Drainage of the Wentlooge Level, Gwent: Excavation and Survey at Rumney Great Wharf 1992, *Britannia* XXV, 175–211.

Gardiner, M. 1988: Medieval Settlement and Society in the Broomhill area and Excavations at Broomhill Church, in Eddison and Green (eds) 1988, 112–27.

Hall, D. and Coles, J. 1994: *Fenland Survey: An essay in landscape and persistence*. English Heritage Archaeological Report 1.

Hallam, H.E. 1954: *The New Lands of Elloe: A Study of Early Reclamation in Lincolnshire*. Leicester University Department of English Local History Occasional Papers 6.

Hallam, H.E. 1965: *Settlement and Society: A Study of the Early Agrarian History of South Lincolnshire*. (Cambridge University Press).

Hallam, S.J. 1970: Settlement around the Wash, in Phillips, C.W. (ed) *The Fenland in Roman Times*, 22–113. Royal Geographical Society Research Series 5.

Harvey, B. 1977: *Westminster Abbey and its estates in the Middle Ages*. (Oxford University Press).

Jones, M. 1989: Agriculture in Roman Britain: the Dynamics of Change, in Todd, M. (ed) *Research in Roman Britain 1960–89*, 127–34. Britannia Monograph 11.

Leech, R. 1977: Late Iron Age and Romano-British Briquetage Sites at Quarrylands Lane, Badgworth. *Proc Somerset Archaeol and Natural History Society* 121, 89–96.

Miles, A. 1975: Salt-panning in Romano-British Kent, in de Brisay and Evans (eds) 1975, 26–30.

Millett, M. 1990: *The Romanization of Britain*. Cambridge University Press).

Morris, E. 1985: Prehistoric Salt Distribution: Two Case Studies. *Bulletin of the Board of Celtic Studies* XXXII, 336–79.

Murphy, P. 1994: Environmental Archaeology: Third Progress Report. *Fenland Research* No 9, 26–9.

Place, C. 1992: *An Archaeological Desktop Assessment of Land Owned by Chainrock Corporation N.V. in the Area of the Castle Point Local Plan*. South Eastern Archaeological Services unpublished report, 1992/54.

Rackham, O. 1986: *The Ancient Woodland of England: The Woods of South-East Essex*. (Rochford District Council).

Reaney, P.H. 1935: *The Place-Names of Essex*. English Place-Name Society XII.

Reeves, A. 1995: Romney Marsh: the fieldwalking evidence, in Eddison, J. (ed) *Romney Marsh: The Debatable Ground*, 78–91. Oxford University Committee for Archaeology Monograph 41.

Rippon, S. 1994: The Roman Settlement and Landscape at Kenn Moor, North Somerset: Interim Report on Survey and Excavation in 1993/4, *Archaeology in the Severn Estuary 1994*, 21–34.

Rippon, S. 1995: The Roman Settlement and Landscape at Kenn Moor, North Somerset: Interim Report on Survey and Excavation in 1994/5, *Archaeology in the Severn Estuary 1995 (volume 6)*, 35–47.

Rippon, S. 1996a: *The Gwent Levels: the evolution of a wetland landscape*. CBA Research Report 105.

Rippon, S. 1996b: Roman and medieval settlement on the North Somerset Levels: survey and excavation at Banwell and Puxton, 1996, *Archaeology in the Severn Estuary 1996* (volume 7) 39–52.

Rippon, S. 1997: *The Severn Estuary: landscape evolution and wetland reclamation*. (Leicester University Press).

Rippon, S. 1999: The Rayleigh Hills, South East Essex: patterns in the exploitation of rural resources in a 'woodland' landscape, in S. Green (ed) *The Essex landscape: in search of its history*. (Essex County Council).

Rippon, S. Forthcoming: The Transformation of Coastal Wetlands: exploitation and managmeent of marshland landscapes in North West Europe during the Roman and Medieval Periods. (London: British Academy/Oxford University Press)

Round, H. 1903: The Domesday Survey, *Victoria County History of Essex* volume 1, 333–598.

Sheail, J. 1972: The distribution of taxable population and wealth in England during the early sixteenth century, *Trans. and Papers of the Inst. of British Geographers* 55, 111–25.

Simmons, B.B. 1979: The Lincolnshire Car Dyke: navigation or drainage?, *Britannia* 10, 183–96.

Smith, J.R. 1970: *Foulness: A History of an Essex Island Parish*.Essex Records Office publication 55.

Smith, R.A.L. 1939: Marsh Embankment and Sea Defence in Medieval Kent, *Econ Hist Rev* 10, 29–37.

Smith, R.A.L. 1943: *Canterbury Cathedral Priory: a study in monastic administration*. (Cambridge University Press).

Tatton-Brown, T. 1988: The Topography of the Walland Marsh area between the Eleventh and Thirteenth Centuries, in Eddison and Green (eds) 1988, 105–11.

Thirsk, J. 1967: *The Agrarian History of England and Wales IV. 1500–1640*. (Cambridge University Press).

Todd, M. 1993: Charterhouse on Mendip: an interim report on survey and excavation in 1993. *Proc Somerset Archaeol and Natural History Soc* 137, 59–67.

Ward, J. 1987: 'Richer in land than in inhabitants'.South Essex in the Middle Ages, c.1066–c.1340, in Neale, K, (ed) *An Essex Tribute: Essays presented to Frederick Emmison*, 97–108.

Whittick, G.C. 1982: The earliest Roman lead-mining on Mendip and in North Wales: a reappraisal. *Britannia* XIII, 113–123.

Wilkinson, T.J. and Murphy, P.L. 1995: *The Archaeology of the Essex Coast, Volume 1: The Hullbridge Survey*. East Anglian Archaeology 71.

Williams, M. 1970: *The Draining of the Somerset Levels*. (Cambridge University Press).

Williams, M. 1982: Marshland and Waste, in Cantor, L. (ed) *The English Medieval Landscape*, 86–125. (London: Croom Helm).

Williams, M. 1990: Agricultural Impacts in Temperate Wetlands, in Williams, M. (ed) *Wetlands: a threatened landscape*, 181–233. (Oxford Institute of British Geographers/Blackwell).

10. The Changing Landscape and Coastline of the Isles of Scilly: Recent Research

Jeanette Ratcliffe and Vanessa Straker

New information about the early environment of the Isles of Scilly has come to light as a result of a palaeoenvironmental assessment of organic material exposed in the low cliffs and intertidal zone that fringes the present islands. Midden and peat deposits dating from the late Mesolithic to the Early Medieval period have yielded valuable data relating to the vegetational history and past land use of the archipelago. As well as confirming previous evidence for a Mesolithic/ Neolithic deciduous forest which by the late Iron Age at least had become transformed into an open landscape of cultivated fields, pasture and heathland, it has established for the first time a range of early Bronze Age to Iron Age crops. In addition, the intertidal sediments have been shown to have potential for testing the existing model for sea level change in Scilly. Though detailed biostratigraphic analysis is necessary before sea level index points can be established, preliminary results obtained during the analysis suggest that sea level rise over the last 5000 years may have been less dramatic than previously suggested.

Introduction

Located twenty eight miles (45 kilometres) south west of Cornwall, the Isles of Scilly is a tiny granite archipelago teeming with archaeological remains, including the houses, fields and ritual and burial sites of its earliest inhabitants (Fig. 10.1). An important aspect of Scilly's archaeology is the presence of remains below high water, the result of the gradual submergence of a once much larger land mass. Submerged stone remains (such as field walls, hut circles and cist graves) have been documented since the eighteenth century, but it is only in recent years that intertidal peat deposits have been recognised. As sea level continues to rise, erosion around the edge of Scilly's existing islands continually exposes archaeological structures and layers in the low cliff face. Though ultimately having a destructive effect, this process provides informative cross sections through many sites, including prehistoric (and later) settlement remains consisting of stone round houses and midden deposits.

Over a five year period from 1989–1993, with funding from English Heritage, Cornwall Archaeological Unit (in conjunction with the Ancient Monuments Laboratory and Bristol University) implemented a small-scale recording and sampling programme to assess the palaeoenvironmental potential of these early coastal sites (Ratcliffe and Straker 1996). With the intertidal peat deposits, the aim was to test their potential for enhancing understanding of the vegetational history of Scilly and as a means of testing and refining the current model for sea level change. For cliff-face sites, the main aim was to assess their potential for yielding information on the subsistence economy and diet of the early inhabitants of the islands, with particular emphasis being placed on sampling for plant macrofossils which, apart from charcoal, were virtually unknown for Scilly. A total of twelve sites were assessed. The locations of these are shown on Figure 10.2, and Table 10.1 summarises the environmental work carried out at each.

Early settlements exposed in the cliff face

The sites

Nine sites were located on both the outer and inner-facing shores of the present coastline, the cliffs in which remains were exposed being only 0.5–3.0 metres high, making them particularly vulnerable to coastal erosion, but also, on the whole, very accessible, and easily recorded and sampled from the beach below. The degree to which the archaeological remains could be interpreted in each case depended on the way in which the cliff had eroded in relation to them. It was easier to define and interpret a straight and vertical cliff face than one that had eroded differentially along its length or slumped, been undercut or burrowed into by rabbits and rats.

The majority of sites were early settlements. At most of these, ruined stone-walled buildings were exposed in the cliff face, together with occupation and post-occupation layers and, in some cases, features such as hearths and stone-lined drains. A trend recorded at four settlement sites was the disposal of domestic waste within buildings

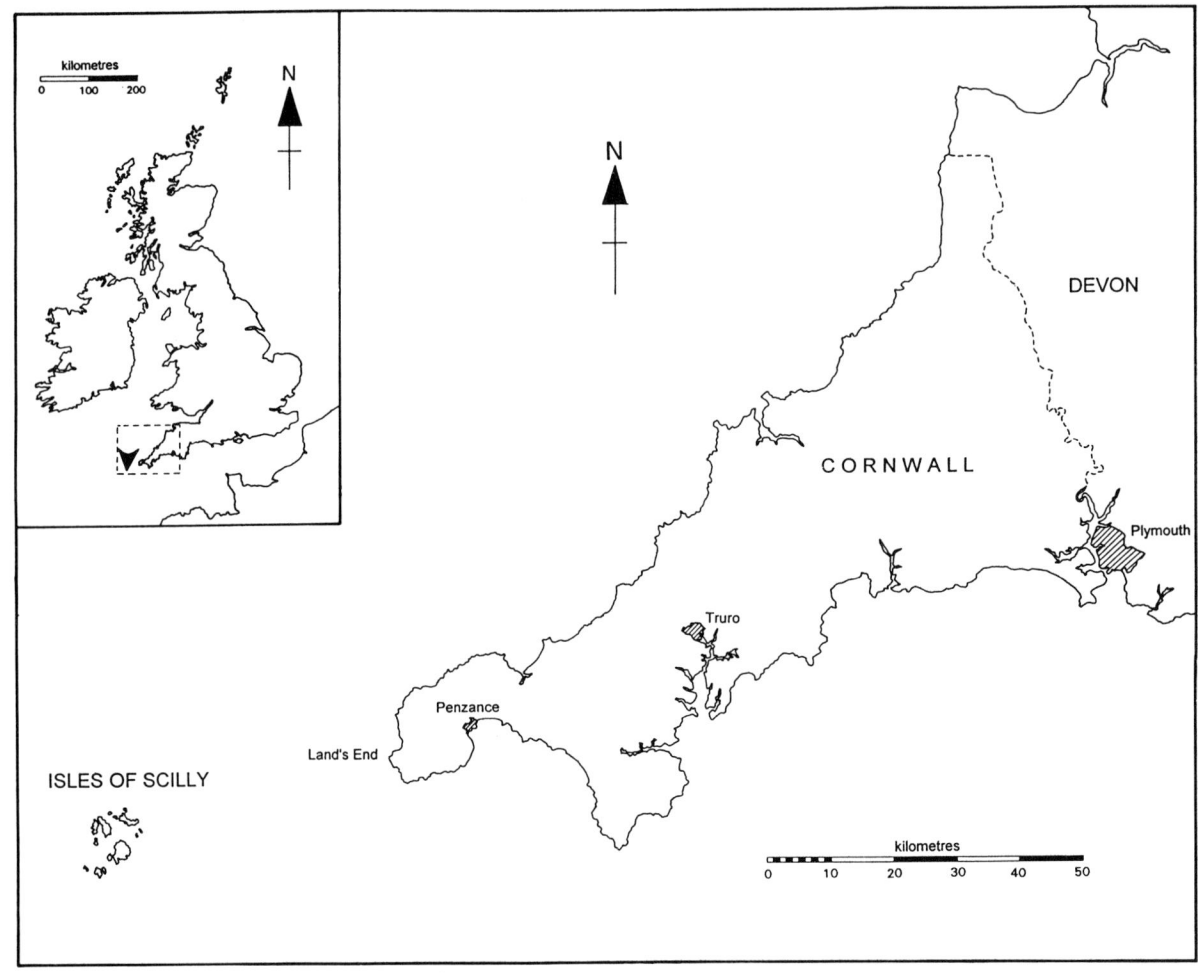

Figure 10.1 Geographical location of the Isles of Scilly.

that had gone out of use, the part of the site which generated the rubbish either having been already eroded away or perhaps still surviving inland. Middens dominated by limpets were a feature of three of the sites and in two cases (at Porth Killier and on Tean) provided the alkaline conditions necessary for good bone preservation. With the exception of Shipman Head, all sites yielded artefacts – pottery, flints and stone objects, such as saddle querns. Of particular note is pottery of a form dateable to the late Bronze Age/early Iron Age found at West Porth, Samson. This is the first identification of such pottery in Scilly. The Neolithic potsherds and flints from the otherwise Bronze Age site of Bonfire Carn are also important, as evidence for Neolithic occupation is very rare in the islands.

Sampling and recording methods

The sampling method consisted of taking bulk samples of limpet middens and other archaeological layers. Occasional spot samples were taken for pollen assessment and Kubiena boxes for soil analysis. Owing to the fact that care had to be taken not to undermine the cliff section, the samples were smaller than those usually taken from excavations. In order to provide a context for the environmental sampling, a detailed section drawing was made of the cliff face in each case (see, for example, Fig. 10.3). Recorded layers and features were assigned context numbers and described on site context forms. Artefacts collected were allocated unique finds numbers and were marked on the section, as were the positions of the samples taken. A full photographic record was also made of the cliff face (Fig. 10.4).

Assessment of the environmental samples

All the bulk samples were processed by flotation, and the resulting floats and residues were completely sorted through. Animal bone, marine shell, charcoal and plant macrofossils were extracted. Further study of the shell has not yet been completed, but the bone was identified, together with those charcoal samples submitted for radiocarbon dating. For the plant macrofossils, owing to the small size of the samples, it was possible to make full counts of these.

Both charred and mineralised plant remains were preserved. The discovery of mineralised seeds is significant, since it emphasises that the potential of archaeo-

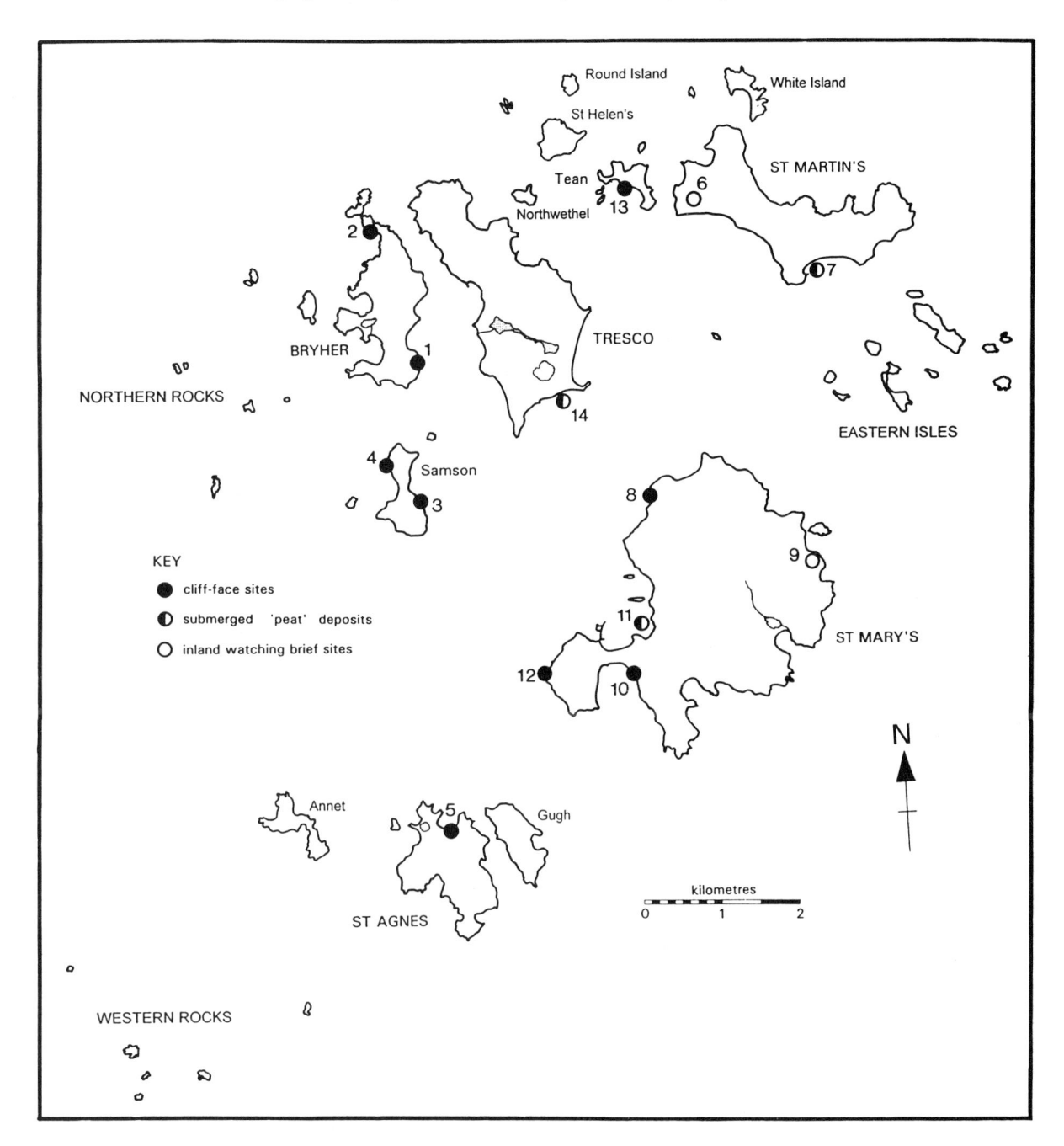

Figure 10.2 Location of sites at which palaeoenvironmental work was carried out between 1989 and 1993 (see Table 10.1 for site names and dates and summary of work carried out at each site).

logical deposits in Scilly to preserve information on past flora and land use is not confined, in dry soils, to charred plant macrofossils, which are inevitably biased towards arable activities. It also means that adequate provision must be made to recover this information when future sampling and recovery programmes are planned. A wide variety of animal bones were also identified, including very small fish, bird and amphibian bones.

Radiocarbon measurements were obtained from all of the cliff-face sites, except Shipman Head, where suitable organic material was not present, and Steval Point, where radiocarbon dating was not appropriate for such a late site. Charcoal, charred grain, animal bone and limpets have all been successfully used to obtain radiocarbon determinations (a marine offset being applied when calibrating determinations obtained from material of marine origin). The calibrated date ranges provide a near continuous sequence from the early Bronze Age to the late Iron Age, with a few Romano-British and Early Medieval (6th-8th century AD) date ranges in addition. This provides a chronological framework for the palaeoenvironmental evidence and for the other types of data

Table 10.1 Palaeoenvironmental work at sites in Scilly: 1989–1993.

No	Date of Sampling	Site	Date of context	Diatoms	Pollen	Seeds	Charcoal	Wood	Foraminifera	Molluscs	Animal bones**	Soils, sediments	RC dates
1	1993	Bonfire Carn	Late Bronze Age			√	√						√2
2	1989, 1993	Shipman Head	Iron Age		√								
3	1990	Samson, East Porth	Early Bronze Age			√							√1
4	1990	Samson, West Porth	Late Bronze Age/Early Iron Age			√	√						√2
5	1989	Porth Killier	Mid to Late Bronze Age			√	√			√M	√		√3
6	1992	Lower Town*	Early Medieval			√				√L & M	√		√3
7	1990/1	Par Beach	Mesolithic to Early Medieval	√	√	√	√	√			√ teeth	√	√10
8	1991	Halangy Porth	Early to Middle Iron Age			√	√						√2
9	1992	Mount Todden*	Prehistoric		√								
10	1991	Porth Cressa	Mid to Late Bronze Age			√	√			√M			√2
11	1992	Porth Mellon	Late Neolithic/Early Bronze Age	√	√	√		√	√				√4
12	1990	Steval Point	Post-medieval, 17th century			√					√		
13	1989	Tean, East Porth	Late Roman to Early Medieval			√				√M	√		√2
14	1990/1	Crab's Ledge	Prehistoric to Romano-British	√	√	√						√	√8

* Developer-funded watching brief   L = land snails, M = marine molluscs   ** including fish and bird bones

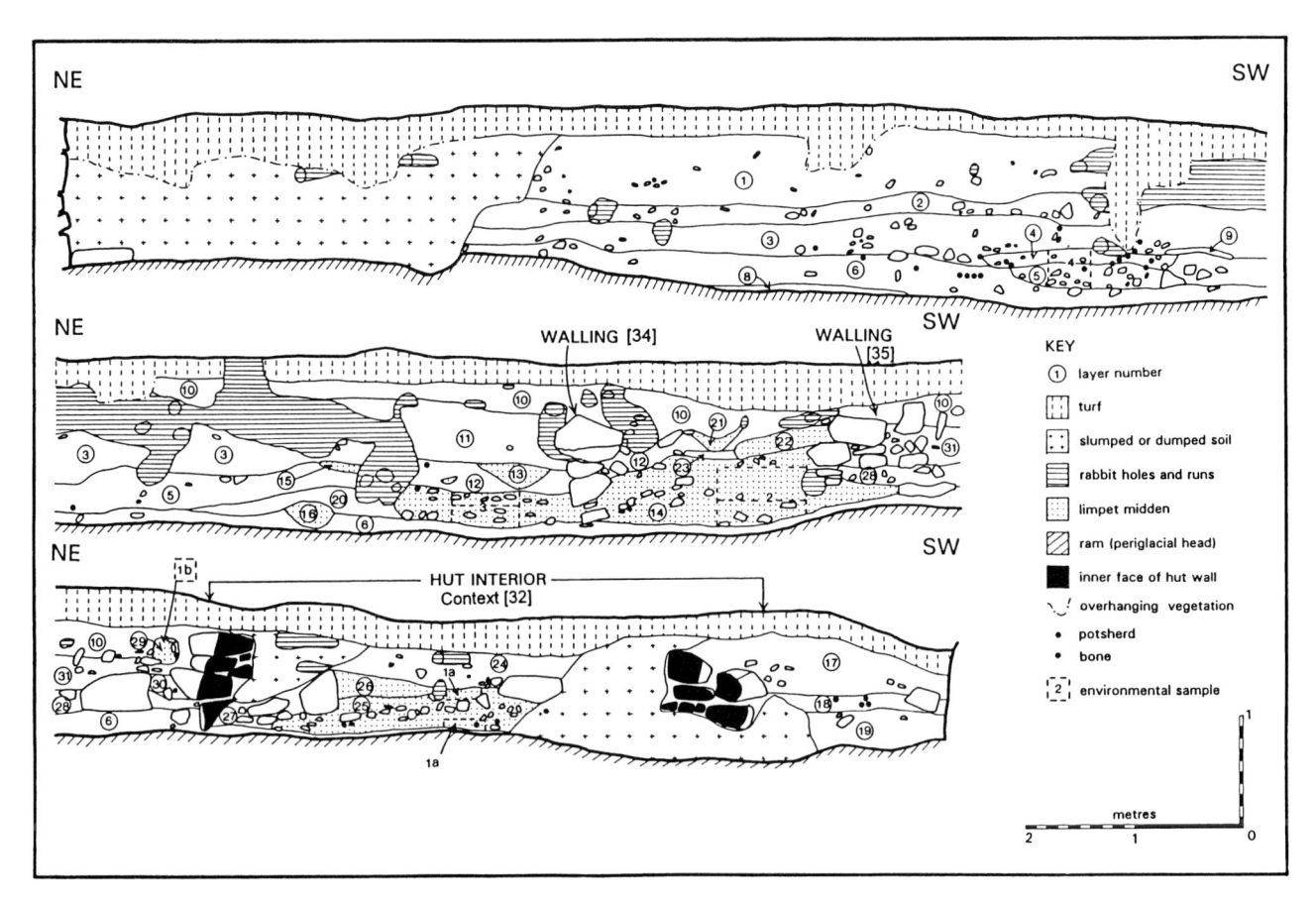

Figure 10.3 Section drawing of the cliff face at Porth Killier showing the location of samples taken (1989).

collected, and it increases the number of radiocarbon-dated settlement sites in Scilly from four to eleven.

New evidence for prehistoric crops and arable weeds

Prior to 1989, the most abundant source of evidence for the subsistence economy and diet of early Scillonians were assemblages of animal bone and shell from excavated settlement sites. The 1989–93 assessment project has provided additional bone evidence. For example, for the Bronze Age it has added seven new fish and ten new birds to the list of species identified for Scilly. However, the key environmental gain from the cliff-face sites has been the establishment of a range of crops for the Bronze Age and Iron Age. These are naked and hulled barley, emmer wheat and celtic bean. The identification of naked barley in an Iron Age Scillonian context is important since as well as apparently being confined to westerly and northerly locations in the British Isles, it also tends to be found more commonly in a Bronze Age context. Accompanying the arable crops was a range of plants typical of cultivated and disturbed ground, such as fat hen, knotgrass, black bindweed and chickweed which are commonly found elsewhere in Britain. One or two have specific habitat requirements that provide additional information on soil conditions. Corn spurrey, for example, is characteristic of acid soils such as those that would have developed over the granite after woodland clearance, while ploughman's spikenard is typical of calcareous soil. The addition, either intentionally or accidentally, of shell sand would have created suitable conditions for calcicoles.

Intertidal peats

The sites

All three sites at which intertidal peats were recorded and sampled are located on inner facing shores, on the edge of the lagoon which (according to the present model for sea level change in Scilly) was a low-lying plain during prehistoric times. As well as shelves of peat exposed on the surface of the beach (Fig. 10.5), buried bands were also recorded. A total of ten deposits were identified – five on Par Beach, three at Crab's Ledge and two in Porth Mellon. Most of these are not true peats but minerogenic intertidal sediments containing varying amounts of organic matter (humic silts, sands and sandy silts). Wood content is low or absent and the deposits appear, therefore, to be different in character to the submerged forest beds documented around the Cornish coast. All exposed areas of peat have been truncated by marine erosion and

Figure 10.4. One of the Bronze Age limpet middens exposed in the cliff face at Porth Killier.

Figure 10.5 Late Neolithic peat exposure on Higher Town (Par) Beach, St Martin's.

probably also by peat cutting for fuel, since this is known to have been carried out until recent times on Scilly's downs and inland mires. On all three beaches prehistoric stone remains (field systems, hut circles and a stone row) had a direct or indirect relationship with the peat deposits.

Sampling and recording methods

Exposed remains were surveyed and levels taken and related back to a known Ordnance Datum (OD) height in order that both the horizontal and vertical position of each exposure and each sample point could be recorded (for example, see Fig. 10.6). Samples were taken from the exposed areas of peat in monolith and Kubiena tins, blocks and bulk samples (the latter at consecutive 4 or 5cm intervals), once a clean section had been produced by cutting back the eroded edge of the peat or excavating a pit through its surface. These samples were later subdivided in the laboratory for specialist assessment and radiocarbon dating. A powered percussion auger was used to locate and sample buried deposits – pollen and radiocarbon subsamples being taken from two of the auger columns.

Assessment of the environmental samples

The peat samples were assessed for pollen, and some were also assessed for plant macrofossils, diatoms and foraminifera. Full counts were made for the plant macrofossils, but not for the other types of evidence. The few pieces of wood collected were identified to species.

For most of the samples pollen preservation was good and concentration was high. Preservation of plant macrofossils was more variable, this material being poorly preserved in deposits located higher up in the intertidal zone and susceptible to more extensive drying out between high tides (the best results being obtained from Porth Mellon where the peat exposures are located at mean low water). For at least a third of the samples assessed for diatoms, the diatom abundancy, preservation and species richness was such as to warrant more detailed analysis, and the assessment has confirmed that such analysis will provide data on the salinity conditions under which the various sediments accumulated. Unfortunately, foraminifera preservation was generally very poor. However, since this was probably the result of a combination of *a)* aerial

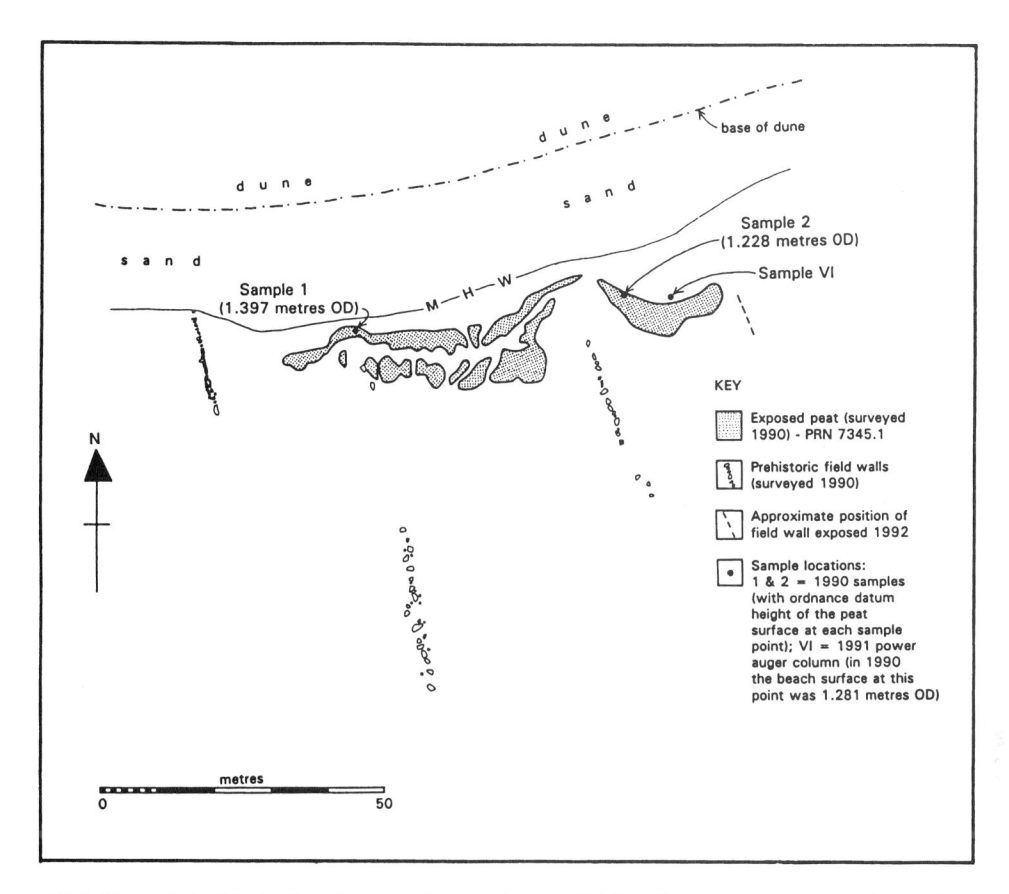

Figure 10.6 Plan of Crab's Ledge showing the prehistoric field walls, peat exposure and sample points.

exposure at the site and *b)* prolonged storage of the samples in a wet state at room temperature, better results may be obtained in the future by more targeted sampling and more careful storage.

Radiocarbon measurements were obtained from peat and wood samples from the intertidal sediments (from the base and top, and sometimes the middle of these). Samples taken from the exposed areas of peat produced good results, with calibrated date ranges spanning the late Mesolithic to the beginning of the Early Medieval period (5th–7th century AD). However, the measurements obtained for samples taken from the auger cores are problematic. The dates for the different peat layers do not correspond to their relative stratigraphic positions and it is assumed that some contamination must have taken place during the sampling process.

Enhancing Scilly's vegetational history – the intertidal pollen evidence.

Palynological evidence previously collected in Scilly (during the 1960's and 1970's) came almost exclusively from St Mary's, primarily from the inland mires of Higher and Lower Moors (Scaife 1984). The pollen sequence from Higher Moors is the longest from Scilly and dates back to the 6th millennium cal BC. At this time the surrounding vegetation consisted of mixed oak woodland. This was subsequently partially cleared for cultivation (probably during the Neolithic), but during the middle Bronze Age or later there was a period of forest regeneration, though some land remained open. However, from the late Bronze Age or early Iron Age there was extensive woodland clearance. This general picture of a deciduous forest which by the Iron Age had been transformed into an open environment of cultivated fields, pasture and heathland, was confirmed by the pollen evidence from Lower Moors and soil pollen analysis on St Mary's and on Nornour. However, it was unclear to what extent it reflected the vegetational and land-use history of Scilly as a whole. The sampling of intertidal peats during the 1989–93 project allowed for the collection of evidence from a wider area, though it should be noted that this new pollen evidence is based on assessment counts only, and should therefore be regarded as provisional.

By and large, the intertidal evidence corresponds with that from Higher Moors. The earliest of the deposits examined, at Par Beach, St Martin's, was dated to the late Mesolithic or early Neolithic (the late 5th/early 4th millennia cal BC). These provided evidence for the existence of mixed deciduous woodland (oak, hazel, birch, lime, elm, holly, alder and willow), broadly similar to that identified at Higher Moors for the earlier Mesolithic. By the late Neolithic (3rd to 4th millennia cal BC), at Porth Mellon on St Mary's, this woodland was still a major feature of the local vegetation. This deposit may tentatively be correlated with the start of the second phase at Higher Moors, as may an insecurely dated late Neolithic deposit on Par Beach. Here there was charcoal and only low levels of tree and shrub pollen, suggesting that at this location some clearance took place at this date.

It has been suggested that the high percentage of birch pollen in the initial forest phase at Higher Moors represented scrub regeneration resulting from anthropogenic disturbance and abandonment by Mesolithic gatherer-hunters (Scaife 1984, 39). However, birch was also common in the Neolithic woodland at Par Beach and Porth Mellon and it may in fact have been a major part of the postglacial climax woodland, which in Cornwall is usually dominated by oak and hazel. Whatever the significance of the high levels of birch, these late Mesolithic to Neolithic deposits provide a useful environmental context for the artefactual evidence of these periods, previously rare in Scilly, but now (especially in terms of Neolithic material) more commonly identified.

There is currently no pollen evidence from elsewhere in Scilly for the mid to late Bronze Age forest regeneration recorded at Higher Moors. Neither is there any indication of it in the archaeological record – indeed the two middle to late Bronze Age settlements sampled as part of the 1989–93 project produced evidence for arable and pastoral farming. The Higher Moors evidence may reflect a local vegetational change and not necessarily the situation elsewhere in Scilly. Equally, the only dated pollen evidence for the start of the main phase of woodland clearance still comes from Higher Moors, where radiocarbon dating places it in the late Bronze Age or early Iron Age. However, given the picture emerging from settlement sites of fairly intensive occupation throughout the Bronze Age, this could have occurred earlier in other parts of Scilly.

The other intertidal deposits date from the Late Iron Age to the 7th century cal AD and the pollen assessments from these concord with the evidence from High Moors. At Crab's Ledge woodland and scrub had been largely replaced by the end of the Iron Age/beginning of the Romano-British period by areas of saltmarsh and open ground. By at least the early Medieval period the area around Par Beach was an open landscape, with plants of disturbed ground, sand dunes and heathland represented in the pollen record.

Sea level change and the submergence of Scilly

Today the Isles of Scilly comprise two hundred individual rocks and islands, but it is not difficult to imagine these as part of a much larger land mass which has become gradually submerged. At low tide, extensive sand flats are exposed on the inner facing shores of the northern half of Scilly, making it easy to visualise former plains fringed by low granite hills and sand dunes. Bryher, Tresco and Samson are still joined at low astronomical tide (LAT) and the water is so shallow between the islands that a drop in sea level of less than 10 metres would re-unite all except St Agnes and Annet.

The current model for sea level change

An archaeological model for the submergence of Scilly has been published by Charles Thomas (Thomas 1985, 17–64). In the absence of radiocarbon dates from the intertidal zone, he calculated sea level change since 3000 BC using the vertical positions of submerged archaeological sites which could be broadly dated from artefactual evidence or by analogy with sites elsewhere. He assumed that these sites were originally located just above the contemporary shoreline, at 1.8 metres above high astronomical tide (HAT) (5.3 metres above mean sea level (MSL)), and that the tidal range in Scilly has remained constant for the last 5000 years – that is 6.4 metres between HAT and LAT. Having plotted the vertical positions of the dated sites in relation to present MSL, he was able to calculate the height of the latter for the periods when the sites were in use, by subtracting 5.3 metres in each case (Fig. 10.7, Lines A and B; Thomas 1985, Fig. 2). Thomas then adjusted the results of this calculation by introducing a downward deflection of 2 centimetres at 1000 AD and doubling this deflection at 5 century intervals. In this way he changed his sea level/age line into a curve, which indicated that around 3000 BC MSL was almost 17 metres below that of today (Thomas 1985, Fig. 3). The curve for Scilly is much steeper than that for Newlyn or the Bristol Channel. Thomas suggests that this difference is the result of a very localised downward displacement of Scilly's granitic laccolith in addition to more general isostatic movement.

According to Thomas, his model represents an average yearly rise in sea level of 2.1–2.6 millimetres, which means 21–26 centimetres every 100 years and 2.1–2.6 metres every 1000. However, although Thomas' model assumes that the submergence of Scilly was a gradual process, he recognised that there may be an alternative scenario, which could have involved more dramatic events such as tidal surges (the displacement of huge volumes of water in a particular direction).

Perhaps the most controversial aspect of Thomas's model is his suggestion that today's islands did not finish forming until relatively recent times. He postulated that until the end of the Roman period all of them (excluding St Agnes, Gugh and Annet) were joined together at high water, and that as recently as the 11th century AD the position was still the same at low water, and that separation was not complete until the early Tudor period. He has used the distribution of Cornish and English coastal and shore place-names to support this hypothesis. The

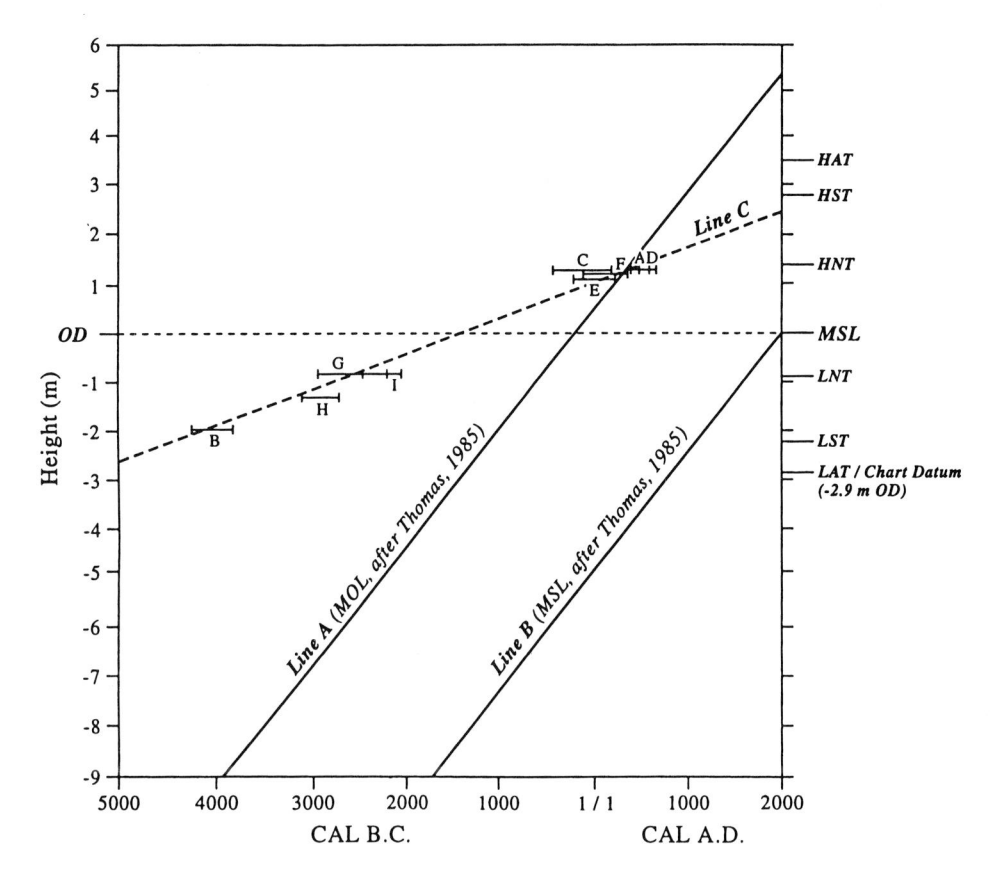

Figure 10.7 Sea Level change in Scilly – Lines A and B after Thomas 1985, Fig 2; Line C, based on calibrated date ranges for selected intertidal peat samples (A-B = Par Beach, C-F = Crab's Ledge, G-I = Porth Mellon).

early pre-16th century Cornish forms are restricted to the outer coasts and rocks of today's islands, while the later English names populate their inward facing shores.

Results from the intertidal 'peats'

One of the key aims of the 1989–93 project was to assess whether the intertidal peat deposits could be used to test and refine Thomas' model. The assessments of the peat indicate that this should be possible provided that detailed analyses are carried out. The preliminary results suggest that sea level rise in Scilly was more gradual than Thomas' model suggests. However, there are problems with making such comparisons because different data has been used and for both types of data there are difficulties in ascertaining what the evidence actually means in terms of the evolution of the present coastline. In the case of Thomas' model, he has had to assume that his dateable sites were located at the contemporary minimum occupation level (MOL) and also that MOL has consistently been 5.3 metres above mean sea level. In addition, most of his sites are only very broadly dated and some could belong to different periods than those chosen by him. As far as the intertidal peats are concerned, the extent of marine influence on the formation of these is varied and can be unclear. At Par Beach, for example, the deposits seem to have formed in and around the edges of freshwater pools, and marsh and fen conditions existed, perhaps developed in wet dune slacks. In contrast the deposits sampled at Crab's Ledge are more likely to have formed under saltmarsh conditions or were at least subjected to marine inundation, though the exact nature of this needs clarifying. At Porth Mellon, although dunes may on occasion have protected the area, there is evidence for it having been subjected to marine inundation and salt spray.

A tentative first attempt to refine the curve for sea level change in Scilly is shown in Figure 10.7 (Line C), but it should be noted that detailed biostratigraphic analyses are required to confirm this. The 2 sigma calibrated date ranges for selected radiocarbon measurements obtained from the intertidal sediments have been plotted against their respective OD heights, and a best fit line (estimated by eye) drawn through them (Line C). This is shallower in gradient than lines A and B, which are taken from Thomas (1985, Fig. 2) and recalculated to OD rather than chart datum (CD). The intersection of

Line C around AD 2000 appears to suggest that the present intertidal sediments accumulated close to the high Spring tide (HST) level. In order to facilitate comparison with Thomas' data, the (possibly erroneous) assumption must be made that the difference between MSL and HST has remained constant, with MSL being *c.*2.8 metres below HST. Then it can be seen that between about 1 and 500 AD, MSL may have been at about 1–1.6 metres below the present level, compared with Thomas' estimate of *c.*3.5–4.7 metres below it. At about 1000 BC, Thomas' model suggests a figure of about -7.25 metres OD for MSL, which is in the order of 4.7 metres lower than that which the recent work might point to. It is clear that the land exposed above HST was formerly more extensive in Scilly, but tentative though the figures suggested above may be, it is unlikely that the land area was as great as Thomas has suggested.

The suggestion that the intertidal peats originally occupied a position between high normal tide (HNT) and HST gives a tentative context, which could be examined by looking at the relationship of Scilly's present inland mires to OD/CD. Examination of the coastal (and other) processes affecting these mires may also be relevant to the study of the submerged deposits.

It is clear from the preliminary results presented in this report that the potential exists to establish sea level index points for Scilly. Detailed biostratigraphic analysis is now required to explain the submergence of the islands.

Future Work

Against the background of a continually rising sea level and diminishing land mass there is clearly a need for further work around Scilly's coast, where sites have been shown to be rich in palaeoenvironmental and other types of evidence. More work is required not just at cliff-face and intertidal sites, but also inland (particularly at High and Lower Moors and other inland mires and pools) and within the marine area between Scilly's present islands, where stone remains and peat deposits have been identified but not yet recorded or sampled.

Acknowledgements

Many contributions to the project were made by Alex Bayliss (Radiocarbon calibration and analysis), Nigel Cameron (diatoms), Mike Godwin (Foraminifera), Henrietta Quinnell (artefacts) and Frank Turk (animal bones).

References

Ratcliffe, J and Straker, V. 1996: *The early environment of Scilly: Palaeoenvironmental assessment of cliff-face and intertidal deposits, 1989–1993* (Cornwall Archaeological Unit, Cornwall County Council).

Scaife, R.G. 1984: *A History of Flandrian Vegetation in the Isles of Scilly: Palynological Investigation of Higher Moorsand Lower Moors Peat Mires, St Mary's*, in Cornish Studies 11, p. 33–47.

Thomas, C. 1984: *Exploration of a Drowned Landscape: Archaeology and History of the Isles of Scilly* (Batsford, London).

# 11. Stress at the Seams: Assessing the Terrestrial and Submerged Archaeological Landscape on the Shore of the *Magnus Portus*

David Tomalin

Since the publication of 'Statement on England's coastal heritage; a survey for English Heritage and the RCHME' (Fulford, Champion and Long 1997), much attention has been given to the weakness of the artificial seam which divides the familiar territory of terrestrial archaeology from that part of the Britain's cultural resource which is concealed and preserved below mean low water mark (MLWM). For archaeologists, planners, coastal protection authorities, harbour authorities and offshore operators, much emphasis has been recently placed on the wisdom of a 'seamless approach' to the on-shore and off-shore heritage (ibid). This optimistic proposal has sought to overcome some of the substantial problems, which arise at the mean low water boundary (DOE 1993). This paper presents the results of work on the Wight shore of the Eastern Solent to develop underwater and intertidal survey and assess the potential of the resource.

Background to recent intertidal and sub-tidal investigations on the Wight/Solent coast

Regular revisions of the Admiralty charts show that MLWM is a fluctuating watershed that can advance and retreat over the intertidal zone. Unfortunately, this watershed has been used, quite inappropriately, to impose a perceptual division across a landscape that offers a single and seamless history. As an impediment to the protection of the national heritage, this boundary is particularly perturbing for it is here that the curatorial powers of Local Authorities, the remit of their Town and Country Planning Acts and the attendant obligation to gather SMR data are all rendered impotent.

In the submerged dimension of England's coastal heritage the genius of destruction can be swift and sure. The powers of near-shore and off-shore natural processes are ever active, while the technical and commercial aspirations of human communities make an ever-increasing impact upon the submerged and unseen hills and valleys which are the setting of the archaeological landscape of the seabed.

Since 1994, many off-shore operators including Port and Harbour Authorities, navigational and capital dredging agencies and water and sewage utilities have adopted a voluntary code for the protection of archaeological remains (JNAPC 1995). Unfortunately, these agencies generally lack the necessary archaeological expertise to recognise, assess and record coastal remains as they come to light. On the other hand, curatorial archaeologists of the County and District authorities have the ability and the data base systems to inspect and record coastal archaeological remains, but they are generally constrained by the current structure of the Standing Spending Assessment from casting their vision across the meandering boundary drawn at mean low water mark.

Beyond this boundary, it has been assumed, imprudently, that environmental issues are adequately handled by the 'sectoral controls' which are currently applied to off-shore operations (DOE 1993b). However, without the active participation of English Heritage and a statutory input from the compilers and curators of coastal Sites and Monuments Records it is difficult to see how offshore operators and regulators can be provided with the information and guidance they require to achieve best practice in the sub-tidal zone.

The seamless approach

Since 1991 there has been a growing awareness that erosion has been destroying archaeological sites of all periods in many coastal areas of Britain while little concerted research has been organised to resolve this problem (Wainwright 1991). Recently, it has been emphasised that ancient landscapes can extend seamlessly from dry land, through the intertidal zone, and into the sub-tidal dimension. In all of these areas, the principles set out in Planning Policy Guidance 16 (PPG16) need to be applied with equal consistency (Fulford, Champion & Long 1997, 225–227).

This seamless approach, advanced by English Heritage, is a timely and adroit one for it anticipates an urgent need to identify and rank coastal archaeological sites in advance of a new timetable of coastal change. The need to identify and assess the environmental significance of coastal sites and to interpret their relationship with past sea-levels becomes ever more pressing as our present shorelines become stressed and altered as a result of global warming and sea-level rise (RCHME/EH 1996,4).

Other burgeoning issues must also be resolved. Not least are some disturbing requirements of the Global Agreement on Trade (GAT). Concerns are now felt that these may free overseas commercial dredging interests to seek and exploit English coastal marine aggregates whilst denying local coastal protection authorities the opportunity to withhold and conserve such deposits in order to fulfil the shoreline management needs.

In 1991, English Heritage announced that the nation's seabed was under greater threat than ever before. The need to develop underwater survey was boldly advocated; especially where organically preserved remains of prehistoric occupation might survive (Wainwright 1991, 44). By this time it had already become evident that the Solent presented one of the most needy and the best preserved areas where the extent and vulnerability of a submerged archaeological landscape might be tested.

A detailed intertidal survey of the Wight shore of the eastern Solent was conducted between 1990 and 1995. The intertidal and onshore dimension of the study was principally funded by English Heritage. Supportive subtidal work was also carried out to a distance of 1.5 km offshore. This work was funded by the Isle of Wight County Council supported by the University of Southampton and the Hampshire and Wight Trust for Maritime Archaeology. It allowed the submerged archaeological landscape to be examined to a depth of 20 metres below sea level.

The on-shore coastal environment of Wootton Creek

In designing the Wootton-Quarr coastal survey, an opportunity was seized to investigate one of the lesser creeks of the Solent region. The level of prehistoric, Roman and later activity in and around this creek has since proved to be surprisingly intense and it has revealed a remarkably long ancestry. This can be traced back to early Neolithic activity in the 4th millennium BC when wooden trackways were laid across the coastal saltmarsh.

During the field survey of the hinterland and catchment area around the creek, it became evident that the level of prehistoric interest in this location might exceed the generally sparse evidence of human activity which might be traced throughout most of the natural zone of northern Wight. General archaeological and palaeo-environmental investigations in this zone suggested that, prior to medieval times, relatively little human disturbance had been imposed on the natural habitat of the northern coastlands. This meant that, in contrast with the arboreal history of the other natural zones of the island, the natural woodland cover over this Tertiary clayland had remained relatively rich.

This perceived difference at Wootton has suggested that the natural attributes of the creek may have been sufficient to attract particular human activity to the shore and the shoulders of the drowned river valley in Neolithic times. It might be proposed that before the close of the Neolithic period, particular attributes of this location might have become sufficiently important to enable the inhabitants to distinguish themselves as a specific coastal community.

In the Wootton-Quarr study area, palynological evidence has been gathered from the shoreline environment and from a focal point of human activity on an adjacent hilltop overlooking the creek. Activity on Puck House Hill is attested during late Neolithic times and it is succeeded by the construction of a small round barrow cemetery (Fig. 11.1). A cemetery such as this is certainly an unusual feature within the northern Tertiary clayland zone of the Isle of Wight. Its presence might be explained by the growth of a successful maritime community developing its interests around the mouth and margins of the creek.

From a tiny localised peat mire lying within 0.8km of the Puck House Hill barrow cemetery comes vital palynological evidence revealing an episode of substantial reduction of tree cover (Scaife 1986 & forthcoming). Concurrent with this event is a progressive increase in cereals. Although an absolute date is still awaited for this event, the evidence seems to suggest that extensive deforestation on and around the hilltop may have occurred at a time when the cemetery was in use. The dating of this event is based on a contemporary decline in the growth of *tilia*. Elsewhere, in the Isle of Wight this is an event attributable to Late Bronze Age times but at this site a Neolithic date is suspected. (Scaife 1986 & pers com).

A further source of environmental information has been the creek head sedimentology. For the past 700 years the innermost kilometre of the tidal reach has served as an inter-tidal millpond constrained and protected by a large earthen dam. At the head of millpond, a stable brackish wetland has blanketed and preserved earlier deposits that can be traced, by coring, to a total depth 6 metres below the present surface of the alluviated valley. An investigation of the pollen, diatom and particle size of these sediments has yielded a record of the long-term history of environmental changes within the creek.

The intertidal evidence of coastal change

Evidence of the post-glacial evolution of the coastline has been recovered from two distinct shoreline morph-

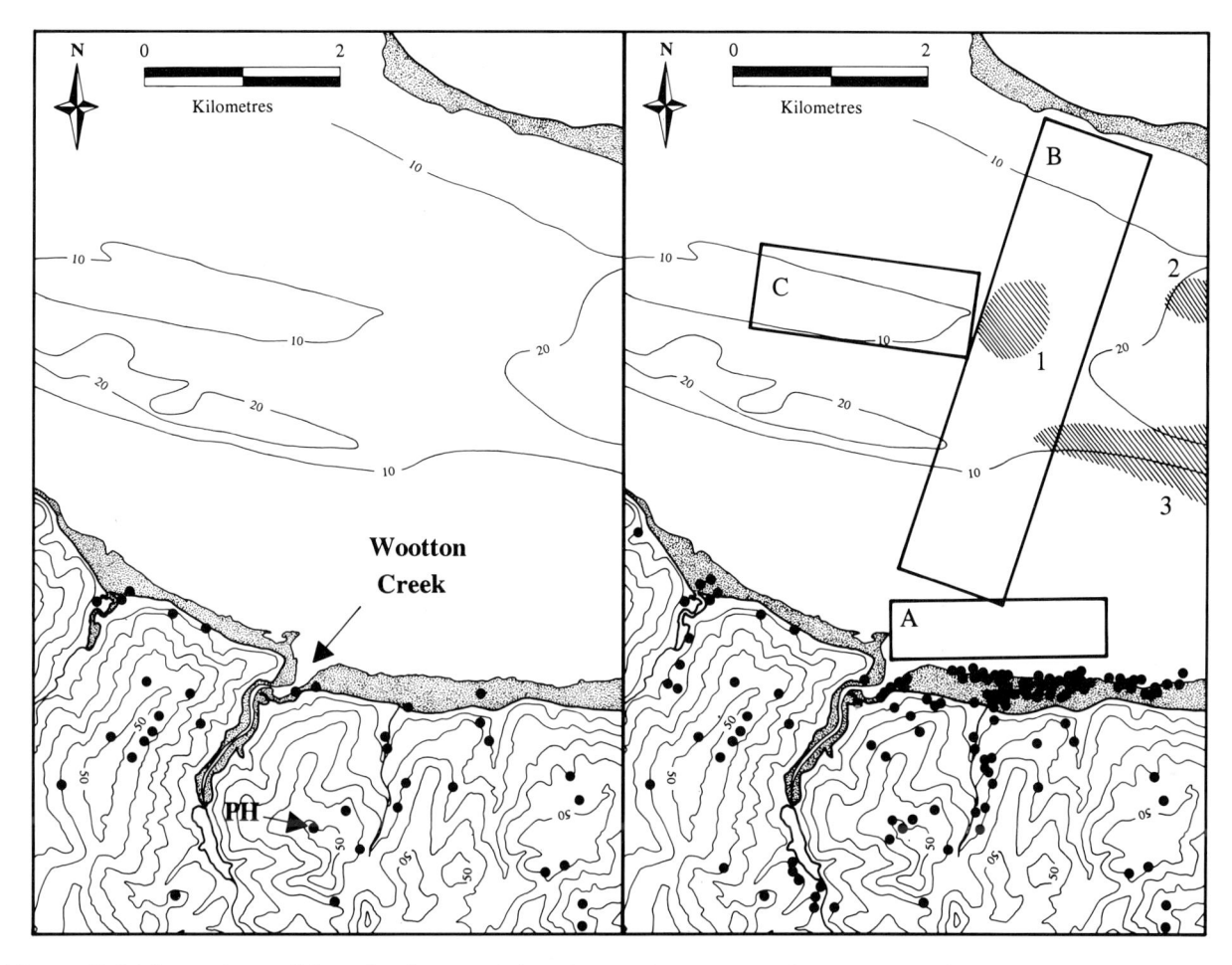

Figure 11.1 The onshore-offshore landscape of the Wootton-Quarr coast showing- Left: the perceived archaeological resource before new survey. (PH = Puckhouse Hill). Right: the seamless view including 161 archaeological structures in the intertidal zone and artifact strews (1) and historic anchorages (2 & 3) in the sub-tidal zone. Sub-tidal survey zones A-C and seabed loci 1–3 are described in the text.

ologies within the study area. On the open alluvial shore of the Solent a flat intertidal zone some 200 metres wide is largely composed of accreted silts with intercalated peat. Evaluation of these deposits reveals a phase of post-glacial saltmarsh followed by the growth of reed swamp, a phase of colonisation by an expanding Neolithic forest followed by renewal of saline conditions and the accretion of further marine silts.

Low fetch and low wave energy on this coastline have generally favoured the accretion of silt held in dynamic equilibrium with a post-Glacial rise in sea level. There is, however, evidence of a recent loss of equilibrium (Bray *et al* 1991). On the open coast, between the mouths or palaeochannels of the drowned creeks, a wave-cut platform has advanced at present mean high water mark. Wave attack is also responsible for the truncation of the earlier accreted deposits and entombed archaeological features at the low water level of the platform.

Within the sheltered estuarine environment of the creeks or rias on this coast, a more extensive history of accretion and sedimentation can be detected. These old drowned river valleys are feeders to a major submerged palaeovalley known as the '*Solent River*' (Fox 1861; Everard 1954). On the intertidal strandline at Quarr, the archaeological team has been able to auger one of these feeder palaeochannels to a depth of -7.5m OD.

At the mouth Wootton Haven, a large shingle bar, has provided a further opportunity to identify, by augering, the deep succession of Holocene sediments which have accrued whilst human activity has progressively exploited the neighbouring shoreline. It is evident that both of these sequences of ancient intertidal sediments are threatened, respectively, by the renewed process of wave attack and by human intervention through navigational dredging.

Methods of assessing the off-shore environment and its submerged landscape

In order to extend a seamless vision over the submerged landscape as well as the on-shore terrain, the study area for the Wootton-Quarr project was projected some 5km off-shore (Fig. 11.1). This allowed the submerged late Pleistocene and Holocene landscape to be examined to a depth of 30m below Ordnance Datum. This study area transected the floor of the Solent at a point where the gravel bed of the Pleistocene palaeovalley had been already traced across the seabed (Dyer 1975).

A variety of techniques were used to evaluate the submerged dimension of the study area. In the nearshore sub-tidal area, geo-acoustical survey by Dr Justin Dix and Anthony Hanks of the University of Southampton, Department of Oceanography and Archaeology was executed to reconstruct the coastal palaeochannel system and the landsurface of Pleistocene and earlier Holocene times.

In area A, use was made of a 3.5 kHz ORE sub-bottom profiler to investigate the stratigraphy of the sub-strata and the basement geology of a zone measuring 3km × 0.5km. Survey lines were aligned parallel to the coast and were set at 50m intervals. Survey was pursued inshore into the minimal surveyable water depth which proved to be a little less than 5m. Position fixing was achieved with the help of a Sercel NR 108 Differential GPS system. This provided a real time accuracy of ±m. This machine provided a single analogue printout.

In area B, further sub-bottom profiling was carried but in this case a high resolution swept frequency 2–8 kHz Geo-Chirp unit was employed. Survey lines at 100m intervals were run in a 6km transect across the Solent from Stokes Bay, on the Hampshire coast, to Wootton Creek. This superior unit, manufactured by Geo-Acoustics, was capable of penetrating the seabed to a maximum of 30 metres whilst producing a vertical resolution of ±200 mm. The results could be captured and stored digitally and were capable of subsequent filtering, manipulation and interrogation. Improved position fixing with a Trimble 3000 SE differential GPS provided a real time accuracy of ±1 metre.

In area C a sidescan sonar survey was conducted over a submerged island or shoal known as Ryde Middle Bank. This was an area where the presence of historic shipwrecks was suspected on the steep sides of the ancient shoal. An area measuring 3km × 0.85km was surveyed along east-west tracks set 50m apart. The object was to compile a three dimensional bathymetric relief map of the shoal and to use fine resolution of the sidescan to identify shipwreck or other artefactual remains which might be betrayed by their acoustic shadow.

The equipment used over the Middle Bank was a Honeywell Elac LA4100 portable hydrographic echo-sounder and a Waverley sidescan sonar system with a WE3000 processor unit operating at 100 kHz. An analogue record was directly printed on a WE 3700 thermal linescan recorder. The sidescan unit was set to cover a 75m swathe each side of the towing vessel. Position fixing was achieved with a Trimble 4000 SE differential GPS. The sidescan unit had a capability of detecting upstanding anomalies more than 100mm high.

Targeted underwater archaeological inspection down to a depth of 20 metres was also used as a means of verification in area C of the offshore zone. Paired underwater archaeologists, assembled in either a team of four or six, operated from the 30ft pilot cutter. This procedure proved to be useful on the Middle Bank and also on the shallow shelf known as the Mother Bank. Further inspection is planned on areas of the Mother Bank shelf where the soft surficial sediments are known to contain well preserved portions of Neolithic wooden trackways which have otherwise been traced on the low water boundary with the intertidal zone.

A further means of obtaining seabed environmental evidence proved to be a controlled trawl over an area which was otherwise frequently scoured by fishermen. This exercise was primarily planned to gain direct knowledge of the environment in which Roman and post-Roman artefacts had been commonly recovered in the nets of oyster dredges. This exercise was organised by the Hampshire and Wight Trust for Maritime archaeology and the Isle of Wight Council and was conducted on 28–29 February 1995. It proved to be an efficient means of sampling bottom conditions and bed forms in areas which two areas that are known to have served as historic anchorages.

The archaeological trawl was conducted with a standard A-frame oyster trawling rig controlled by an experienced two-man fishing crew. The vessel was a 20 ton steel-hulled motor fishing vessel equipped with a Furuno Navstar GPS system with VDU and logger. Twin oyster trawl nets were operated by one crew member whilst the contents were checked and recorded by two archaeologists. By carefully overlapping the lowering and the raising of the trawl nets, virtually contiguous samples were recovered from the seabed. The use of non-standard heavy winch gear allowed the trawl to be lowered, if necessary, to a depth exceeding 30 metres.

The archaeology of the on-shore and intertidal landscape

The first evidence for human activity in the margins of the ria inlets, and on the open alluvial shores between them, is provided by a generous array of flint picks. These have been recovered from a variety of derived positions below mean high water mark. A date in the late 5th millennium or early 4th millennium BC is suggested for these artefacts which are more often to be found on the beach in close proximity to one or other of a number of burnt flint scatters. Some of these deposits have been found to contain a small number of microliths and charcoal. An absolute date is now awaited.

By the mid 4th millennium BC, saltmarsh conditions had developed on the margins of the inlets and on the intervening open coast. By now, sufficient human activity had arisen on this shoreline to promote the construction

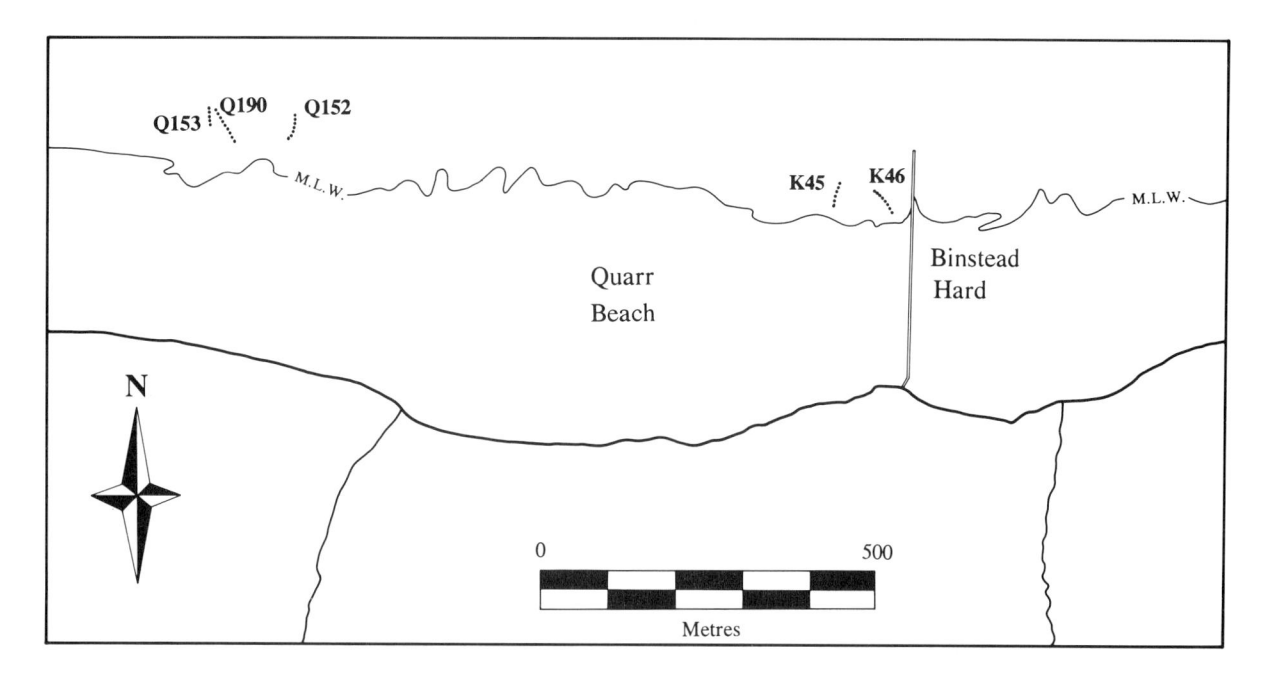

Figure 11.2 Neolithic trackways entering the sub-tidal zone on the open coast at Wootton-Quarr.

of wooden trackways. These have since been traced below mean low water mark into the sub-tidal zone where they now await underwater inspection (Fig. 11.2).

The construction of further Neolithic wooden structures, ostensibly for fishing purposes, can also be traced on the margins of the Quarr palaeochannel. Ashore, on the summit of Puck House Hill, we can detect that a community using Grooved Ware had established an interest in this region in late Neolithic times. This hill subsequently accommodated a small, yet significant, round barrow cemetery in early Bronze Age times.

Early Bronze Age coastal activities are attested at the mouth of Binstead Creek where a variety of contemporary wooden trap-like structures were constructed during the early second millennium BC (Fig. 11.3). During the later Bronze Age, larger wooden structures were erected on the soft sediments on the margin of this creek and a small array of domestic potsherds was scattered in their vicinity (Fig. 11.4). At the mouth of Wootton Creek the conditions for preservation have been less conducive yet here we find that a substantial longshore alignment of stout oak posts was erected around 800 BC. This is provisionally identified as a fish weir.

By the latter part of the 1st century BC, the mouth of Wootton Creek seems to have attained the status of a useful haven for shipping. On the eastern shore we find a modest scatter of local late Iron Age coarse wares and imported Gallo-Roman fine wares entombed within the intertidal silts.

During the Roman period we can identify a substantial increase in the rate of artefact-loss at this favoured landing place. By now the Haven seems to be supporting a maritime community which is handling out-going goods such as beef supplies. These seem to be attested by a butchery and salt-making industry that has been detected on the shore. The character of the pottery strewn across the shore and the loss of a group of coins during or after AD 380 suggests that the natural assets of the creek ensured its continuing use by mariners until the close of the Roman period.

Documentary evidence for maritime activity

The archaeological evidence for prosperity of the coastal community in Roman times is repeated by a second floruit during the High Medieval period. This renaissance of maritime activity can be readily attributed to the growth of the Cistercian abbey of Quarr after the arrival of its founding community from Savigny in AD 1132. Some of the ships of Quarr are recorded during the 14th century. These include *la Mariote* which was transporting Isle of Wight corn to Scotland in AD 1303 and a single-masted cog, *la Seinte Marie*, which was carrying a similar cargo to the Landes coast of Gascony in AD 1347. In AD 1365 *la Anne* and *la Martha* and 'other ships of the Abbey' are named in a special grace allowing them to enter port free of all prisage of wine. Another ship ferrying Gascony wine is the *la Katerine* of Quarre which is cited in AD 1396 (Hockey 1970 & 1991).

A further ship of this period to be made known to us is *la Nicholas*. This was anchored at *Falleye* [Fawley] in AD 1327 when it was raided by men from Southampton (Hockey 1970). We are told that this ship was the property of the Abbot of Quarr and on this occasion seems to have been leased to some Southampton merchants who were transporting goods to Sluys in Denmark. This account

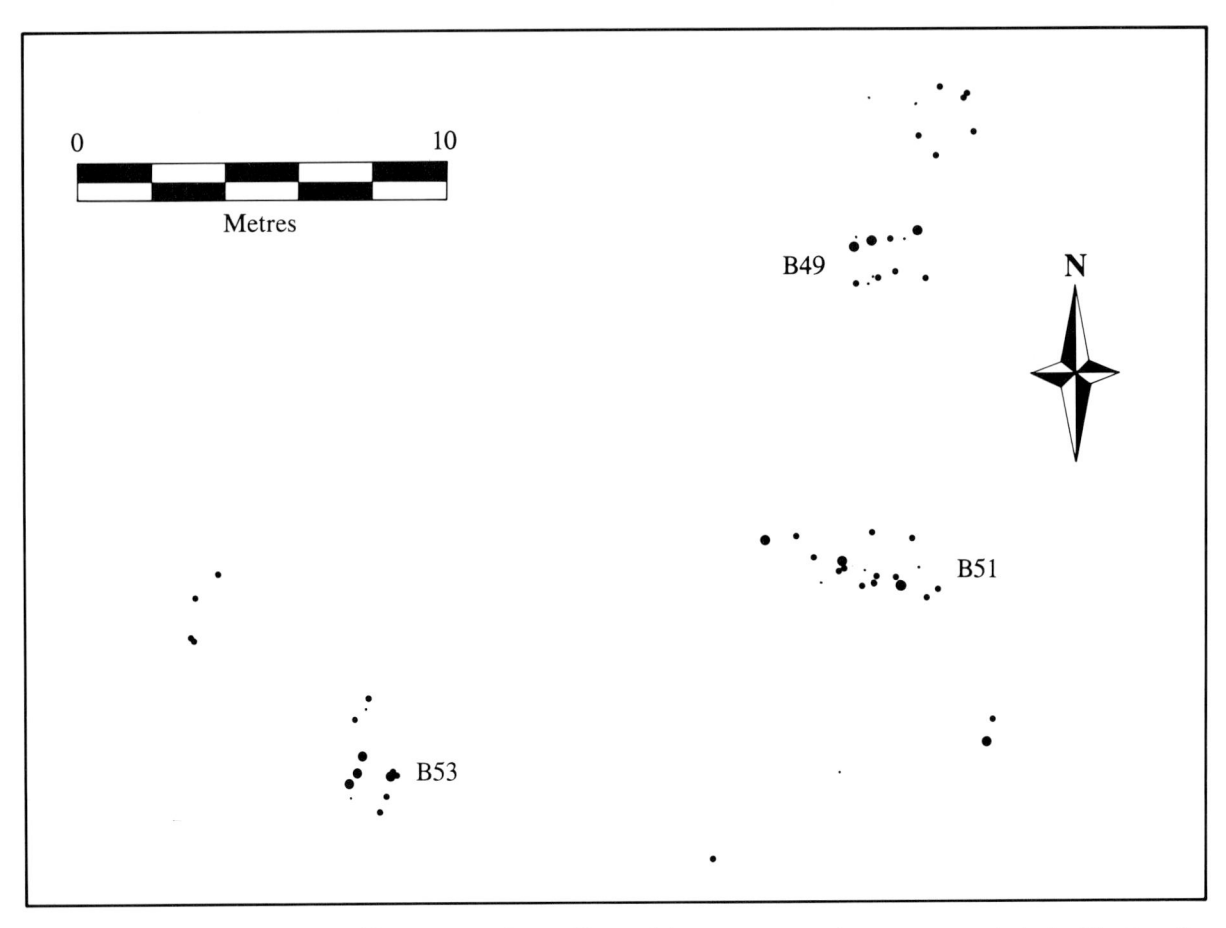

Figure 11.3 Early Bronze Age trap-like structures located beyond the present mean low water margin in the Wootton-Quarr study area at Binstead.

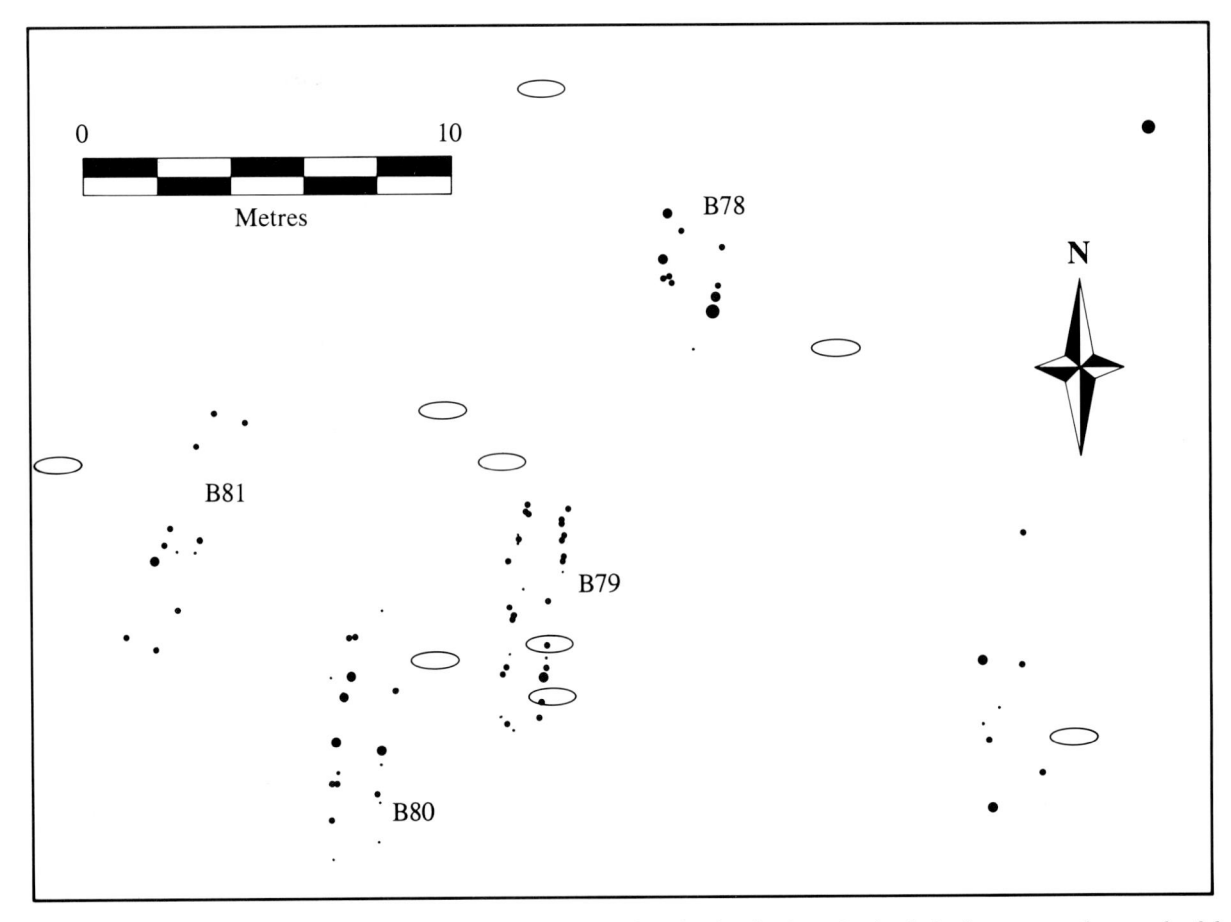

Figure 11.4 Later Bronze Age posts in settings which are postulated to be the feet of raised platforms near the mouth of the Binstead palaeochannel. Oval symbols denote the distribution of Later Bronze Age ceramics.

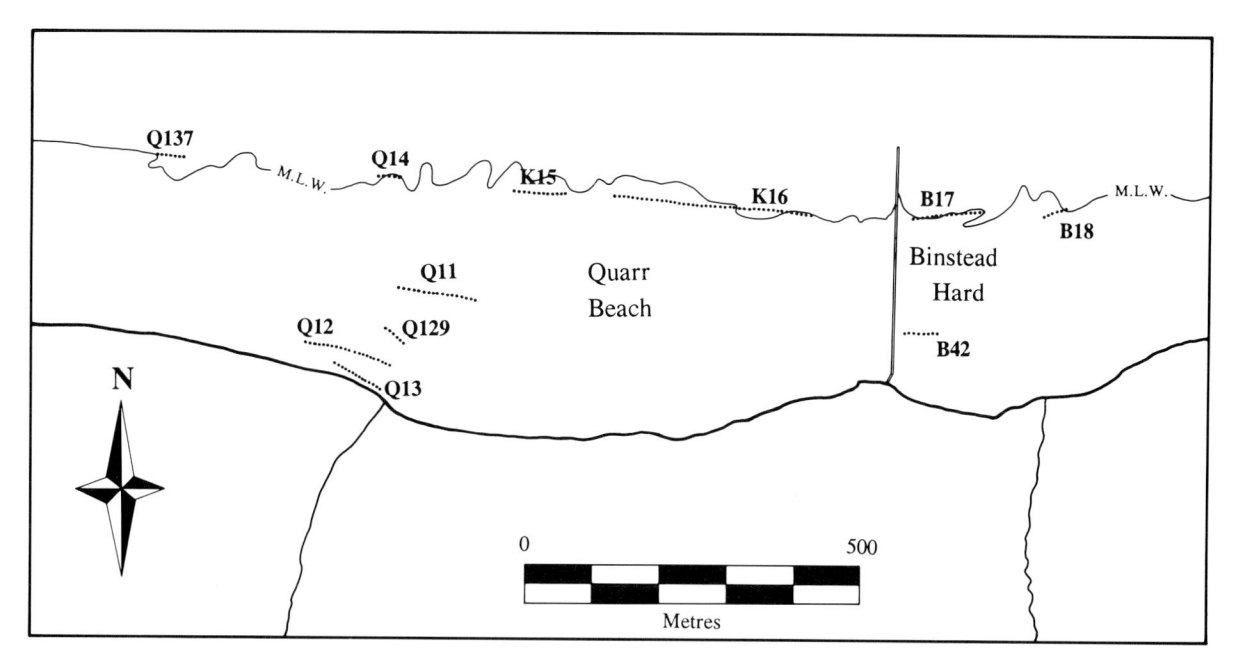

Figure 11.5 Multi-period array of longshore stake alignments on the Wootton-Quarr coast.

confirms that the boats of the abbey included those of ocean-going capability and that sufficient of these craft were used in lucrative leasing or hiring arrangements.

It is uncertain whether such ships were manned by a monastic crew but the seizing of the *La Nicholas* could imply that the Southampton raiders of AD 1327 considered such a crew to be an easy target. Evidence suggesting that *La Nicholas* carried out long-distance trading expeditions is confirmed by the destinations recorded for *la Mariote, la Seinte Marie* and *la Katerine*. The evidence offered by all of these ships confirms that the Haven was used for more than local trade in medieval times.

The brethren of Quarr are also known to have maintained other maritime interests. These included a warehouse in Portsmouth, a merchants house in Southampton, property in Honfleur and wharfage in Great Yarmouth (Hockey *ibid*). With interests such as these it seems hardly surprising to find that a high proportion of imported ceramics had also become entombed in the intertidal mud on the east shore of the Haven.

More surprising is the archaeological evidence offered by the alignments of wooden posts that survive in the intertidal zone of Wootton-Quarr (Fig. 11.5). These were first erected parallel to the shore in Iron Age times. During the 8th-9th century a very substantial longshore alignment of wooden stakes was erected on the open alluvial coast. With its outlying portions this structure seems to be approximately 1 km in length and it represents considerable investment of human energy. It is mostly composed of oak stakes, some 0.25m to 0.40m in diameter. These have been driven into the intertidal sediments close to the present mean low water mark. The stakes are generally set between 0.5 and 2m apart and they are aligned parallel to the shore. The surviving tips of these stakes have been found to penetrate up to a depth of 1m into the mud but in a number of instances no more than 0.3m of the sharpened tip has survived.

It is currently assumed that an alignment of this type was erected as a fish weir and, given that the present tidal range is 4.7m, it could easily have stood proud of the seabed to a height of 2m or more. During the high Medieval period similar, but rather shorter, alignments of this type were erected further up the beach where their siting may have been better adjusted to a rising sea-level. These alignments perhaps served the requirements of the Cistercian community and some of the needs of the contemporary force of quarrymen and stoneworkers who are known to have been working the limestone pits in the vicinity of the church at Binstead. Standing just 200m inland from the fish weirs, the siting of this church suggests the presence of a sizeable community settled in the coastal woodlands of Binstead in Late Saxon and early Norman times.

The archaeology of the off-shore zone

The earliest submerged structures to attract our attention are the five Neolithic trackways that have been identified on 3km of coast between Wootton Haven and Binstead Beach. Each of these trackways is situated on the open coast and has been traced, by wading, up to a maximum depth of -2.9m OD in the sub-tidal zone. The evidence assembled during the coastal survey has shown that, above mean low water mark, these structures have been virtually eradicated by wave action. In the sub-tidal zone however,

Figure 11.6 Ptolemy's location of the Magnus Portus *as depicted in one of the many medieval editions of his* Cosmographia.

they can be exposed on the seabed as remnant pegs, as exposed platforms or they may be probed beneath some 0.3m of sediment.

The distance for which these trackways extend offshore across the Mother Bank shelf and the depth to which they descend is clearly important not only for their interpretation but for the calculation of regional sea-level rise and coastal change. The survival of these types of structure in the sub-tidal zone is by no means assured for they can be afforded no formal protection from navigational or capital dredging regimes. At Quarr these structures are currently being damaged by cockle trawling.

Scatters of artefacts of Roman and post-Roman date have proved to be an unusual feature of the sub-tidal zone. A principal strew of ceramics has been identified at a depth of 10–20m at the eastern foot of the Ryde Middle Bank (Fig. 11.1 area C and locus 1). Here, fragments of 17 Roman vessels, 64 medieval vessels and 175 post-medieval vessels have been recovered.

These ceramics might be attributed to the persistent use of two historic anchorages lying east of the bank. These are Spithead anchorage (Fig. 11.1 locus 2) and Mother Bank anchorage (Fig. 11.1 locus 3) both of which

are scoured each day by a westward current leading to the foot of the Middle Bank. The movement of bed-load along this path is not currently understood but it is hoped that this may be elucidated by examination of bed-forms revealed by sidescan sonar and by further studies of sediment transport carried out by the University of Southampton Dept of Oceanography.

It has been particularly helpful to find that the relative quantities and the sources of foreign medieval ceramics derived from these anchorage strews make useful comparison with the accounts of foreign shipping recorded in the early port books of Southampton. A further comparison with the strewn material found at the landing place at Wootton Haven has yet to be made. Other archaeological material obtained from the controlled trawl has included leatherwork, human remains, glassware and a small array of items provisionally attributed to post-medieval shipwreck.

The off-shore zone and the Magnus Portus

The occurrence of Roman material in what appears to be a derived anchorage context in the off-shore zone prompts us to consider the true antiquity of the two historic anchorages which are known to us from post-medieval times.

The presence of a 'great harbour' on the Wessex seaboard was first recorded by Ptolemy in his *Geography* of *c*. AD 140–150 (Rivet & Smith 1979, 408). Medieval maps considered to be copies of lost Roman maps accompanying Ptolemy's text all show this 'great port' to lie between the island of *Vectis* and the neighbouring mainland (Fig. 11.6).

Rivet comments that Ptolemy obtained much of his information from earlier works and that coastal details of Britain were probably acquired from records of the later 1st century AD. These, it seems, included at least one official survey (Rivet & Smith 1979, 116–7). Elsewhere in his 'geography', Ptolemy provides a list of coastal names in which he excludes the proper names of places but includes descriptive ones. It is for this reason that Rivet argues that the *Magnus Portus* recorded by Ptolemy in his inventory, and displayed on the associated maps, is best interpreted as a description of the whole of the sheltered coast between the Isle of Wight and the mainland.

Once we accept that the name *Magnus Portus* is descriptive of a section of coast, rather than a specific coastal settlement, we are prompted to question how large this anchorage and coastline might be. Rivet suggests that the whole of the Solent and Southampton Water might be included. While this might indeed be the case, our growing knowledge of historic anchorages in this area suggests that it would only be favoured creeks and sheltered 'roads' or moorings that would be actually utilised by visiting craft.

Ptolemy's description of a 'great port' prompts us to

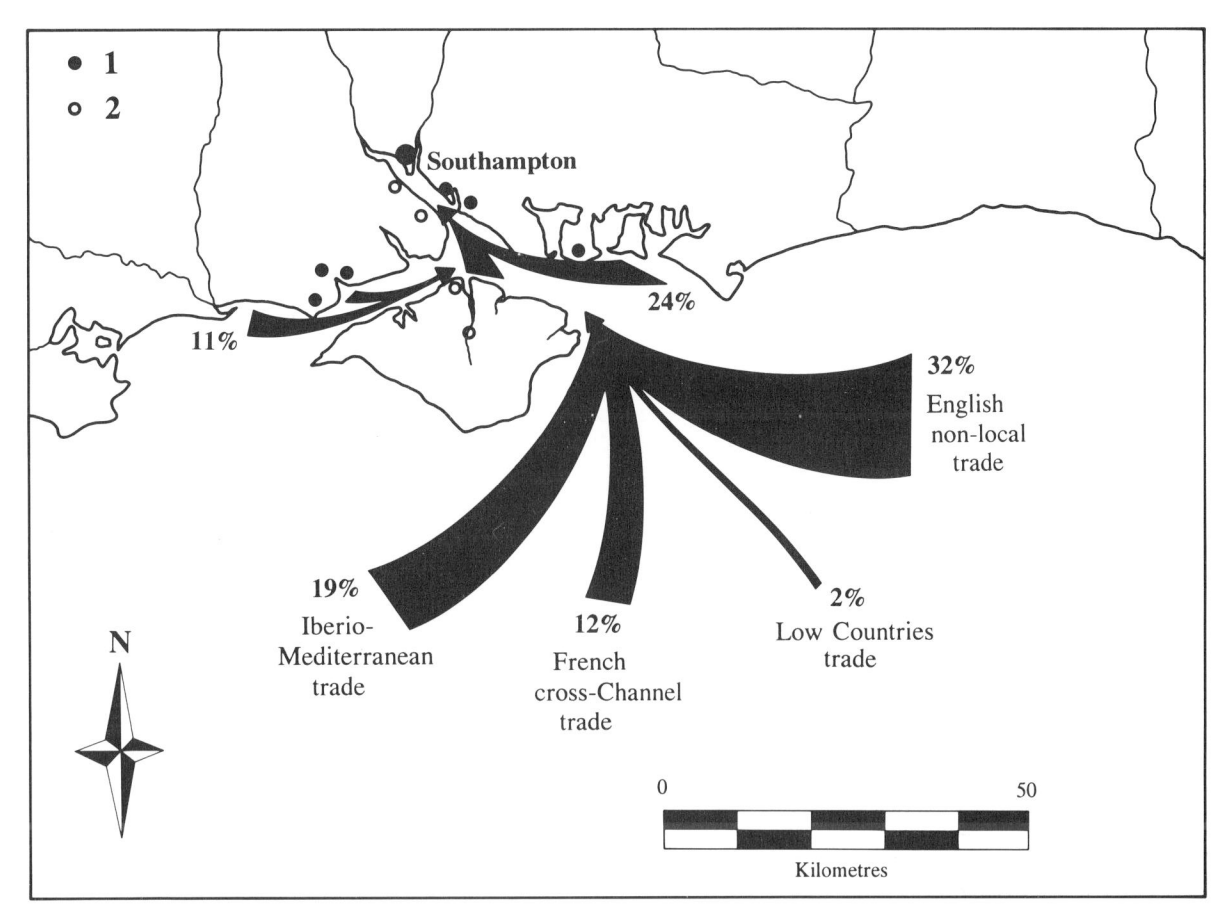

Figure 11.7 Networking of local craft via the port of Southampton in AD 1435–6. The sources of alien craft and the member ports of the collective customs system or 'liberty' are also shown. Member ports are identified as – 1 documented, 2 probable.

consider another classical descriptive reference that might be applied to the coastline of our region. This is the reference made around the mid 1st century BC to the market or '*emporion*' used by *Venetic* seafarers conveying goods from Armorica to Britain. Attempts to identify the location of this 'market', cited by Strabo, have resulted in appealing claims for Hengistbury Head where significant quantities of Armorican imports have been found (Mays 1981; Cunliffe 1987). As a descriptive term however, 'the market' might be applied, collectively, to a broad array or confederation of receptive and intercommunicating coastal communities. One possible setting for such a coastal market might be the *ria* coast between Hengistbury and the Chichester Channel. A broader interpretation might include Lulworth and Selsey.

In either of these cases it can be argued that the great natural port or seaway presented by the Solent was a pivotal point in nurturing a local coastal trading network in which Gallic traders might participate. The relative importance of these favoured anchorages, harbours and landing places in different parts of the network might change over time. This could allow early economic successes at Hengistbury to be eclipsed by more effective hinterlands served by the Roman system of roads and later by the requirements of Saxon settlement. A later model of such a network survives in the unification of ports within the liberty of Southampton as recorded in the port books of the 14th and 15th centuries. An analysis of a one year shipping account recorded in the port book of AD 1435–6 for Southampton reveals the extent and frequency of local coastal traffic collaborating in this confederated system (Fig. 11.7).

For later prehistoric times and the Roman period, a somewhat similar history may await determination by means of a thorough investigation of the anchorage strews which are now known to survive on the floor of the Solent. These strews offer an appropriate complement to the historical evidence of post-medieval times. This shows that the natural maritime amenities of the eastern Solent were readily seized upon as a great port or anchorage ideally suited to the needs of foreign craft. It is due to the appraisal of submerged and intertidal landscapes encompassed within the Wootton-Quarr project that the potential of this seabed evidence can be finally grasped.

Conclusion

The rapid survey of concealed and submerged archaeological resources on the Wootton-Quarr coast has drawn our attention to a variety of new issues.

1. The survey has revealed that favourable depositional environments in the intertidal and sub-tidal sections of a sheltered coast can contain extensive and well preserved evidence of prehistoric coastal activity which need not necessarily be reflected in the archaeological evidence available immediately onshore. The chemical and biological stability of these environments requires careful management and monitoring.
2. The survey has demonstrated that natural harbours and their hinterlands deserve special consideration as the focal points at which early maritime communities can develop. Such considerations and safeguards should extend to the identification of concealed archaeological deposits preserved below mean low water mark.
3. Archaeological appraisal of the submerged landscape in the offshore zone demonstrates that anchorage strews and palaeoshoals are an important archaeological resource capable of revealing the prehistory and history of national and international trade.
4. Experiments in the seaward dimension of the study area have revealed a need to develop and deploy geo-acoustical survey, monitored trawling and underwater inspection as means of identifying, quantifying and protecting the national archaeological resources concealed in a submerged landscape.
5. The quantity of archaeological material regularly recovered by fishermen from the submerged landscape has emphasised the need to ensure that liaison, monitoring and recording on a seasonal basis can be built into the operation of the local Sites and Monuments Record (SMR). Unfortunately a present lack of statutory recognition for local Sites and Monuments Records discriminates against coastal authorities who may seek to remedy this problem.
6. Palaeoenvironmental investigations carried out over the intertidal zone, the *ria* floor and the catchment of the creek have been particularly rewarding. These attest the value of deploying diatom analysis, palynological and sedimentological studies as a means of establishing the history of human coastal settlement and the nature, scale and pace of erosional changes to the coastal landscape.
7. The project has identified a number of disturbing flaws in the level of management and protection that can be offered to certain elements of the archaeological landscape in the coastal zone. In the sub-tidal zone, archaeological deposits were found to be denied formal protection from the destructive effects of navigational dredging and were poorly served by the exemptions awarded to harbour authorities.
8. At the mouth of Wootton Creek it was found that early wooden structures of Bronze Age and subsequent dates were subject to highly active and destructive effects of wave action and draw-down. Rich cultural strews in the intertidal zone were subject to similar destructive processes. These processes could be associated with maintenance dredging for the adjacent ferry channel.
9. In the sub-tidal zone of the Solent's southern shore, it was found that the archaeological safeguards required by PPG16 and PPG20 could not be applied to the building of an off-shore island and marina until the primary stage of dumping and build-up had brought the new island clear of mean low water mark. At present this proposal is in abeyance but the flaw in the intent of PPG16 makes this proposal a continuing threat.
10. On the open intertidal coast, the loss of a rich array of earlier prehistoric structures has been provisionally attributed to a recent cessation of sediment accretion and a contemporary die back of the stabilising and protective blanket of *Spartina* grass. This is a change which has been observed since the 1950's and it appears to be coincident with an increase in the discharge of nutrient-rich sewage into the Solent and an increase in the passage of large container ships through the Eastern Solent (Tubbs 1991).

The final comment on this coastal landscape must address the development of a Shoreline Management Plan (SMP). These plans are a recent non-statutory initiative prompted by central Government through MAFF. Government considers that these *'need to be consistent with, and provide an input into, statutory development plans under the Town and Country Planning Act 1990'* (DOE 1992). On the Wight coast the formulation of such a plan is led by the Isle of Wight Council which is a Unitary Authority charged with coastal protection responsibilities. Shoreline Management Plans advocate a holistic yet voluntary approach to the management of the coast and their guidelines advise that archaeological and historic features are important assets that should be recognised. Presumably, these considerations can gather greater force if they are identified in the input Government recommends into statutory development plans.

These guidelines also recognise that some plans may need to address the effects of commercial offshore dredging and the dredging of harbour entrances (MAFF 1995 2.14 & 2.15). Unfortunately these guidelines seem to fall notably short of earlier coastal protection advice advocated by MAFF. This emphasised that all sites should be assumed to have at least four components of environmental significance, including archaeology, and that a lack of quantitative data should not lead to the archaeological interest being overlooked (Penning-Rowsell *et al* 1992).

Due to coincidental and very substantial support from

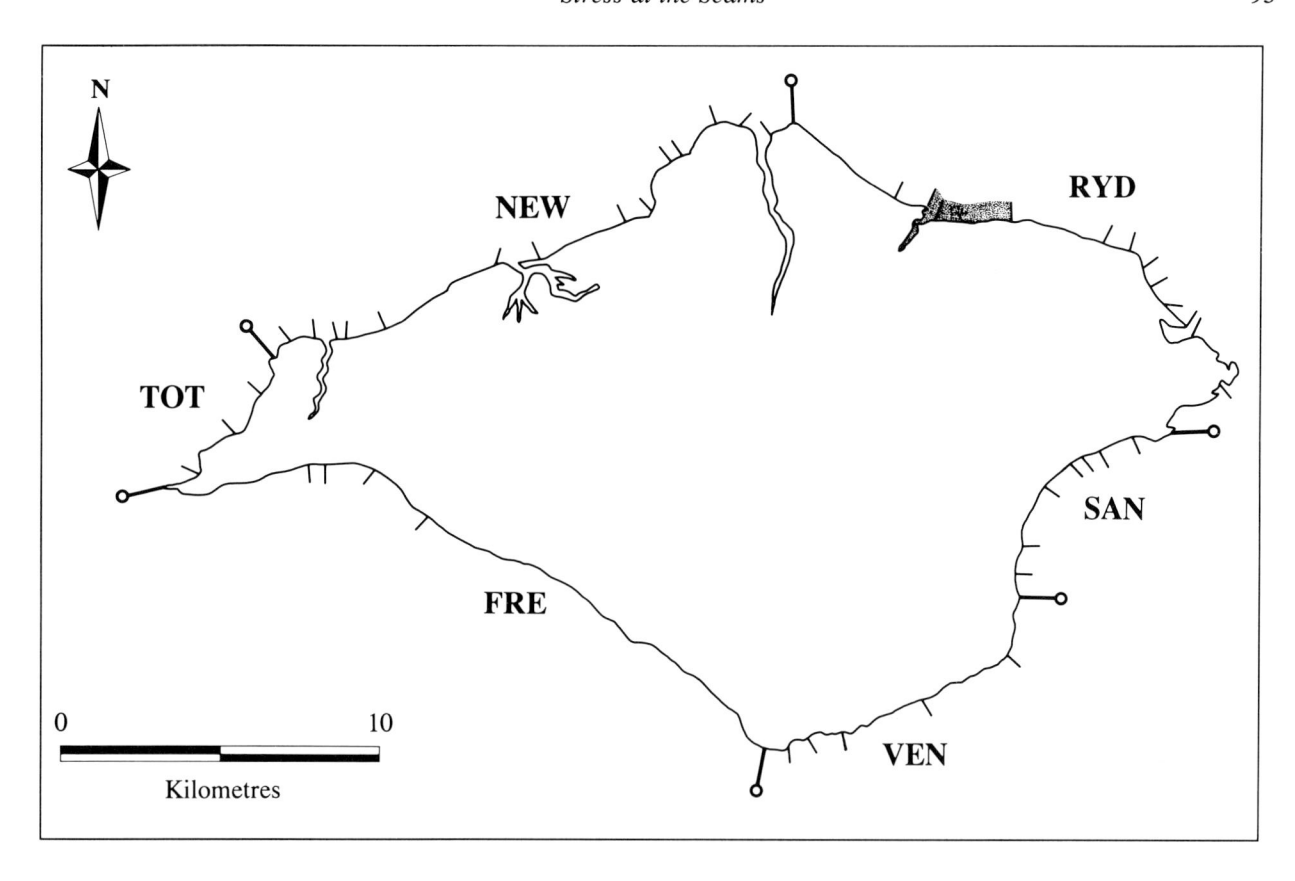

Figure 11.8 The eroding coastal landscape of Wight divided into its coastal process units and management units. All 52 management units are due to receive 75 year management and protection prescriptions yet only 6% (shaded) have received field evaluation of cultural heritage loss. In these surveyed units the number of archaeological sites has been increased by 1800%.

English Heritage it has been possible to make a well informed evaluation of the archaeological resources of the Wootton-Quarr coast. It is particularly fortunate that this evaluation has preceded the assessment by the Coastal Protection Authority of the management needs of the 'coastal process unit' which embraces this portion of the coast. Nevertheless, the standard set of shoreline management options offered by Government and MAFF can still relegate these cultural resources to progressive destruction by means of 'managed setback'. This weak prescription can arise because the cultural resource, whatever its national or international importance may be, can only be classified as an 'unquantifiable benefit'. This cannot score vital points in the general formula for prioritising the needs of coastal protection (Penning-Rowsell *et al* 1992).

The archaeological evidence at Wootton-Quarr nevertheless suggests that prior to very recent events, the intertidal zone has been historically stable and that a long history of accretion has preserved features of great antiquity. This prompts the question as to whether archaeological investigation should be generally employed as a means of establishing a shoreline history that should be considered prior to the choice of shoreline management option. In this particular case it might be argued that the archaeological evidence suggests that a stable and accreting coastline has only been destabilised during a recent episode which is marked by increased human impact. In this case a soft engineering option might be sought as a means of 'holding the line' and re-establishing accreting conditions.

Elsewhere on the coast of the Isle of Wight, a total of fifty two individual 'management units' have now been identified where prescriptions for coastal defence seem likely to proceed on the basis of a desk-top assessment of the cultural resources of the shoreline (Fig. 11.8). The concealed archaeological landscape unmasked in the Wootton-Quarr project shows just how wide the chasm between desk-top perception and reality can be. The evidence assembled in this new coastal survey provides a salutary warning of the pit-falls which await an unwary environmental consultant who may be tempted to use the random and possibly archaic gatherings of a Sites and Monuments Record to determine the management needs of the cultural heritage within the intertidal and sub-tidal zones.

In a changing administrative climate where desk-top appraisal of old data can be more economically appealing than investment in primary field survey and research, there is an ever-present danger that non-statutory provision for our coastal heritage can appear as an eminently soft target in the predatory search for 'efficiency savings'. The Wootton-Quarr project reveals a rich and vulnerable segment of the national cultural resource in the coastal zone. Here, English Heritage and the local authority have been able to glimpse heritage loss in the sub-tidal zone. They are, however, currently denied any empowerment to stray across the artificial seam that is perceived to lie along the wavering mean low water boundary.

Over the past decades some remarkable misapprehensions and presumptions have gained common acceptance when plans have been made to protect the environment of the sub-tidal zone. Not least has been the subliminal persuasion offered by successive generations of maps on which the topography of the underwater landscape has been so seductively mis-represented as a sterile plain of beguiling blue. Here, historic shipwrecks have been scattered like decoys to allure the attention of our legislators away from the wider vision of the submerged national archaeological resource.

The seamless view of the coastal archaeological landscape at Wootton-Quarr confronts many assumptions. In particular, it demonstrates that an absence of field-validated evidence should never be accepted as evidence of archaeological absence in the intertidal and sub-tidal zones. This is a lesson that cannot be over-emphasised when we come to assess future environmental impacts and changes on our European coastline.

Acknowledgements

Generous grant and technical aid by English Heritage has enabled the Isle of Wight Council to expand the coverage and vision of its sites and monuments service over a key section of its coastal zone. We are grateful to the Isle of Wight Council for its initiative in promoting this primary research and we are especially thankful to Frank Basford, Rebecca Loader, David Motkin, Ivor Westmore, Alan Brading, Kevin Trott and Nick Blake who all have persisted with primary fieldwork in the worst imaginable conditions.

Environmental studies have been co-ordinated by Dr Rob Scaife and carried out by Dr Antony Long, Dr Nigel Cameron, Dr Mark Robinson, Matthew Canti and Jean Dean. Monitoring of the intertidal depositional environment has been planned and executed by Mike Corfield of the Ancient Monuments Laboratory and Paul Simpson of the Museums and Heritage Service of the Isle of Wight Council.

Geophysical analyses cited in this text have been carried out Dr Justin Dix, Robin Edwards and Anthony Hanks. Absolute dating has been co-ordinated by Jennifer Hillam and Alex Bayliss. Off-shore underwater inspection has been co-ordinated by Brian Sparks, Sarah Draper and Gary Momber of the Hampshire and Wight Trust for Maritime Archaeology. The direction of the on-shore project has been guided by Paul Gosling, Steve Trow, Clare de Rouffignac and Sarah Reilly of English Heritage.

A mosaic of access requests have all been kindly acceded by the residents of the Wootton-Quarr area. Especial thanks are due to the Abbot and community of monks of the modern Abbey of Quarr who have generously helped in a wide variety of ways to ensure the success of this project.

References

Bray, M.J., Carter, D.J. & Hooke, J.M. 1991: *Coastal sediment transport study; report to the Standing Conference on problems associated with the coastline (SCOPAC).* Vol 3, the Solent & Isle of Wight. (University of Portsmouth and Isle of Wight Council).

Cunliffe, B. 1987: *Hengistbury Head, Dorset. Vol 1: The prehistoric and Roman settlement, 3500 BC–AD 500.* Oxford University Committee for Archaeology Monograph 13.

DOE. 1992: *Coastal zone protection and planning: Government's response to the second report from the House of Commons Select Committee on the Environment.* (HMSO).

DOE. 1993a: *Planning in the coastal zone.* Department of Environment: Welsh Office. (HMSO).

DOE. 1993b: *Development below low water mark: a review of regulation in England and Wales.* Department of Environment: Welsh Office. (HMSO).

Dyer, K.R. 1975: 'The buried channels of the 'Solent River' southern England'. *Proceedings of the Geological Association,* 86, 239–245.

Everard, C.E. 1954: 'The Solent River, a geomorphological study'. *Transactions of the Institute of British Geographers,* 20, 41–58.

Fox, W.D. 1861: 'When and how was the Isle of Wight severed from the mainland'. *The Geologist,* 5, 452.

Fulford, M., Champion, T.C. & Long, A. 1997: *England's coastal heritage; a survey for English Heritage and the RCHME.* English Heritage Archaeological Report 15. (London).

Hockey, S.F. 1970: *Quarr Abbey and its lands 1132–1631.* (Leicester University Press).

Hockey, S.F. 1991: *The Charters of Quarr Abbey.* (Isle of Wight County Council).

JNAPC. 1995: *Code of Practice for Seabed Developers.*

MAFF. 1995: *Shoreline management plans: a guide for coastal defence authorities.* (London).

Mays, M. 1981: 'Strabo IV 4.1: a reference to Hengistbury Head?', *Antiquity,* 55, 55–57.

Penning-Rowsell, E.C., Green, C.H., Thompson, P.M., Coker, A.M., Tunstall, S.M., Richards, C. & Parker, D.J. 1992: *The economics of coastal management; a manual of benefit assessment techniques.* (The yellow manual). (Belhaven Press. London).

RCHM/EH. 1996: *England's Coastal Heritage: A Statement on the Management of Coastal Archaeology.*

Rivet, A.L.F. & Smith, C. 1979: *Place-names of Roman Britain.* Batsford. (London).

Scaife, R.G. 1986: *Palaeoecological investigations in the Isle of Wight.* Unpub. PhD thesis. University of London.

Tomalin, D.J. 1993: 'Maritime archaeology as a coastal management issue; a Solent case study from the SCOPAC coast'. *Proc Littlehampton Conference on the Regional Coastal Groups after the House of Commons Report. October 1992.* Standing Conference on Problems Associated with the Coastline (SCOPAC). (Isle of Wight County Council).

Tubbs, C.R. 1991: *The Solent; a changing wild-life heritage.* Hampshire & Wight Wild Life Trust. (Romsey).

Wainwright, G.J. 1991: *Exploring our past: strategies for the archaeology of England.* (English Heritage. London).

12. The Langstone Harbour Intertidal Archaeological Project: Building a GIS for Data Integration

Dominic Fontana, Peter Collier and Alastair Pearson

This multi-disciplinary project aims to develop a Geographic Information System (GIS) to hold and display archaeological and environmental data for the analysis of an inter-tidal zone: Langstone Harbour on the south coast of Hampshire, England forms the study area. The project is being carried out with the support of The Royal Society for the Protection of Birds (RSPB) and Hampshire County Council. Metric aerial photography and analytical photogrammetry are employed to create a detailed topographic base. The photogrammetric models were fitted within a control network established using a high precision differential Global Positioning System (GPS). Recorded three-dimensional co-ordinates of archaeological finds and structures will allow the comparison between environmental and locational contexts of coastal archaeological structures. This will greatly enhance the available archaeological data, adding value to it, as well as assisting the study of sea level change and wider coastal processes. Conversion and integration of other historical and environmental data is adding further data layers to the GIS.

Aims and Objectives

The development of the Geographic Information System (GIS) for integrating environmental, archaeological and historical data from Langstone Harbour resulted from the timely conjunction of several individual projects and the recent availability of appropriate computer technology.

From an archaeological perspective Langstone Harbour is an area of considerable potential importance (Allen *et al* 1993). Undoubtedly, it has long been an attractive site for much human activity. The proximity of plentiful food supplies including fish, wildfowl and shellfish, allied to the relative ease of coastal or international transport must have played a major part in ensuring its continual use. Limited archaeological field investigations in the past around the northern shoreline and within the intertidal zone have discovered archaeological sites and finds of all periods. These range from the later Mesolithic, around 7th-6th millennia BC, to those of very recent historical interest, including much material from the Second World War.

It seems likely that there are built structures and considerable accumulated detrital deposits associated with these coastal activities, and it is anticipated that archaeological evidence will survive in other, uninvestigated, areas of the Harbour. Indeed, because most of the Harbour's intertidal zone consists of a muddy and waterlogged environment much of the organic archaeological material should be surrounded by an anaerobic matrix and hence should remain in good condition. Certainly, this is the experience of much other maritime and intertidal archaeology notably the *Mary Rose* site in the Solent (Rule 1982), the *Wasa* in Stockholm and the London waterfront excavations of the 1980s (Milne 1985).

The archaeological aims of the initial stage of the project are straightforward. They are to detect archaeological remains and, together with known archaeological records, provide a full database of all surviving evidence. In so doing it should be possible to map known archaeological resources by period and to expose biases within the database.

Langstone Harbour is also a site of considerable environmental importance. The Harbour is a designated Site of Special Scientific Interest (SSSI) and has international status in combination with Chichester Harbour as a Ramsar Site for its important intertidal wetlands. It is also a Special Protection Area (SPA) which supports internationally significant numbers of migrant and over-wintering waders and wildfowl. The north of the Harbour contains an RSPB reserve, which provides secure nesting sites for many waders including Little Tern, Lapwing and Redshank. The harbour has provided a study site for marine biologists and geographers for many years. Extensive studies of the vegetation cover were conducted by the department of Geography at Portsmouth Polytechnic in the late 1970s and early 1980s (Budd 1980;1981;1982;1983). There is considerable continuing interest in the study of the harbour environment and there are several projects now being undertaken in the harbour by the University of Portsmouth.

The environmental aims of the project are therefore, equally clear: to record and examine evidence for erosion in the harbour; to map the current vegetation cover in the harbour and to create compatible digital maps from historical vegetation data for the harbour and to integrate the Low Water Bird Count Data provided by the RSPB.

The availability of the various existing data sets and the possibility of new data covering aspects of the environment, history and archaeology of the harbour offered a significant opportunity for developing a study which crossed the traditional boundaries of academic disciplines.

It is therefore important that the project should be able to link the results of these archaeological, environmental and biological studies with further research into the history of the harbour. Each of the separate data sets assists in compiling a research tool which more closely models the interactive complexity of the harbour system than any single study's data set. A Geographic Information System (GIS) provides the vehicle to fulfil these aims of joining these disparate data sets together in a meaningful way.

Geographic Information Systems (GIS) and archaeology

The ability of GIS to integrate different data sets, using geographical position as a common spatial framework, is of considerable potential benefit to many individual areas of research – archaeology, biology, geomorphology, history and geography to name but a few.

Until recently, typical analytical methods such as spatial auto-correlation, cluster analysis, variance to mean ratios amongst others, have been used to analyze social organisation and spatial clustering. However, opinions vary as to the success of these methods when applied to archaeology. Indeed, recognition of their limitations is not a recent phenomenon. During the height of their use Paynter *et al* (1974) contended that "Analytical methods such as spatial auto-correlation and the mapping of principal components have not been able to provide understandable answers to the questions asked of them."

Classic statistical models are generally not designed for three-dimensional spatial analysis. GIS models space mathematically and include a graphic component that models spatially referenced data. Archaeologists are beginning to view GIS as providing a range of methods and techniques that through description and interpretation of the data facilitate problem solving and thus make possible "the true integration of natural and cultural factors in modelling and recreating past cultural landscapes." (Green 1990, p.356) The overlay, correlation and comparison of multi-dimensional maps is seen as a primary requirement in the study of archaeological landscapes. Analysis and display of hard copy maps is viewed as problematic and the mathematical manipulation of the mapped data is also difficult. One of the key problems highlighted is the inflexibility of hard copy maps. Classifications and intervals have to be established and are relatively inflexible in comparison to reclassification functions of GIS. However, savings in time are relatively insignificant in comparison to the benefits it provides in terms of how archaeologists can think about and interpret space (Green 1990).

Considerable attention is being drawn to the fundamental analytical functions of GIS. Its potential to interrelate spatially referenced data as map overlays and manipulate and analyse these data-maps is reasonably well known (Burrough 1986). However, the successful application of GIS to both the coastal environment and archaeology depends on several key components beyond the mere capability of the hardware and software. The biggest stumbling block in its application has been the lack of data of suitable metrical accuracy, completeness and consistency. Consideration of the provision of high quality spatially referenced data therefore forms the bulk of this paper.

In addition to the need for appropriately high quality data a multi-disciplinary team was seen as essential for the Langstone Harbour Project. It consists of marine archaeologists, terrestrial archaeologists, surveyors, photogrammetrists, GIS specialists, marine biologists and geomorphologists.

Secondary data sources

In the case of Langstone Harbour secondary data sources consist of available topographic and geological maps. Other documents relating to past research on the ecology and surviving archaeology also have to be included.

Archaeological records

For known archaeological data the county Sites Monuments Record (SMR) is a crucial starting point as it should provide information on the nature, extent and shape of known sites and provide an indication of the likelihood of remains surviving in areas apparently devoid of significant archaeology.

The SMR situation in Hampshire is relatively sophisticated as its SMR is managed by an ORACLE database supported by a GIS using ARC/INFO. In fact, many SMRs have computerised their records over the past two decades in an attempt to maintain and analyse their data more efficiently. As with most organisations given the responsibility of maintaining and managing inventories, archaeological organisations have computerised existing card indexes to improve the efficiency of data entry, storage and retrieval. However, this has been undertaken with little view to expanding the capability of the database to link to available and associated site plans and maps. Indeed, Harris and Lock (1990) comment that "a regrettable feature of the computerisation of the archaeological discipline over the past two decades is that the process has tended to exclude the full locational component from the archaeological record." As a result even the best of the SMRs are insufficiently spatially referenced. It is this "full locational component" which is of prime importance in the study of intertidal coastal archaeology if the full potential of the archaeological record is to be realised. The study of sea-level change and coastal morphological change necessitates such precision, as the data needs to be compared over a far wider area than is covered by any single county SMR.

Topographic mapping

In order to provide the geographical context for the archaeological and environmental data a highly accurate base map is used as the fundamental framework of the GIS being developed for Langstone Harbour. This will be used in modelling the environmental and archaeological distributions within three dimensions.

Available mapping

The Ordnance Survey mapping across the entire harbour is available at a maximum scale of 1:2,500 and for the Portsmouth coast at 1:1,250. The Admiralty chart of Langstone and Chichester Harbours is available at a scale of 1:20,000. A prototype map integrating the Admiralty chart data with O.S. mapping has recently been published for Langstone Harbour at a scale of 1:25,000.

The use of Ordnance Survey maps or Admiralty charts for building a coastal zone GIS presents significant problems. Understandably, these maps are designed to meet the needs of a broad user base. However, they were not produced with the assessment of change or three-dimensional modelling as an intended application. As a result much of the information is of insufficient accuracy and detail to support the aims and objectives of this study.

Maps are not normally the product of one hand and one time (Collier *et al* 1994). Due to the complex nature of the map production process, it is inevitable that many different individuals will be involved in the production of any single map sheet. Individual map sheets rarely result from a single survey. Usually they have evolved through a series of revisions to their present form. Where the map is at the basic scale for that area it should represent a reasonable picture of the situation on the ground at the time of last revision. However, where the map has been compiled from larger scale maps of that area, the state of revision may vary across the sheet. Consequently it will not represent the situation on the ground at any one point in time. Additionally, the revision methods will have varied over the years. This means that the resultant map cannot be used as a reliable baseline for any studies which attempt to look at change over time.

Problems concerning the use of secondary map sources are not peculiar to those mapping the intertidal zone. However, the physical characteristics of the intertidal zone, typically flat with little appreciable change in relief, places particular demands on existing topographic maps.

A popular use of historical maps has been to map and measure change in the landscape. Studies have typically taken a stretch of river or a coastal spit and attempted retrospective change monitoring. Such an approach is fraught with difficulty, as the detected change may be largely the result of cartographic error. Adequate field verification is therefore required to substantiate map evidence. Successful application of such methods is limited to areas where change is likely to be of a macro rather than micro scale. Unfortunately, such methods are unlikely to yield valid or verifiable results in the relatively stable environment of Langstone Harbour where change is expected to be significant but subtle. It is therefore even more difficult to determine whether detected change in planimetric position reflects geomorphological processes or merely cartographic error. In the studies carried out on Langstone Harbour it has been found that most of the apparent changes in the mudflats and channels as shown on various maps are due to differences in the surveys and depictions of the features rather than actual changes in the features themselves. This makes it extremely difficult to use topographic maps to study past changes in any quantitative way though it does not preclude their use as a very soft data source that must be very carefully interpreted.

The nature of the intertidal zone is also problematic when we consider the modelling of its surface. Even large scale O.S. maps do not contain adequate height data for the three-dimensional modelling of environmental and archaeological distributions. The 1:2,500 O.S. mapping is restricted to a few spot heights and the 1:10,000 series has 5–metre contouring. As all heights in the harbour are below 5 metres no contours appear on the maps. The Admiralty charts have more height and depth data shown but as these relate to chart datum, which itself is related to Lowest Astronomical Tide (LAT). Unfortunately, LAT differs with specific location and therefore the exact height of a particular location is difficult to ascertain and will not result in sufficient precision for the exacting needs of the project.

The Ordnance Survey use a single height datum for the UK based on six year's observations of mean sea-level at Newlyn, Cornwall between 1915 and 1921, whereas the Hydrographic Office relate their Chart Datum (heighting) to the "lowest expected astronomical tide". This method of determining a datum will ensure that a mariner using the chart will always be able to keep sufficient depth of water beneath his vessel but does not allow the establishment of the height of a specific point. In the case of the Langstone and Chichester Harbours (chart No. 3418) there is nothing shown on the chart itself to indicate a potential problem. However, the difficulty of fixing heighting to a particular point in space is amply illustrated in the "Outer Approaches to The Solent" Chart No. 2045 (Edition 19th October 1990) which includes a table giving the relationship between Chart Datum (C.D.) which is based on LAT and Ordnance Datum (Newlyn) (O.D.). The figure for Portsmouth Harbour is that C.D. is 2.73 metres lower than O.D. but that the figure for Hurst Point is just 1.83 metres below O.D. and that C.D. is 3.05 metres below O.D. at Bognor Regis. Thus, there is a 1.2 metre difference in the vertical position of C.D. from West to East across the Solent in relation to the single fixed height of O.D.. If one is attempting to match height data sets from across a wider area than a single locality of a few square kilometres in size then this inability to define a height position becomes a significant difficulty. The problem of handling the variable height datum within and between sheets is one that even the Ordnance Survey and the Hydrographic Office have found difficult to resolve in their recent experimental attempt at a coastal zone map.

It can be seen then that both the Ordnance Survey maps and Admiralty charts are inappropriate for such a detailed study. The acknowledged limitations of available map sources are acute when we consider the intertidal zone. Interest in the coastal zone in terms of its perceived economic development potential and conservation needs are, after all, a relatively recent development and it is not surprising that such problems exist.

Mapping from primary data sources

To overcome the difficulties inherent in the existing mapping it was decided to use aerial photography as the primary data source. Photography has a number of advantages over maps due to the way in which the "product" is produced. As mentioned above, a map may be a composite of data collected over a considerable period of time whereas a photograph represents one particular moment in time, when the shutter was opened and the exposure made. Also, a photograph displays raw, uncontaminated data, as no attempt has been made to classify or structure the data contained within the image. A photograph may be used successfully by any number of specialists, each of whom can take from the image what he or she finds appropriate. This is undoubtedly a most significant feature of air photographs when applied to a multi-disciplinary study. Though the accuracy of the resultant mapping is, to a large extent, dictated by the type of photogrammetric instruments available, the content can be determined by the user. Should this user decide at some later date that additional or higher resolution information is required, the data still exists in its raw form on the photograph for that work to be carried out with relative ease.

Another major advantage of using photogrammetry is that the mapping of the harbour could be carried out, to a large extent, away from the site. The study area consists of a large expanse of tidal mud flats with limited accessibility and is an important breeding site and feeding ground for birds. Limiting damage was of prime importance. Given the environmental sensitivity of the location and the potential danger of surveying on mudflats, mapping had to be carried out with a minimum of ground survey. As an alternative, the possibility of using depth sounding equipment mounted in a boat was considered. However, many areas of the harbour are only 1–2 metres deep at high tide and access even with a small inflatable boat can be somewhat problematic. The photogrammetric mapping option was therefore chosen.

Air photography and provision of ground control

Stereo 1:5,000 scale colour photography was flown at low water spring tide by Cambridge University Committee for Aerial Photography in late July 1992. This provided the base data set for the mapping.

Highly accurate (±20 cm) photogrammetric mapping requires good quality ground control. To achieve this a control network of surveyed points, each visible in the photographs, was measured. It is standard practice to provide 2 (preferably 3) plan points, and 4 height points for each model. However, the availability of an analytical plotter and aerial triangulation software minimised the required number of control points. Ground control was therefore provided for only the beginning, middle and end of each strip of photography.

The Wild 200 system, a high precision Differential Global Positioning System (GPS), was kindly lent by Leica U.K. to establish accurate control points. This equipment fixes positions from U.S. Military Navstar Satellites to a claimed accuracy of 5mm + 1ppm. Supplementary ground control points were added using a Total Stations electronic theodolite.

The control network was fitted to a single O.S. triangulation pillar to ensure that the GIS map was internally precise. Any positional discrepancy in the fit of the survey to the National Grid could therefore be related to that single point. This would allow a simple global correction factor to be applied if required.

Once the control network had been constructed the photogrammetric plotting of the map data began. This was carried out using a data specification developed in the Langstone Harbour Project Research Design by the project team for Hampshire County Council (Pearson & Fontana 1993). This consisted of a form of progressive sampling whereby a 20–metre grid of spot heights was collected for the whole Harbour and a 10–metre grid was applied over areas of special interest. Positional accuracy of better than ±10 cm in Eastings and Northings and ±15 cm in height were achieved despite some problems in resolving the precise surface on the featureless mudflats.

In addition to the grid data, "hard" features and breaks of curve were collected to assist with the Digital Terrain Modelling (DTM) from which the contours were to be interpolated. At the same time the all the drainage lines were mapped along with the top and bottom edges of all major channels. All information was recorded on-line in x, y and z co-ordinates.

Ground control for the 1992 photography also provides control for mapping from earlier or later sets of air photography. This allows a direct comparison of the drainage patterns between photography dates to detect any mobility, scouring or filling of the channels. The height values from these linear features could also be used in the creation of the DTM, which would assist in building a higher precision representation of the changing ground surface.

Archaeological Data Collection

The archaeological data is collected using a hierarchical collection strategy. Firstly by field walking using a general rapid walkover technique and, in inundated areas, a rapid swimover technique. In both cases only limited quantities of diagnostic artefacts were collected. Secondly by transect sampling of the substrata using a hand auger across sections of the harbour. And thirdly by more detailed collection of artifactual evidence in selected 50 m x 50 m areas which themselves contain 1 m × 1 m total collection quadrats. These areas were selected on the basis of known occurrences of artifacts and the rapid walkover. In the 1m × 1m quadrats all of the archaeological evidence is systematically collected and recorded. This approach enables both a qualitative assessment of diagnostic material and a quantitative appraisal of the archaeological potential for the whole harbour. Each of these auger transect points, major find spots, detail areas and quadrats were surveyed into the control network using a Total Station theodolite so that all of the data that they contain is recorded as accurately as possible in X, Y and Z.

It is this precise recording of three dimensional coordinates of finds and structures that will allow the comparison, particularly by relative height, of any coastal structures and finds within Langstone Harbour or with those on other published sites across the U.K. as a whole. This will, potentially, greatly enlarge the available archaeological data set as well as adding value to it. It could, for example, contribute to the study of sea level change and wider coastal processes.

In Langstone Harbour there are a number of enigmatic timber structures which bear a resemblance to an Anglo-Saxon fish weir found in the River Colwick, Nottinghamshire and others of different dates on the Severn Estuary (Salisbury 1988). In order to function, coastal fish weirs needed to be built in certain locations such that they were only covered by water at high tide. They therefore offer an opportune means by which to estimate sea level for their period of construction and use. Additionally, as they are located close to the modern shoreline (within 30m) they give a good indication for the maximum extent of that part of the coast. This should assist in the assessment of coastal erosion for that locality. However, it must be recognised that the presence of the structure may itself have altered the process of change. Each structure may have been in use for an extended period and rebuilt many times hence it is important that any indications of prevailing sea level from one site are comparable, by height, to those from other places. As yet these structures have not been objectively dated, but it is intended to use dendrochronological dating methods on samples from these structures in the near future. The triangulation of their function, period and height location will be necessary to draw out any firm conclusions.

Wider triangulation will only prove possible if other studies adopt the recording of accurate positional data that relates to National Grid and Ordnance Datum (Newlyn). If this is achieved then it will be possible to add new data to a growing data set over many years and yet still retain the relative spatial relationships between finds discovered at different times. It seems unlikely that any one project will have sufficient funds available to collect enough data on its own. Therefore, it will be extremely important that non-aggregated, well-located data is passed on by this and other projects for future researchers. In a coastal environment it is these spatial relationships spread over a very wide geographical area which will illuminate as much of the past as the local context and physical nature of the finds themselves.

Collecting vegetation data

The mapping of vegetation patterns and the comparison between vegetation distributions of different dates comprise another data layer for the project. This information will assist in the detection of environmental change over time. Because vegetation cover is dependent upon many factors, including erosion, deposition, sediment type, exposure duration, salinity etc., it is anticipated that the study of the vegetation coverage will assist in understanding the interaction of the many variables.

For the contemporary mapping of the vegetation cover the harbour was flown in the summer of 1994 with photographs taken at 1:10,000 scale as colour infra-red diapositives. These show the main areas of different vegetation types and will provide evidence for vegetation cover mapping which will be mapped from the air photos using photogrammetric and photo-interpretative techniques. In addition to the cover derived from the 1994 air photographs the project has used data already collected and mapped from the Budd (1980,1981,1982,1983) surveys of the early 1980s. The vegetation maps from this study have been digitised to ensure compatibility with the GIS and will enable the areas to be compared by species in each year of the study with the current vegetation cover and the archaeological information. One major potential of this data integration is the ability of the GIS to use the height mapping to divide the areas of vegetation by contour height zones. This will enable the calculation of area cover of specific species within a single height zone across the harbour. For instance, this will give a total area figure for *Entromorpha s.p.* contained within the +0.5 – +1.0 metre zone which could then be further sub-divided into smaller areas of the harbour, thus, allowing the comparison of vegetation cover by height zone with, say, the RSPB's Low Water Bird Count data. The analysis of the vegetation cover maps can be carried further as each area has a percentage cover attribute attached to it. Hence, using biomass data collected in the field by quadrat sample, it will be possible to calculate total biomass by species, by height zone, by aspect, by slope, by specific location, for a sector of the harbour, for the harbour as a whole, or indeed, any combination of these factors. This will greatly increase the range of views of the data available to researchers.

Some interim results

Based upon a tentative reading of the initial data, it does appear that "Spartina dieback", which was of concern to the RSPB, is not responsible for erosion of the islands in Langstone Harbour. The foreshore of the areas being eroded is made up of well-consolidated sediments that do not appear to be subject to remobilisation. The archaeological evidence further supports this view. Considerable quantities of archaeological material (Mesolithic and Bronze Age) are being released from the cliff sections in the eroding areas. As such, it would strongly indicate that these areas of the islands have been disturbed by human activity in the past and that this has resulted in increased local susceptibility to erosion. Indeed, the environment here is quite different from the channels as they contain unconsolidated sediments, which could be readily remobilised, and which still maintain healthy Spartina cover. It is possible that detailed study of localised vegetation cover and erosion will prove to be an important factor in understanding the distribution and appearance of archaeological material and vice-versa. This is particularly evident on the southern shore of North Binness Island where several sherds of a late Bronze Age pot (Allen *et al.* 1994) were found on the surface of the mud in conjunction with a hearth (F112). That they were surface finds in an intertidal zone strongly suggests that the locality had been relatively recently denuded.

In other areas of the harbour the integration of historical research with vegetation cover suggests that the presence of *Fucus s.p.* can be related to past oyster culture activities. Shingle placed on the mud in the mid 1800s to act as hold-fasts for young oysters is now providing the same service to *Fucus s.p.*. Hence, past human activity, which has modified the locality, directly affects the current flora by alteration of the natural environment.

Conclusion

Integration of erosion-monitoring mapping and vegetation cover data together with the archaeological and historical data will extend the value of the whole database beyond that of each individual set. The archaeological finds can, in the right circumstances, develop a chronological index for past coastal states. Likewise, the erosion mapping and study of vegetation cover may assist in the location of further archaeological sites and finds by indicating areas of greater potential.

The key to this integration of the different data sets is the effective and precise geographical location of all information. It is essential that all of the data collected for such a study is surveyed to an appropriate accuracy and recorded so that spatial relationships are maintained. The ability to cross reference to other sites is critical. This can only be achieved by using a national co-ordinate system and height datum.

It is also very important that mapping of sufficiently high quality is used to provide the locational context for the data layers. Without such a map, misleading impressions of the topographical surroundings of archaeological sites and finds and vegetated areas will be given. The map will provide the baseline for studying the erosional and depositional events in association with the other data layers.

Acknowledgements

The following organisations contributed staff and resources to the Langstone Harbour Project: the Hampshire County Archaeologist; the Hampshire and Wight Trust for Maritime Archaeology; Wessex Archaeology; University of Portsmouth, Department of Geography and Department of Biology.

References

Allen, M., Gardiner, J., Fontana, D.J.L., and Pearson, A.W. 1993: "Archaeological assessment of Langstone Harbour Hampshire" *Past*, No. 16. December 1993.

Allen, M., Fontana, D.J.L., Gardiner, J., and Pearson, A.W. 1994: *The Langstone Harbour Archaeological Survey Project: The Assessment, 1993.* (Report for Hampshire County Council).

Budd, J.T.C. 1980: *Survey of the Intertidal Vegetation of Langstone Harbour.* (Internal Report, Southern Water Authority, Worthing).

Budd, J.T.C. 1981: *Survey of the Intertidal Vegetation of Langstone Harbour.* (Internal Report, Southern Water Authority, Worthing).

Budd, J.T.C. 1982: *Survey of the Intertidal Vegetation of Langstone Harbour.* (Internal Report, Southern Water Authority, Worthing).

Budd, J.T.C. 1983: *Survey of the Intertidal Vegetation of Langstone Harbour.* (Internal Report, Southern Water Authority, Worthing).

Burrough, P.A. 1986: *Principles of Geographical Information Systems for Land Resources Assessment.* Monographs on soil and resources survey No. 12., Oxford Science Publications. (Clarendon Press, Oxford).

Collier, P., Fontana, D.J.L. and Pearson, A.W. 1994: 'The use of multi-temporal Aerial Photography as a data source for an Ecological GIS' *Proceedings of The International Geographical Union: Regional Conference Prague, August 1994*

Green, S.W. 1990: 'Approaching archaeological space: an introduction to the volume' in Allen, K.M.S., Green, S.W. and Zubrow, E.B.W. (eds) *Interpreting Space: GIS and archaeology.* (Taylor and Francis, London).

Salisbury, C.R. 1988: 'Primitive British fishweirs' in Good, G.L., Jones, R.H. and Ponsford, M.W., (eds) 1988 *Waterfront archaeology, Proceedings of the third international conference, Bristol.* CBA Research Report No. 74.

Harris, T.M. and Lock, G.R. 1990: 'The diffusion of new technology: a perspective on the adoption of geographical information systems within U.K. archaeology' 33–53 in Allen, K.M.S., Green, S.W. and Zubrow, E.B.W. (eds) *Interpreting Space: GIS and archaeology.* (Taylor and Francis, London).

Milne, G. (ed) 1985: *The Port of Roman London.* (Batsford, London).

Paynter, R.W., Green, S.W. and Wobst, H.M. 1974: *Spatial clustering: techniques of discrimination.* Paper presented to the annual meeting of the Society for American Archaeology., Washington D.C.

Pearson, A.W., and Fontana, D.J.L. 1993: *The Langstone Harbour Project: An integrated research design for the study, mapping, and interpretation of the archaeological resource of the inter-tidal zone.* Report for Hampshire County Council and The Hampshire and Wight Trust for Maritime Archaeology.

Rule, M. 1982: *The Mary Rose: the excavation and raising of Henry VIII's flagship.* (Conway Maritime Press, London).

13. Sea Ponds, with reference to the Solent, Hampshire

Christopher Currie

This essay identifies the extensive use of ponds and other features on the sea shore for keeping fish, crustaceans and shellfish fresh. These features were well known in antiquity, and are recorded in detail in Roman literature. Numerous examples are recorded in the Solent from the medieval period onward. Details of the fishing industries supplying these ponds are given. It is felt that similar features can be identified in other localities, and local fieldwork is encouraged.

Introduction

In recent years a growing interest in the archaeology of the maritime foreshore has led to a number of unidentified features being recorded. Fish weirs are amongst the most common features to be recognised to date, but the identification of other features associated with sea fisheries is still in its infancy. This essay looks at the various containers constructed on the foreshore to keep captured sea food alive while awaiting sale. Despite being much favoured by the Romans, these features have been largely ignored by post-Roman scholarship. Most research to date has concentrated on freshwater ponds (e.g. Roberts 1986; Aston 1988). Although Hockey (1970, 50) and this author (Currie 1988, 283–86) have made brief comment on their maritime equivalents, this essay looks at the subject in more detail.

Sea ponds in Roman literature

The earliest literature on the artificial keeping of fish in ponds can be traced to the 1st century BC. Marcus Terentius Varro (*De Re Rustica*) and Marcus Tullius Cicero (*Ad Atticus*) are amongst the better-known authors to discuss the subject. Lesser known works can be traced back to Hazo of Carthage c. 88 BC.

These show that fishponds were well known to the Romans in the 2nd century BC. The later writer, Lucius Junius Moderatus Columella, tells how Cato sold his ward's fishponds for "*the immense sum of 400,000 sesterces*" (Ash et al 1948–55, 402–05). It is not clear which Cato is referred to here, Marcus Porcius I (who died in 149 BC), or Marcus Porcius II (who died in 46 BC). Both Varro and Pliny the Elder (AD 23–79) refer to 2nd century personalities associated with fishponds (Hooper 1934, 522–29).

Varro tells of two sorts of ponds, freshwater and saline. The former were commonplace by the time he wrote because they were "*open to common folk, and not unprofitable*". Sea ponds were reserved for "*the nobility*" and "*appeal to the eye more than to the purse, and exhaust the pouch of the owner rather than fill it*". It is recorded that they were both built and stocked at great cost. Hirrus is recorded as taking 12,000 sesterces from the buildings around his fishponds, but he spent all that income on food for his fish (Hooper 1934, 522–23).

It would seem that the elaborate construction of ponds on the seashore to retain marine fish was considered a form of status symbol. Cicero (106–43 BC) sneered at those who followed this fashion and "*who think they can touch the sky with their finger, if they have barbed mullets in their ponds which are tame enough to come when called*" (Hooper 1934, 525n).

Columella, writing in the 1st century AD, gives a hint how this extravagance had probably developed from more utilitarian needs. He tells how the natives around Rome had not only constructed ponds themselves, but had collected certain fish spawn from the sea and had stocked these ponds with it. It is not possible to identify the exact species referred to here but some sea fish are tolerant of freshwater and vice-versa, so this practice was not impossible. Both ancient and modern applications of this interchangeability are discussed elsewhere by this author (Currie 1986a, 47–48). It is then recorded that "*...an age followed which abandoned this method of keeping fish and the extravagance of the wealthy enclosed the very seas...*" (Ash et al 1948–55, 402–03). These wealthy people vied with each other to possess the most exotic species. Where some had "*rejoiced in names taken from conquered nations...(those) who made fishponds their chief interest, rejoiced in the names of the fish they had captured*" (Ash et al 1948–55, 404–05).

Columella found the practice of keeping fish for show

wasteful, and urged villa owners to keep fish as a source of profit: "*But since men's moral sense has become blunted that such behaviour is reckoned not only as customary but also as highly laudable and honourable, we too, lest we should be seen to be out-of-date critics...., will show that the fishpond is also a source of profit which the head of a household can gain from his country estate.*" (Ash *et al* 1948–55, 404–05).

A detailed description of how sea ponds were constructed is given by Columella. This depended on the type of shoreline for which the ponds were proposed; rocky shores needed ponds that were cut out of rock whereas on flat muddy shores embankments needed to be thrown up to prevent the sea from washing them away (Ash *et al* 1948–55, 404–15). "*We consider...the best pond is one which is so situated that the incoming tide of the sea expels the water of the previous tide and does not allow any stale water to remain within the enclosure. The pond is either hewn in rock, which rarely occurs, or built of plaster on the shore...Channels should be provided for the water on every side of the pond; for the old water is more easily carried away if there is an outlet on the side opposite to that which the wave forces its way in...It will be well to remember that the gratings made of brass with small holes should be fixed in front of the channels through which the fish-pond pours out its waters, to prevent the fish from escaping*" (Ash *et al* 1948–55, 406–11). For comment on the supposed tidelessness of the Mediterranean, one is referred to Hooper 1934, 528–29n.

At Caesarea rock cut tanks have been discovered associated with an Herodian promontory palace. These were first identified by Flinder as piscine and although subsequent excavation has not fully upheld this view, it would appear that these features may have been converted into fishponds at a post-Herodian date (Levine & Netzer 1986, 158–60, 176–77).

Sea Ponds in England, with reference to the Solent in Hampshire

The status given by Romans to sea ponds seems to have been transferred to freshwater ponds in medieval England. Sea fish were not regarded as status food here, although they retained their prestige in parts of Germany away from the coast (Jones 1960). In England, the status of freshwater pond fish seems to have been associated with land ownership, whereas the sea, according to statute, was common to all men. Despite the lower status of sea fish, it would appear that there was still considerable demand for them across a range of social classes. Preserved sea fish were particularly useful as a 'penance' food at Lent, whereas freshwater fish were generally reserved for high status aristocratic feasts (Currie 1989). It was still considered worthwhile, therefore, for fishermen on the coasts to have sea ponds for keeping their captures.

Hockey gives an example owned by Quarr Abbey at Fishouse on Wootton Creek on the sheltered north side of the island (1970, 50). Its mode of operation was not given, and Hockey was unsure whether they were pools for keeping fish alive or some sort of tidal trap. He suggests that they may have even been oyster ponds, which were common in the Solent in the 19th century. There is a large inlet on the eastern shore of Wootton Creek today that may be the site of this pond. Hockey further records that such ponds were not unique to monastic orders. The d'Insulas and the Trenchards both owned similar structures, known locally as "lucks", near Fishouse and Shalfleet respectively (1970, 50).

On Hayling Island, where there are no permanent freshwater streams, a late 13th century account of the alien priory there records 4d for '*fishes brought for the pool*' (Longcroft 1857, 208). It is thought that the priory had a sea pond on the east coast of the island, where there is an inlet called 'My Lord's Pond' (King 1961, 44). In 1725 a Mr Till is recorded as leasing the sea fishery at Hayling together with '*the fish-pond there*' (Longcroft 1857, 289).

"FWL", writing about the Solent fishermen on the shore near Titchfield Abbey *c.* 1900, recalls seeing cod swimming in ponds in the River Hamble estuary. He says local tradition ascribed these to the nearby abbey (FWL 1939, 5–6). Although there is no proof for the latter statement, his observations can be confirmed by the presence of ponds shown on early Ordnance Survey maps, where they are marked as lobster ponds (OS 6" map, 1859 edition, sheet 74). In the early 19th century the Hamble boasted a fishing fleet of 20 well and sail boats going to the West Country for lobsters and crabs (Hewitt 1912, 468). When the local fishing industries were in terminal decline in the 1930s, a series of nostalgic articles appeared in the local press that described the life of the fishermen. These described the 'well' boats as being capable of keeping their catch alive in water-filled compartments in the ship's hull until delivered to the sea ponds in the estuary. Many of the fish caught by Hamble fishermen were taken off the Irish Coast (HRO 93M94/47/6).

There appears to be a close relationship between some coastal Domesday fisheries and the well-documented later sites, and also the proximity of salterns. The lands of Jumieges Abbey on Hayling Island, mentioned above, contained a salt house and two fisheries (Munby 1982, 10.1). At Crofton in 1086 a fishery with two salt houses at 100d is recorded (ibid, 18.1).

On the Meon estuary near Crofton was a fishery known as the 'Breach'. This was probably created in its present form *c.* 1607 when it is recorded that the lord of the manor of Brownwich owned a fishery there (HRO 5M53/1076). A letter of the 1740s describing this unusual sea pond indicates it had similarities to those described by Columella. The main difference was that the 'Breach' was an inlet off the main Meon estuary that served as a form of tidal trap, allowing fish in of their own accord before they were fished for, whereas Columella's ponds were stocked artificially. *"...when there were plenty of mullet and bass...they would often come into the Breach in great sholes as there was nothing to hinder the fish passing out of one water into another....what with the hard winter's kill there is a scarcity of fish....but if care is taken to encourage round fish as they used through the hatches from the sea as this is how the fishery is stocked"* (HRO 5M53/1114).

The very nature of the type of pond described here, close to the shore, makes their survival doubtful as time and tide would, quite literally, wash them back into the sea. The above-mentioned 'Breach' only survives because of its protection behind the sea wall built by the Earl of Southampton in the early 17th century. Its recognition was only made through the chance discovery of the 18th Century documents concerning disputed ownership.

In 1583 the Admiralty Book for the port of Southampton records that the fishermen of Eling were presented for catching illegal fry in their weirs 'for their own stores' (Welch 1968, 112). The word 'stores' was a common abbreviation in historic times for store-ponds, where fish were kept for growing on to edible size. This reference suggests that the fishermen of Eling had sea ponds, although their sites are unknown. Again, Domesday Book records a fishery and salt house at Eling (Munby 1982, 1.27).

To demonstrate that the Solent is not unique in having sea ponds, another well-documented example survives at Anthony in the Plymouth Sound, Cornwall. This was described by Carew in his Survey of Cornwall *c.* 1600 as being a 'fishfull pond'. Remains of the banks are still currently visible (Cornwall and Scilly SMR no SX45NW 17). Like many of the Solent sites, a saltern is to be found nearby (Cornwall and Scilly SMR no SX45NW 9).

Tide mills and fish ponds

Another type of site that combines its function with the keeping of sea fish in ponds is the tide mill. Many of these mills existed on the Solent shores, and a number of them can be shown to have used the mill pond as a fishery. The best example is recorded in 1250 when Juliana, daughter of Richard de Walleys, granted Quarr Abbey the right to construct a pond and mill on the tidal River Medina at Claybrook (Hockey 1970, 50). This mill is now known as East Medina Mill, one of two large tide mills on the Medina. A lease of 1517 to John Pocock includes Claybrook 'with its pond and stream called le Luck, with fishing and game rights' (Hockey 1991, no. 391). An earlier lease records the fishpond's value as 20d per annum (Hockey 1991, no. 390).

Other containers for keeping fish alive

At the Admiralty Court for Southampton in 1585 it is recorded that Edmund Legat of West Hook *'toke upe a store poot with contayne suygens or conger yealls in him'* (Welch 1968, 125). These store pots are wooden containers, often baskets, in which captured fish are kept alive by lowering them into the water. Wicker 'cages' for keeping fish alive on the Rhine are described in the 1630s (Bereton 1844, 45). The bishop of Winchester's Pipe Roll for 1299 records a 'fysh which' or fish box for keeping captured fish alive (Roberts 1986, 136). The 'store poot' reference shows that these features were used in the Solent. They range from simple tethered baskets, to larger fixed cages made of hurdles attached to stakes. The remains of stake-type features that could have been fixed cages have been identified at low tide in Wootton Creek on the Isle of Wight (Tomalin pers. comm.; Tomalin this volume).

Oyster farming in the Solent

Oyster fisheries were recorded in the Solent from at least the medieval period at Emsworth, on the mainland opposite Hayling Island, and at Hamble (Hewitt 1912, 468). There are detailed records of oyster fishing in the Solent in the 16th century. These are to be found in the Admiralty Court Book for the Port of Southampton, which once claimed jurisdiction over the greater part of the Solent. This records the struggle the authorities had to bring the produce of local fisheries to market in Southampton. Many local fishermen preferred to avoid paying market tolls, and the black market trade evaded attempts to suppress it.

According to the Admiralty Book, the licensed oyster fishermen were required to bring a boat load of oyster fry to be 'layed' in oyster beds controlled by the town (Welch 1968, 8). A number of people with land on the shores of the Solent estuaries set up their own oyster beds or 'coves', as they were known locally, and ignored orders to destroy them. In 1577 it is recorded that John Watering, Arthur Fry, John Dallimore and Gyles Hault had two illegal coves each in the Hamble estuary, whilst William Arnolt, James Hamson, Thomas Neuds and William Ayles had one each (ibid, 87–88). Fishermen from the Isle of Wight were accused of bringing quantities of 40,000 oysters at a time to Watering and Arthur Fry, who sold them on 'into the country' (op. cit., 88). By 1584 Fry had increased this to 300,000 oysters a week at Lent (Welch 1968, 118).

That these 'coves' are some sort of artificial oyster bed or pond is attested by the fact that John Fry is accused of buying oysters from local fishermen *'and kepes them in his cove and selleth them againe having no craft at sea at all'* (ibid, 69). Welch (op. cit., 128) thought that a cove is *'a kiddel, part of a weir where fish could be caught'*. This seems to come from a reference in the early 1580s to a Mr Pett of Staplecourt, near Botley (on the tidal Hamble). He had a fish weir that *'all the coves of the ware doth spill much fish by reason that keping of the ware and doth bring it out by Shoterlls'* (op. cit., 101). It may be that coves were kept adjacent to weirs, but it is unlikely that they were themselves weirs. If so it would pose the question why fishermen were bringing oysters that had already been caught to the Hamble estuary to put them in a fish trap or weir. It is more likely that some 'coves' were located near weirs, so that fish-keepers could keep their resources close together. From the evidence given in other sources, it would seem that 'coves' are a type of artificial oyster pond or bed, similar to those shown on late 19th-century Ordnance Survey maps.

In 1585 the Admiralty Book talks of oyster 'laying' in 'Hamble Houke', a tidal creek on the east side of the Hamble estuary (Welch 1968, 125). This practice continued into the 18th century as a lease of 1748 shows. Here John Brett of Hook Valence in the parish of Titchfield came to an agreement with the Duke of Portland for the 'laying' of oysters in Hook River. This gave him the right of 'carrying and laying Oysters to Grow and fatten in the River or Lake called or Commonly known by the name of Hook River or Lake' (HRO 5M53/1423). A similar lease was needed in 1836 between a consortium of oyster merchants and Sir George Grey, the Commissioner of the Portsmouth Dockyard, to lay oysters therein (HRO 20M50/248). Comparable leases were required from the lord of the manor for keeping oysters within the land-locked sea inlets either side of Hayling Island (Longcroft 1857, 142).

By the time of the first large scale Ordnance Survey maps *c.* 1870, many of the prime Solent pond sites seem to have been converted for the breeding and fattening of oysters. A number of 19th-century saltern sites are shown containing oyster ponds. On the east side of Hayling Island 'Mengham Salterns' are marked, but close inspection of the maps show that the large ponds here are marked as oyster ponds (OS 25" map, 1908 edition, sheet 84.12). However, the Domesday entry, referred to above, suggests there had been a saltern and fishery in close conjunction here much earlier.

Large-scale commercialism came to the oyster fisheries of Hayling Island in 1865 following the creation of the South of England Oyster Company. This created oyster beds stretching over 900 acres in Langstone Harbour, and had a smaller area near the salterns on the east side of the island, reusing part of a derelict saltworks. This latter is described as a 'park' by Trigg (1892, 75): *'A 'park' was formed on the latter [east] side by laying down 2000 hurdles upon which was placed a quantity of clean, coarse ballast, the oysters being laid on this. The beds are so enclosed that by means of sluices the water is maintained at any depth according to the season.'*

However, it can be shown that smaller scale oyster farming had occurred before this on Hayling Island. In a court hearing of 1841 Henry Cribs and Edward Clark were summoned for stealing oysters from a 'bed' at Mill Rithe owned by Charles Fleet. The latter claimed that he had staked out a bed here for twenty five years paying the Lord of the Manor 5/- a year, and had put down young oysters every winter. Witnesses came forward to testify that oysters had been kept on the island for many years. James Hoar attested that he had held the adjoining bed for many years, and Moses Barnett, fisherman, swore that he had rented beds there from 1800 (Thomas 1961, 128).

At Pennington, near Lymington, amongst earthworks and ponds that the modern OS maps mark as 'salterns', a large fish pond is shown in conjunction with extensive oyster beds (Fig. 13.1). Lloyd (1968, 12–13) gives no indication that the ponds at Lymington were used for anything but salt making. He argues that the conversion to fish and oyster ponds came after the closure of the salterns in 1865. As evidence he quotes from page 64 of E. King's 'Round Lymington and through the New Forest', published in 1877. This states that: *'On the site of the latest [saltern] that were kept in work (up to 1865), there is now an oyster breeding establishment, in connection with ponds for the preservation of salt-water fish for the inland markets: a scheme set on foot about 1870.'*

This apparently conclusive statement does not match up with the evidence of the Lymington tithe map of 1845 (HRO 21M65/F7/150/1–2). This map shows the same ponds marked as an 'Oyster Bed and Fish Pond'. This throws some doubt on King's statement, and suggests that sea ponds existed within the salterns whilst the latter were still operating. The Victoria County History seems to imply that oyster farming and salterns existed in close conjunction with one another in the estuaries on the Isle of Wight at Newtown and Newport from an early date (Hewitt 1912, 468). It might be suggested therefore that many of the large reservoirs feeding salterns around the Solent in the post-medieval period would have made very suitable store ponds for fish and oysters. It is hard to believe that local people would not have thought to obtain two profitable uses from the same resource, thereby making it difficult to distinguish a saltern feeding reservoir from a pond for keeping sea food.

Bradley (1975, 21–22), writing about the salt industry on the Solent shores in the Iron Age and Roman period, highlighted a similar dilemma in his interpretation of such sites. He suggests that there was probably a connection between these early saltworks and trade in salted fish, but recognises the difficulty in proving it.

He goes on to argue that early salt production could have only been undertaken during the four warmest months of the year. Although by the later post-medieval period there was the option to use of coal-fired evaporation techniques, the early saltworkers would have needed other activities to supplement their income. Seasonal farming and fishing would have been the most obvious ways of doing this. Is seems unlikely to be a coincidence that the oyster fishing season was considered to be a winter occupation well into the present century. This was even formalised in 1843 when an agreement with French fishermen outlawed oyster dredging between May and August every year (Rudkin n.d., 9).

There are records of how the oysters were kept fresh in 'well' boats, similar to those used for fish and

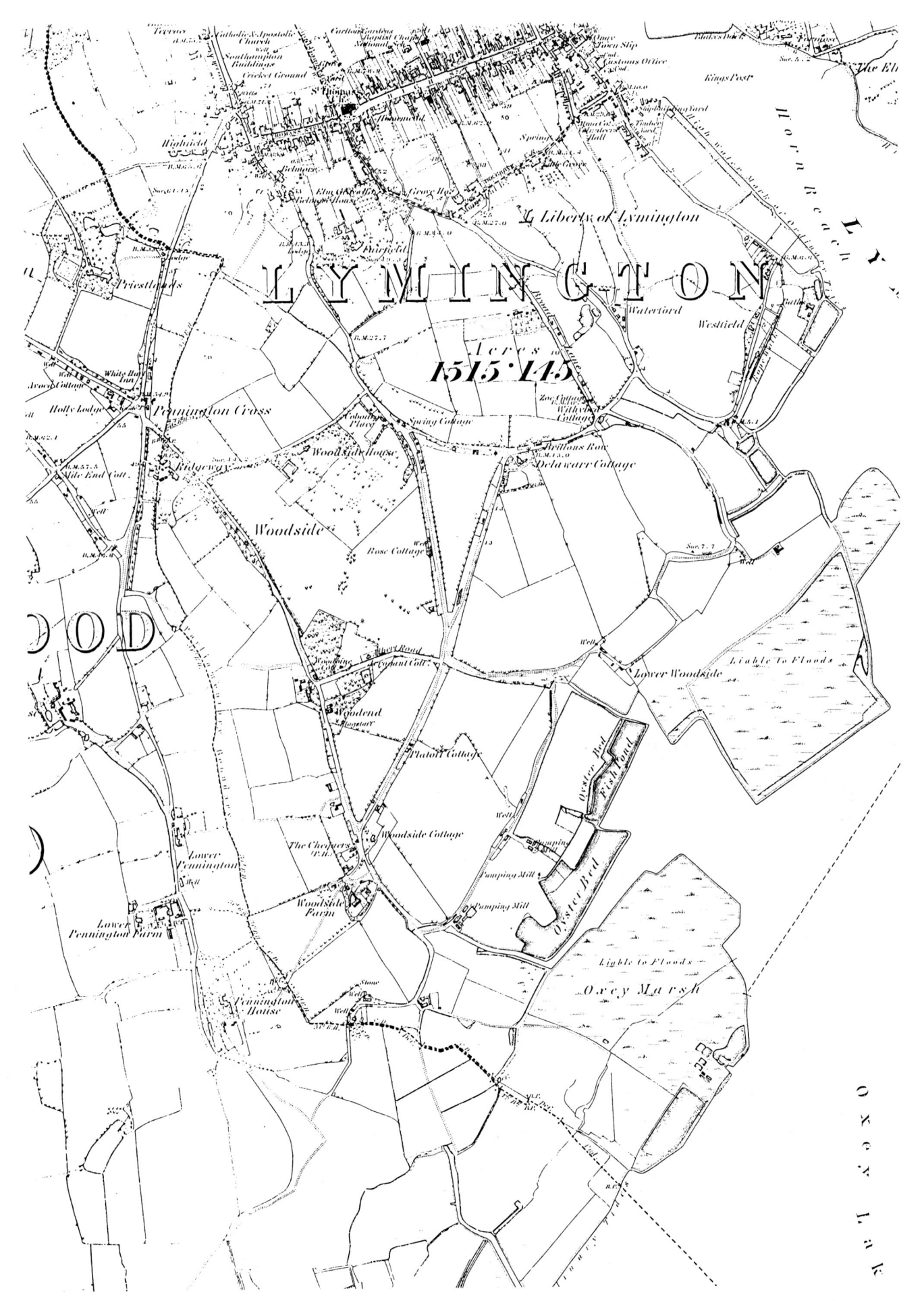

Figure 13.1 Extract from OS 6" sheet 88 (1867 ed) showing ponds and other coastal features near Lymington, Hants.

crustaceans by the Hamble fishermen. Rudkin (1987) has given a detailed description of the oyster catching ship 'Echo', considered to be the 'Queen' of the Emsworth oyster fleet at the beginning of the 20th century. This boat was 110 feet in length, 21 feet 6 inches wide, and had a 'well' in the hull capable of holding 90 tons of fresh sea water (ibid, 6). In the Medina River on the Isle of Wight a wooden houseboat called the 'Ark' was used to store oysters for the market. This had a false bottom with a cradle with perforated sides that allowed water to pass freely over the oysters (Hewitt 1912, 468).

Fish houses

There is evidence for fish houses at a number of sites in Hampshire. An extant freshwater example survives at Meare near Glastonbury in Somerset where fishermen are thought to have lived and stored their equipment during the prolonged fishings evidenced at medieval sites. Another example has been excavated near Byland Abbey in Yorkshire (Kemp 1984, 43–51).

These sites are a little-studied aspect of historic fishing even though place-name evidence throughout England indicates that they were once common. It has already been noted above that there were sea ponds near a place called Fishouse on the Isle of Wight (Hockey 1970, 50). Likewise there is a farm close to the shore at Titchfield that was known as "Fish House" on documents from the 1740's dealing with boundary disputes (HRO 5M53/1110–12). This name survived on maps in the last century, though the name has changed to Solent Court in recent years.

Conclusions

The evidence shows that the artificial keeping of fish and oysters had been going on in the Solent long before the arrival of large-scale commercial activity in the later 19th century. The documents give details of the physical appearance of the sea ponds and oyster beds. Even when the latter were little more than staked out 'beds', it would seem that the remains might be recognised archaeologically by the boundary stakes, and the hurdles laid on the floor of the sea to take the ballast on which the oysters were deposited. The maritime foreshore all over the UK seems to be littered with hurdles and stakes, many of which have been associated with fish weirs. Now that documents explain another use of such equipment, it is possible that artificial oyster beds will be recognised in many other places besides the Solent.

Likewise, the identification of sea ponds here as a common feature of the foreshore will hopefully inspire fieldwork in other localities. It is possible to look forward to a time in the near future when they are as common a feature on County Sites and Monuments Records as their freshwater counterparts.

Sites of fish and oyster ponds marked on early Ordnance Survey maps of the Solent (Fig. 2)

In compiling this list, the difficulty in distinguishing fish ponds from saltern feeding ponds is recognised. It is possible that the two uses often coincided. An Ordnance Survey marking as a fish pond should not preclude the possibility that the site was once a saltern reservoir, and vice-versa. The Mengham site is well documented as being a saltern reservoir that was converted to commercial oyster beds in 1865. Conversely, the Shalfleet Salterns appear to be on, or near, the site of a medieval sea pond.

1. Hampshire side

SU 715035 North Hayling, large complex of 'oyster breeding ponds', eroded remains still visible on foreshore.
SU 740054 Emsworth, complex of small oyster beds, now gone.
SU 681039 Farlington, one large pond of unknown origin.
SZ 733992 East Hayling, large inlet called 'My Lord's Pond', still extant; contained oyster beds in 1871.
SZ 737987 East Hayling, North's Salterns, 'Feeding Pond' shown, now boating lake.
SZ 737992 Mengham's Salterns shown with feeding pond and series of oyster breeding ponds.
SZ 682995 Eastney, 'The Glory Hole', possible site of fish pond, now gone.
SZ 675995 Eastney, ponds shown on north side of channel, now gone.
SZ 676018 Great Salterns Lake, possible saltern reservoir.
SU 581053 Saltern's Quay, Fareham, a number of unspecified ponds shown in 1870.
SU 491054 Warsash, Rising Sun Public House, 'Lobster Pond'.
SU 486058 Warsash, Hamble Saltern, 'Lobster Pond'.
SU 485066 Hamble, unspecified ponds and oyster beds.
SU 466035 Ashlett, saltern 'feeding pond'.
SU 433070 Sylvan Villa, unspecified pond.
SU 424082 Hythe, two unspecified ponds.
SZ 418978 Beaulieu River, Warren Farm, large pond and subsidiary channels.
SU 418003 Beaulieu River, Witcher's Copse, 'Tidal ponds', two ponds shown.
SZ 328938 Pennington, Oxey Marsh, two very large 'Oyster beds' and one large 'fishpond' shown. Marked as 'salterns' on present maps.
SZ 320931 Pennington, Oxey Marsh, complex of nine unspecified ponds shown on saltern site.

2. Isle of Wight

SZ 552925 Wootton Creek, Fishouse, inlet on creek possible site of medieval pond.
SZ 510920 East Medina Mill, site of medieval fishpond, now marina.
SZ 415915 Hamstead Saltworks, large pond and salt drying cisterns.

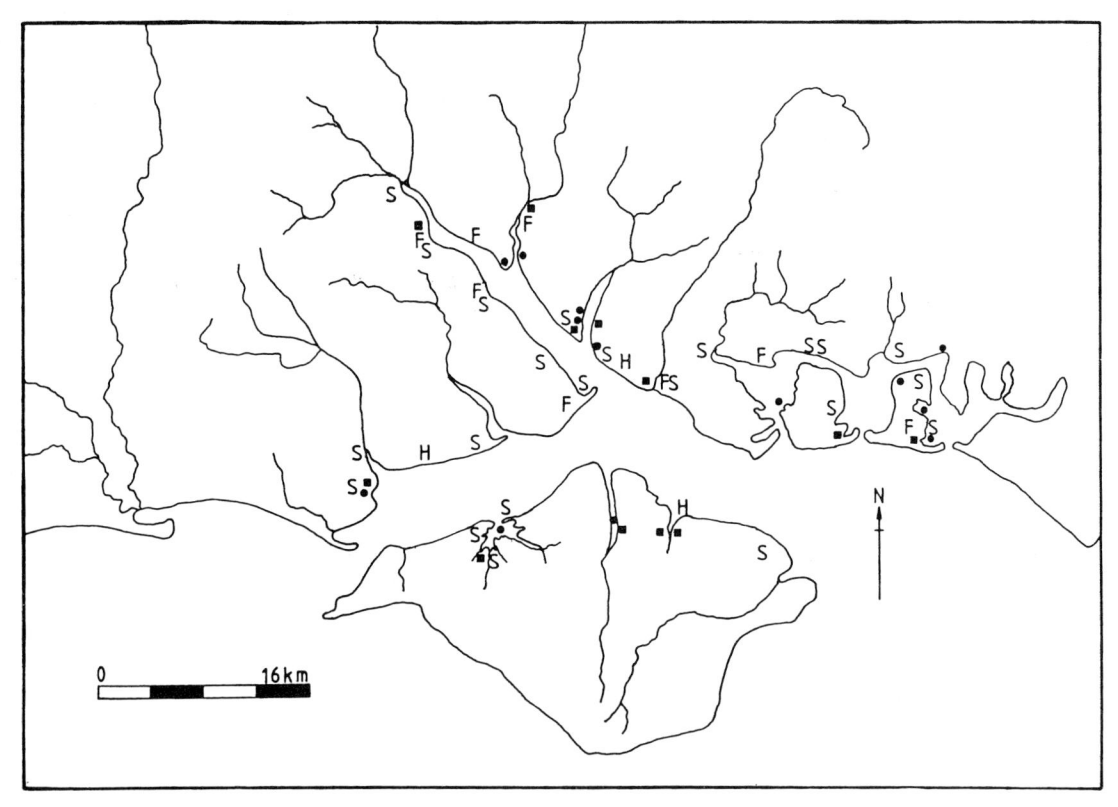

Figure 13.2 Sites with evidence of the fishing industry in the Solent. Key: S – Salterns; F – Recorded Fisheries; H – Recorded fish houses; ● Site of oyster ponds; ■ Site of fishponds.

SZ 414907 Shalfleet Saltworks, five large ponds shown, salt drying cisterns marked separately. Medieval fishponds recorded at Shalfleet.

SZ 419911 Newtown Saltworks, large pond shown, oyster fishery recorded at Newtown.

References

Original sources held in the Hampshire Record Office (HRO):

HRO 20M50/248 Lease for laying oysters in Portsmouth Dockyard, 1836

HRO 5M53/1076 Wriothesley papers concerning the Breach

HRO 5M53/1110–1114 Letters concerning the Earl of Portland's estates in Hampshire, with particular reference to Titchfield parish

HRO 5M53/1423 Lease for laying oysters in Hook River, Titchfield, 1748

HRO 21M65/F7/150/1-2 Tithe map & award for Lymington, 1845

HRO 93M94/47/6 Extract from Hampshire Advertiser, 1933 entitled 'Hamble, its charm and its story' by 'GHS'

Published references

Ash H.B., Foster, E., and Heffner, E. (eds) 1948–55: *Res Rustica* by Lucius Columella, (London)

Aston, M.A. (ed) 1988: *Medieval fish, fisheries and fishponds in England*, (BAR British series 182, Oxford).

Bereton W. (ed) 1844: *Travels in Holland, the United Provinces, England, Scotland, and Ireland, 1634–35*, (Chetham Society, vol. 1,).

Bradley, R. 1975: 'Salt and settlement in the Hampshire Sussex borderland' in Colchester Archaeological Group (ed), *Salt: the study of an ancient industry,* (Colchester).

Currie, C.K. 1986: 'Salinity tolerance', *Carp Fisher*, 11, 47–48.

Currie, C.K. 1988: 'Hampshire fishponds' in Aston, M.A. (ed) *Medieval fish, fisheries and fishponds*, 267–90

Currie, C.K. 1989: 'The role of fishponds in the English monastic economy', in R. Gilchrist & H. Mytum (eds), *The archaeology of the rural monastery*, (BAR British series 203, Oxford).

FWL. 1939: *A short history of Warsash*, (Fareham).

Hewitt, E.M. 1912: 'Fisheries', in W Page (ed), *The Victoria History of Hampshire and the Isle of Wight*, vol. 5, (London,)

Hockey, S.F. 1970: *Quarr Abbey and its lands 1132–1631*, (Leicester).

Hockey, S.F. (ed) 1991: *The charters of Quarr Abbey*, (Newport).

Hooper, W.D. (ed) 1934: *Res rustica* by Marcus Terrentius Varro, (London,)

Jones, G.F. 1960: 'The function of food in medieval German literature', *Speculum* 35, 78–86

Kemp, R. 1984: 'A fishkeeper's store at Byland Abbey', *Ryedale Historian*, 12, 43–51

Levine, L.I. and Netzer, E. 1986: 'Excavations at Caesarea Maritima 1975, 1976, 1979 – final report', *Qedem*, 21, (Monographs of the Institute of Archaeology, Hebrew University of Jerusalem).

Lloyd, A. 1968: *The salterns of the Lymington area*, (Southampton).

Longcroft, C.J. 1857: *A topographical account of the hundred of Bosmere*, (London).

Munby, J. (ed) 1982: *Domesday Book: Hampshire*, (Chichester).

Roberts, E. 1986: 'The bishop of Winchester's fishponds in Hampshire, 1150–1400: their development function and management', *Proceedings of the Hampshire Field Club and Archaeological Society*, 42, 125–38.

Rudkin, D.J. undated *The Emsworth oyster fleet: industry and shipping,* (Westbourne).

Rudkin, D.J. 1987: *Echo The Queen of the Emsworth oyster fleet*, (Rowlands Castle).

Thomas, F.S. 1961: *The King holds Hayling*, (Havant).

Trigg, H.R. 1892: *A guide to Hayling Island*, (London).

Welch, E. (ed) 1968: *The Admiralty Court Book of Southampton 1566–1585*, (Southampton).

14. The National Trust: Survey and Management in the 'Neptune' Zone

Philip Claris

This paper presents a summary of the development of the National Trust's role and current position in the protection of the historic character of coastal landscapes. Some examples of past practice are examined, and opportunities for the potential expansion of the National Trust's activities are examined: in the application of historical research to coastal zone management generally, and in the role of survey on coasts and islands, and in estuarine, intertidal and offshore areas.

Coastal land holdings

As a result of land acquisitions beginning in the late nineteenth century, and more recently the advent of the Enterprise Neptune campaign, the National Trust now owns just over a sixth of the coastline of England, Wales and Northern Ireland, amounting to some 550 miles in length. We can anticipate that this process of gradual acquisition will continue under the ongoing campaign, perhaps exceeding ultimately the target of 1000 miles set in 1965 when Enterprise Neptune was launched, with the original objective of saving and preserving all remaining "unspoiled" coastal landscapes. A large and growing part of the coastal landscape is therefore being managed on behalf of the nation by the National Trust, with a proportionate effect on the way that landscape and its historic elements are presented and conserved for the future. There is no other category of land or historic site which is targeted on a systematic basis and to the same extent for acquisition and preservation by the National Trust.

While most of this protected coastline extends inland to a moderate degree, often to the skyline, including farm units and many visual and historic landscape features, almost all extends seaward only to the high water mark. The coastal landscape thus perceived as needing protection and therefore acquired to date is mainly dry land, and the seaward zone is normally not specifically protected. In a few areas, such as the Farne Islands, National Trust ownership extends to the low water mark, and this also applies in certain tidal estuaries such as Newtown on the Isle of Wight. Elsewhere a relatively small number of adjoining interests on the foreshore or seabed have been acquired, for example, through some twenty leases from the Crown Estate.

Management of coastal land, however, must inevitably take account of a variety of activities affecting the coastal zone beyond the limits of property boundaries and the high water mark. These include aspects such as recreational and commercial uses, and environmental processes and events, which underline the importance to the Trust of working with other agencies involved in the management of the coastal zone. In this sense the stage is already set for the Trust to take an increasingly active part in maritime research and conservation, steadily improving the emphasis given to historical and archaeological considerations as an integral component of its management and acquisition strategies.

Development of the 'Neptune' philosophy

The philosophical starting point and developing strands of the Trust's 'Neptune' approach can be briefly reviewed in relation to the process of land acquisitions. An aesthetic imperative at the fulcrum of the Trust's early thinking is clear: Dinas Oleu, above Barmouth and overlooking Cardigan Bay, in Gwynedd, Wales, the Trust's first property, was given by Mrs Fanny Talbot in 1895 "to place it into the custody of some society that will never vulgarize it". Management of the coast as a recreational zone, in Victorian terms, was a battle to protect natural beauty from the intrusion of bad taste. Natural historical or ecological criteria were thus also closely linked to this starting point, reflected, for example, in the Trust's acquisition of Blakeney Point, Norfolk in 1912, to protect ecological values, here particularly as a habitat for seals and nesting birds.

Artistic, historical or nostalgic associations have also traditionally influenced perceptions and values, but generally in a secondary role, and quite often most potently when combined together with the primary role of defending areas of beauty. Dunstanburgh Castle, Northumberland, for example, acquired in 1961, is noted in the National Trust Properties Handbook not only for its historic interest but also as providing "outstanding views of adjoining coast and cliff-nesting seabirds". It was painted by Turner, and provides an impressive feature in the wider landscape, also owned by the Trust, which surrounds it. It too is an aesthetic and a romantic object, harmonised with its surroundings through the natural processes of time and ruin. A large number of prehistoric sites, particularly the coastal and promontory forts of the Iron Age, are similarly represented on National Trust coastal land. Indeed, many of the less obvious of these have in a sense merged with their backgrounds, forming part of the scenery but often no longer the focus of attention, their visual impact having faded away.

Specifically archaeological or architectural acquisitions of coastal property are therefore represented in the gradual build up of the 'Neptune' portfolio, but they tend to be secondary to landscape considerations. Where such acquisitions are made on primarily historic criteria, as in the case of Souter lighthouse in Tyne & Wear, built in 1871, these have tended so far to favour the more discrete and 'collectable' of shoreline features.

Survey and management

The identification and recognition of archaeological sites through survey, and more recently a broader appreciation of historic landscape values, have nonetheless become established as axioms of the Trust's approach to the management of all its properties. Archaeological and vernacular building surveys, incorporating land use and landscape studies to varying degrees, have been undertaken since the mid 1980s. The resulting information and recommendations are then absorbed into management – through property management plans, and to a lesser extent acquisition strategy plans; and into presentation and interpretation – through information boards, short publications or guided walk leaflets for visitors. In certain areas monitoring programmes have been initiated to follow the first round of surveys.

An increased awareness of the potential range of historical values and the significance of the many historic features found in the coastal landscape is thus developing, with increasing impact on management objectives and priorities. Areas such as West Penwith in Cornwall have been particularly well surveyed and documented, largely by the Cornwall Archaeological Unit, so that strategies for management and for further acquisition are well-informed. Examples range from the prehistoric and medieval field systems which still dominate the farmed coastal landscape, to the remains of the historic mining industry of Cornwall. The Trust has worked actively to conserve and restore historic features, such as the well-known group of beam engines near Redruth, of which the Levant engine has been restored to steam.

Changing emphasis

A good recent example indicating changes in emphasis of coastal management is provided by the story of the Trust's acquisition and management plan for Orford Ness in East Anglia. This shingle spit and foreland was acquired primarily for its ecological value as an SSSI and RAMSAR site. However, it was also for many years a secret landscape of experimental military activity, the site of trials ranging from ballistics tests in the early twentieth century through to nuclear weapons tests in the 1950s. The legacy of this is most visible in the substantial and extraordinary architectural forms of the test cell buildings used to contain the blast from explosives.

Through survey and historical research the Trust's regional archaeologist Angus Wainwright has begun to build up a record, and establish criteria for assessing the conservation significance of the historic component of the landscape (Wainwright 1994). Rarity, historic association (for example, the first demonstration of the use of RADAR), group value and landscape impact/symbolic value (for example, with reference to the atomic research test cells) are among the criteria, and the analysis of these values is used in combination with an assessment of the aesthetic values of the place. A precise philosophy has been evolved incorporating the principle of non-intervention for several of the most massive concrete structures, which will survive for many generations as coastal landscape features, the contrast between them and their landscape setting only gradually softening with time.

The evolution of new criteria for assessment processes, which clearly go beyond those of the traditional aesthetic used to set the initial target for Enterprise Neptune in 1965, is important for management and for acquisition or protection strategies alike. Just as other relatively modern structures, such as industrial remains or the defensive constructions of the second world war, traditionally seen as eyesores and often neglected, have slowly come to be valued for their historical meaning, so the effect of an acquisition like Orford Ness is to force further re-assessment of cultural values. How long before such a place would be accepted for preservation primarily because of the application of such criteria (and supposing that traditional aesthetic and natural historical interests were absent) is still an open question.

Other changes of criteria have been introduced and have taken effect as primary determinants, but following a less philosophically problematic course more neatly in line with contemporary 'green' thinking, for example, the acquisition of the Trust's 500th mile at Warren House Gill, Co. Durham. Given by British Coal following closure of the mining industry which had been operating since the 1920s, the coal-blackened beaches are destined for restoration, an environmental clean-up to reinstate their natural beauty. This stretch would once not have met the traditional landscape criteria for preservation by the National Trust, but can now be made to do so.

Survey and management of coastal land – examples

Examples of the current approach to the management of the landward side of coastal landscapes, and its basis in survey and recording, can be given. Lundy, for example, in the Bristol Channel, is one of a handful of islands owned by the Trust and in this case leased to the Landmark Trust. A detailed measured survey of the island has been conducted by National Trust staff and volunteers, and combined with historical research by a number of contributors. It is a landscape of strong maritime character and connections, particularly in its defensive and communications features dating from the medieval to the modern periods. These include many gun battery positions such as Brazen Ward – a site which includes a main rectangular building consisting of two chambers. Many such batteries are attributed to the Civil War.

Only one of Lundy's three lighthouses is currently owned by the National Trust, the earliest Georgian 'Old Light': this one having to be replaced historically by the north and south lights. The disadvantage of the Old Light was its location on a cliff so that it was not visible in fog, an unfortunate design problem which must have contributed to the tally of shipwrecks around the island.

These and many more subtle features of the Lundy landscape are, through detailed survey and study, being integrated with increasing success into the management processes of the island. In addition the survey results are being used by English Heritage to inform the Monuments Protection Programme and revision of the Scheduled Ancient Monument designations. A publication of the survey is planned. Surrounding the island underwater are the many known submerged wrecks, of which two are designated under the Protection of Wrecks Act, with most of the rest located within the Marine Nature Reserve. There is great potential for the two Trusts involved on Lundy, together with the other appropriate agencies, further to extend the survey and management principles now being exemplified on land to the underwater historic environment.

If the indivisibility of land and sea is paramount in the histories of island communities, their interdependence is similarly clear in the economic aspects of coastal industries. One example to illustrate this can be shown on the Yorkshire/Cleveland coast where Britain's historic alum industry dominated a large area of coast, from shoreline to hinterland, for some three hundred years until closures of the last alum houses at the turn of the present century. Much of the history and archaeology of the industry was brought to light and subjected to fresh study by Gary Marshall, the Trust's archaeologist in charge of an integrated research and management project (Marshall 1990; Marshall 1994). Conservation and research were undertaken simultaneously on the Trust's alum factory site at Ravenscar, supported by grant-aid from English Heritage, enabling it to be presented and opened to the public by the Trust.

The alum site at Ravenscar is fine example of an industrial coastal landscape linking land and sea. One of many structures surviving as ruins, the winding house, located at the edge of the site on the dramatic Ravenscar cliffs, overlooks the shoreline where ships were berthed in rock-cut docks, bringing coal and urine used in the manufacturing process, and taking out the finished alum crystal. Early rock-cut tramways also survive on the foreshore: these have been included in the Trust's survey and analysis of a complete maritime landscape of related features stretching from the intertidal zone to the inland cliffs from which the alum shale was quarried.

Only rarely has the Trust become involved with archaeological investigations originating specifically in the intertidal zone. One example was the discovery by Gordon Roberts on 21st March 1990 of prehistoric human and animal prints preserved in estuarine silts at Formby Point. The identification and recording of some twenty barefoot human tracks, adult and child, of probable Neolithic date, caused both local and national interest, and Gordon Roberts' research on this subject is continuing.

Future potential

The coastal and maritime inventories being compiled by the Royal Commissions for England and Wales, the Environment and Heritage Service for Northern Ireland, and local authorities, will provide data of significant interest to the National Trust for the management of its coastal landscapes. This new body of information will require analysis and assimilation before its full potential can be known, and ongoing validation and other investigative projects will clearly increase knowledge still further. To date only a brief sample of the results of this work has been examined explicitly in relation to National Trust land holdings, but it is clear that significant concentrations of offshore wrecks do occur in areas adjacent to National Trust land. While National Trust foreshores have already been examined in the Trust's archaeological surveys there is bound to be an increase in the number of identified sites and artefacts recorded by new coastal surveys, both on National Trust land or in the adjacent intertidal areas. The question will then arise as to how to incorporate this data into the National Trust Sites and Monuments Record and property management plans.

The Trust's potential legal interest in the wreck of the sea, derived from its position as lord of the manor in many coastal areas, is another aspect requiring further research. For example, as lord of the manors of Penrose, Carminowe and Winnianton, Cornwall, the Trust may claim wreck occurring "as far out to sea as a flaming herring barrel might be seen on a fair and calm day from the highest point of land". Deeds conveying land to the Trust also raise similar potential interests. For example, another Cornish land parcel conveyed in 1974 includes "all that portion of the foreshore and bed of the sea between High Water Mark (HWM) and Low Water Mark (LWM) ... which abuts on or adjoins the land together with the wreck of the sea and all other rights and easements to the shore belonging".

Recent research has begun to investigate this source of information in more detail. Mike Williams (University of Wolverhampton) and Mike Palmer (South West Maritime Archaeological Group) have discovered important archival evidence mainly arising from nineteenth century surveys and records from the Receivers of Wreck, detailing claims admitted in relation to the relevant manor. This information was compiled by RCHME. Two implications arise for the Trust: first, the potential to exercise claims for conservation purposes; and second, the potential for a considerable increase in historical information, both on the economy of coastal manors and on specific wrecks and ship losses, particularly for the medieval period.

Finally a number of practical and policy initiatives can be pursued. Collaborative links and partnerships with other historical, archaeological and conservation bodies must be a priority, especially to mitigate the question of new costs being added to the Trust's existing conservation bills if its research and management activities are to be usefully extended in the coastal zone.

Second, there is potential to improve contacts with recreational diving groups, so that access arrangements are managed appropriately and conservation guidelines more widely disseminated. Existing Trust guidelines are being updated to take account of the increased interest in wreck diving and to promote good practice among divers.

Training and an expanded brief for the Trust's coastal wardens in future may also prove possible, to assist in the provision of effective controls on identified historic sites. The extension of new conservation leases of the seabed may also be an effective way in some circumstances to implant management of historic sites in the intertidal and offshore areas.

Conclusion

Development of new policy on a broad front for the Trust's future role in marine archaeology will take time, but will certainly build on the Trust's existing support for current initiatives, expressed for example through membership of the Joint Nautical Archaeology Policy Committee. The traditional aesthetic, applied to coastal landscapes, is slowly changing in emphasis, influencing the breadth of survey and management. The acknowledgement of the archaeological value of features of all periods, particularly the less visually appealing sites of more modern times, is particularly significant. The Trust's traditional role in considering for acquisition threatened archaeological sites of national importance will also need to take account of the new inventory data and allied research on maritime sites.

As emphasised at the beginning of this paper, the National Trust has to date adopted only one specifically targeted campaign of acquisitions, the Enterprise Neptune campaign. The 'zone' of this campaign, its criteria and its associated perceptions, have evolved and continue to change in favour of the historic component of the coastal environment. It has proved a highly successful campaign, generating considerable public support. These factors augur well for an extended remit in future, when preservation of the coastal landscape may come to mean preservation of all significant cultural, as well as natural, features of the coastal zone, with the kind of public support and involvement which has made Enterprise Neptune a success.

References

Marshall, G. 1990: The Ravenscar Alum Works – New Evidence from Archaeological and Documentary Sources, *Trans Scarborough Archaeol Hist Soc*, 28, 15–33.

Marshall, G. 1994: *Saltwick Alum Works, An Archaeological Interpretation*, (Scarborough Archaeol.Hist Soc Research Report 11).

Wainwright, A. 1994: Does Orford Ness = Awful Mess? The contribution of Archaeological and Aesthetic survey to the development of a management plan', *National Trust Annual Archaeological Review 1994 (Unpubl)*, 74–9.

Index

Abbot of Quarr 89
Aberg, Alan 1–3
Admiralty Book 109, 110
Admiralty Charts 102
Admiralty Court 29, 109
Allen, John 66
Amsterdam, the 3
Anglo-Saxon period 8, 15, 25, 66, 103
Anne, the 2, 3
Annet (Scilly) 82
Anstruther, Sir John 46
Anthony (Plymoth Sound, Cornwall) 109
Arbroath 44
Ards Peninsula (Co Down) 61
Armorica 93
Arnolt, William 109
Ashlett (Hants) 112
Audley's Castle Quay (Co Down) 62
Ayles, William 109

Ballyhenry Bay (Co Down) 61
Ballyurnanellan townland (Co Down) 63
Banks, William 42
Barnett, Moses 110
Beacon Hill (Harwich) 15
Beauly Firth 51, 53, 54, 56, 57
Beaumont Quay (Essex) 10, 11, 12
Bell Rock (Fife) 43–5
Binstead (Isle of Wight) 91
Binstead Beach 91
Binstead Creek 89
Bishop of Winchester's Pipe Rolls 109
Black Cairn (Beauly Firth) 54
Blackwater, Estuary 8, 9, 15
Blackwater, River 5, 8
Blakeney Point (Norfolk) 115
Blundell, Odo 54
Bognor Regis 102
Bonfire Carn (Scilly) 76
Boswell, John 35
Bradley, R 110
Bradwell power station 10
Bradwell-on-Sea (Essex) 5, 15
Brazen Ward (Lundy) 117
Brean Down 70
Brett, John 110
Brightlingsea (Essex) 10, 12
Bristol Channel 2

British Academy 65
British Marine Aggregate Producers Association 3
Bronze Age period 8, 9, 10, 13, 18, 70, 75–6, 79–82, 86, 89, 90, 94, 104
Bruce, John 51, 53
Brue Valley 65, 70
Bryher (Scilly) 82
Buckhaven (Fife) 32
Buckley, David 1, 5–16
Buglass, John 23
Burgh Records 29
Burnham on Crouch (Essex) 15
Burntisland (Fife) 35
Byland Abbey (Yorkshire) 112

CADW 3, 65
Caerleon 66
Caesarea 108
Cairn Airc (Beauly Firth) 57
Cambridge University Committee for Aerial Photography (CUCAP) 7, 102
Camden, William 5
Canvey Island 10, 13, 71
Car Dyke 69
Carew's Survey of Cornwall 109
Carminowe (Cornwall) 117
Carr Reef/Rocks (Fife) 39, 43
Castleward Bay (Co Down) 61, 63
Castleward Quay (Co Down) 62
Cato, Marcus Porcius I/II 107
Cellardyke (Fife) 32
Chapel Island kelp kilns (Co Down) 62
Chauki Tribe 18
Chichester Harbour 69, 101
Cicero, Marcus Tullus 107
Cindery Island (Essex) 6
Cistercian Order 62–3, 72, 89, 91
Civil War 39, 41
Clacton (Essex) 6, 7, 8
Claris, Philip 1, 115–118
Clark, Edward 110
Claybrook (Hants) 109
Cleveland 1, 23
Cleveland County Archaeology Service 23
Cleveland Maritime Archaeology Database 23, 24, 28
Clyde Navigation Trust 54
Coastal Forum 2

Coastal Protection Authority 95
Collier, Peter 99–105
Collins Creek 9
Colne Estuary 6
Colne, River 5, 6, 10
Columella, Lucius Junius Moderatus 107, 108
Cook, Captain James 25
Cornwall 75
Cornwall Archaeological Unit 75
Cornwall Archaeological Unit 116
Country Site and Monuments Records 112
Countryside Commission 2, 6
Countryside Council for Wales 65
County down 61
Crab's Ledge (Scilly) 79, 81, 82, 83
Crandon Bridge (Somerset) 66
Cribs, Henry 110
Crimdon (Cleveland) 25
Crofton (Hants) 108
Crombie RAF base 32
Crouch Estuary 8, 10
Crouch Valley 13
Crouch, River 5
Crown Estates 2, 115
Currie, Christopher 1, 107–114

Dallimore, John 109
Daniels, Robin 1, 22–28
Day, Wentworth 9
Dengie Peninsula 13
Denmark 17
Dina Oleu (Gwynedd) 115
Dix, Justin 88
Domesday Book 70, 71, 108, 109
Donnelly, William 51
Dumbuck (Firth of Clyde) 51, 53
Dunbar 42
Dunsey Island (Co Down) 62, 63
Dunstanburgh Castle (Northumberland) 116
Durham County Council 23
Durham Plateau 25

Earl of Southampton 109
East Medina Mill (Isle of Wight) 112
East Mersea (Essex) 9
East Mersea Country Park 15
East Neuk (Fife) 39

East Wemyss Fife) 32
Eastney (Hants) 112
Eden, River 33
Edinburgh 41
Eighteenth Century 109
Eling (Hants) 109
Elisenhof (Shleswig-Holstein) 18, 19
Elms Farm (Heybridge, Essex) 8
Emsworth (Hants) 112
English Heritage 1, 2, 9, 75, 86, 95, 96, 117
English Nature 3, 6, 7
Enterprise Neptune 2, 115–118
Environment Agency 10
Environment and Heritage Service for Northern Ireland 117
Environmental Impact Assessments 2
Environmentally Sensitive Areas 15
Eriska, Isle of 51
Erskine Bridge 51
Erskine crannog 53
Erskine Ferry 53
Esbjerg (Denmark) 17
Essex 1, 5–16, 69
Essex Coast 51, 72
Essex Coastal Strategy 15
Essex County Council 5, 10
Essex Mapping Project 7, 10, 13
Essex Marshes 71
Essex Sites and Monuments Record 7

Fanny Crossley, the 61
Farlington (Hants) 112
Farne Islands 115
Fawley (Hants) 89
Feddersen Wierde 18
Fenland 69, 70, 71
Fife 1, 29–37
Fife Council 29
Fife Council Planning Service 31
Fife Enterprise 29
Fife Ness 32, 33, 35
Fife Regional Council 36
Fife Young Archaeologists' Club 35
Fife, East 39–50
First World War 35
Firth of Clyde 51, 56
Firth of Tay 33, 34
Fishouse (Isle of Wight) 108, 112
Fleet, Charles 110
Fontana, Dominic 99–105
Formby Point (Yorkshire) 117
Foulness Island 9, 71
Frazer, James 53
Frisians 18
Fry, Arthur 109
Fulford, Michael 66

Geographical Information Service (GIS) 1, 36, 100
Germany, North 1, 17–21
Global Agreement on Trade (GAT) 86

Goldhanger (Essex) 13
Great Salterns Lake (Hants) 112
Green, Gary 25
Greig, Samuel 35
Grey, Sir George 110
Greyabbey Bay (Co Down) 62, 63
Grooved Ware 89
Gugh (Scilly) 82
Guys Hospital 10
Gwent Levels 66
Gwent Levels Historic Landscape Study 65

Hadleigh (Essex) 15
Hale, Alex 1, 51–59
Hall, Ron 9
Hamble Estuary 109
Hampshire 99
Hampshire and Wight Trust for Maritime Archeaology 3, 86, 88
Hampshire County Council 1, 99, 102
Hamson, James 109
Hamstead Saltworks (Isle of Wight) 112
Hanks, Anthony 88
Hanson, William 53
Harbour Authorities 85
Hartlepool 27
Hartlepool monastery 25
Hartlepool submerged forest 27
Harwich 5, 15
Hastings 3
Hatzum-Boomborg 17, 18
Hault, Giles 109
Havana 35
Hayling Island 108, 110
Hayling, East (Hants) 112
Hayling, North (Hants) 112
Hazo of Carthage 107
Hengistbury Head (Dorset) 93
Heritage Coast 2
Higher Moors (St Mary's, Scilly) 81, 82
Hilda Parnell, the 61
Historic Scotland 3, 29, 32, 33, 47
HMS Campania 35
HMS Success 35
Hoar, James 110
Hockey, SF 108
Hogg, Gavin 47
Holocene era 87, 88
Hook Valence (Hants) 110
Hook, River 110
Hullbridge (Essex) 8
Hullbridge Survey 8, 9, 10, 51
Humber, River 3
Hydrographic Office 101, 102
Hythe (Hants) 112

Ilchester (Somerset) 66
Ingrebourne, River 5
Inverkeithing (Fife) 35

Inverness Field Club and Scientific Society 54
Irish Sea 61
Iron Age period 69, 75, 76, 79, 82, 91, 110, 116
Isle of Eriska 53
Isle of May 39
Isle of Wight 1, 85–97, 109
Isle of Wight County Council 86, 88, 94
Isles of Scilly 75–84

Jaywick (Clacton, Hants) 10
Joint Nautical Archaeology Policy Committee 118
Joint Nautical Archaeology Policy Committee (JNAPC) 2, 85
Jones, Barri 54
Juliana (daughter of Richard de Walleys) 109
Jumieges Abbey 108

Kenn Moor (Somerset Levels) 68
Kent, north 10, 69
Killyleagh Quay (Co Down) 62
Kilsyth, battle of 41
Kincardine (Fife) 32, 33, 34, 35
Kingsbarns Harbour (Fife) 35
Kircaldy (Fife) 35
Kircubbin (Co Down) 62

La Anne 89
La Katerine 89, 91
La Mariote 89, 91
La Martha 89
La Nicholas 89, 91
La Seinte Marie 89, 91
Laing Museum, Newburgh (Fife) 31
Lakeside Shopping Centre 7
Landmark Trust 117
Langbank (Fife) 51, 53
Langenhoe (Essex) 71
Langstone Harbour 1, 99–105
Leas, River 5
Lecale Peninsula 61
Legat, Edmund 109
Leigh Beck (Essex) 13
Leith 41
Leuchars RAF base 32
Lewis, Carenza 1–3
Lindores (Fife) 35
Lion Point (Clacton, Essex) 7
London 10, 15, 71, 72
London Bridge 10
Low Water Bird Count Data 100, 104
Lower Moors (St Mary's, Scilly) 81
Lower Saxony Institute for Historical Research 17
Lundy Island 117
Lymington (Hants) 110, 111

Maclagan, Christian 53–4
Mahee Castle (Co Down) 62

Maitland, Frederick 35
Maldon (Essex) 6
Management for Archaeology Underwater 61
Maritime Fife 29–37, 47
Marshall, Gary 117
Marshhouse decoy 11
Martin, Colin 1, 39–50
Mary Rose, the 99
Meare (Somerset) 112
Medieval period (see also Middle Ages) 69, 89, 91
Medina, River 109, 112
Mendips 66
Mengham Salterns (Hants) 110, 112
Meon Estuary 108
Mesolithic period 8, 25, 75, 81, 82, 99, 104
Mesozoic period 5
Middle Ages (see also Medieval period) 17, 18, 19
Middlesborough Docks 27
Midlands 72
Migration period 18
Mill Rithe (Hants) 110
Ministry of Agriculture, Fisheries and Food (MAFF) 3, 94, 95
Ministry of Defence Hydrographic Office 32
Montgomery, William 62
Monuments Protection Programme 117
Moray Firth 56, 57
Mother Bank anchorage (Isle of Wight) 92
Munro, Robert 51, 53

Napoleon/Napoleonic period 15, 35
National Mapping Programme 5, 7, 10
National Maritime Museum 10
National Rivers Authority 2, 3
National Trust 2, 115–8
National Trust Sites and Monuments Record (NTSMR) 117
Nature Reserves 15
Nautical Archaeology Society 1, 23, 25, 28, 31, 34
Nendrum 62
Neolithic period 1, 7, 8, 17, 25, 79, 81–2, 86, 89, 91
Ness, River 57
Netherlands 17
Neuds, Thomas 109
Newburgh (Fife) 33
Newlyn (Cornwall) 101
Newport (Firth of Tay) 34, 35
Newport (Isle of Wight) 110
Newton (Isle of Wight) 110, 115
Newton Saltworks (Isle of Wight) 113
Nimble 61
Nineteenth Century 10, 32, 33
Norden, John 5

Norfolk 2
Norman Conquest 72
Nornour (Scilly) 81
North Binness Island (Hants) 104
North Sea 17, 18, 20
North York Moors Country Park 23
North Yorkshire County Council 23
Northern Ireland Sites and Monuments Record 63

Oakbank (Loch Tay) 55
Old Hall Marshes (Essex) 11
Old Light' (Lundy) 117
Oldorf (Saxony) 18, 19
Ordnance Survey 11, 28, 32, 62, 101, 102, 110
Orford Ness (Suffolk) 2, 116
Orsett (Essex) 7
Oxey Marsh (Hants) 112
Oxley, Ian 1, 29–37

Paglesham Reach (Essex) 10
Palaeolithic period 3, 7
Palmer, Mike 118
Par (Higher Town) Beach (St Martin's Scilly) 79, 80, 81, 82, 83
Pearson, Alastair 99–105
Peldon area (Essex) 13, 14
Pembrokeshire Coastal Path 2
Pennington (Hants) 110, 112
Penrose (Cornwall) 117
Pittenweem (Fife) 6, 39–42, 46, 48
Planning Policy Guidance 16 (PPG16) 85
Pleistocene era 88
Point Clear Caravan Park (Essex) 6
Poole Harbour 69
Port Authorities 85
Portaferry (Co Down) 62
Porth Killier (Scilly) 79, 80
Porth Mellon (Scilly) 79, 82, 83
Portsmouth Harbour 102
Portsmouth Polytechnic 99
Portsmouth University 1, 100
Pre-Roman Iron Age 17
Princess Augusta, the 35
Pritchard, Peter 25
Proceeding of the Society of Antiquaries of Scotland 53
Protection of Wrecks Act, 1973 27, 117
Ptolemy 92
Puck House Hill (Isle of Wight) 86, 89
Purfleet (Essex) 5, 7
Puxton (Somerset) 66, 69

Quarr Abbey 1, 91, 92, 108, 109
Quiberon Bay 35
Quoile Quay (Co Down) 61

Rains, Mike 36
Ramsar sites 15, 99, 116
Ratcliffe, Jeanette 1, 75–84

Ravenscar (Yorkshire) 117
Redcastle (Beauly Firth) 54
Redruth (Cornwall) 116
Rhine, River 109
Ringhaddy (Co Down) 62
Rinyo-Clacton 7
Rippon, Steven 1, 65–74
River, ALF 92
Roach, River 10
Roberts, Gordon 117
Rodenkirchen (Saxony) 18
Roding, River 5
Rolls Farm (Essex) 13
Roman Iron Age (continental) 18, 20
Roman period 5, 7, 10, 25, 65, 66, 69, 70, 72, 89, 92, 93, 107, 108, 110
Romney Marsh 71
Rosyth RAF base 32
Royal Air Force 7, 10
Royal Commission on the Ancient and Historical Monuments of Scotland (RCAHMS) 29, 32, 33, 36, 53
Royal Commission on the Historical Monuments of England (RCHME) 3, 7, 10, 23, 117, 118
Royal Mary, the 35
Royal Navy 35
Royal Society for the Protection of Birds (RSPB) 99
Ryde Middle Bank 88, 92
Rye 2

Saltburn (Cleveland) 23, 27
Saltern's Quay (Hants) 112
Samson (Scilly) 82
Saxony, Lower 17–21
Scarborough 27
Scheduled Ancient Monument(s) 11
Scheduled Ancient Monuments 117
Schleswig-Holstein 18
Scilly, Isles of 1
Scotia Archaeology 47
Scotland 1, 29, 51
Scott, Sir Walter 43
Scottish Intertidal Zone 52–9
Seaham (Cleveland) 23
Seahenge 2
Seaton Carew (Cleveland) 23, 25, 26, 27
Second World War 7, 9, 15, 30, 99
Seven Years War 35
Seventeenth Century 109
Severn Estuary 65–9, 72, 103
Severn Estuary Levels 66
Severn Estuary Levels Research Committee 3, 51
Severn, River 1, 51
Shalfleet Saltworks (Isle of Wight) 113
Shipman Head (Scilly) 76, 77
Shoreline Management Plans 94
Sites and Monuments Records 85, 94, 95, 100

Sites of Special Scientific Interest (SSSI) 15, 99
Sluys (Denmark) 89
Society for Landscape Studies 1
Solent 87, 113, 102, 107–114
Solent River palaeochannel 87
Somerset 65, 72
Somerset Levels 66
Souter Lighthouse (Tyne and Wear) 116
South of England Oyster Company 110
Southampton 93
Southend 6
Spartina 104
Special Protection Areas 99
Spithead anchorage 92
SSSI 116
St Agnes (Scilly) 82
St Mary's (Scilly) 81
St Monans (Scilly) 39, 46, 48
Staithes (Cleveland) 23, 27
Staplecourt (near Botley, Hants) 109
Steval Point (Scilly) 77
Stevenson, Robert 43
Stokes Bay (Hants) 88
Stour Estuary 5, 6, 10
Stour, River 5
Strabo 93
Strachan, David 10
Strahl, Erwin 1, 17–21
Straker, Vanessa 1, 75–84
Strangford Lough 2, 61–3
Strangford Narrows 61
Strangford Quay 61
Suffolk 10
Sylvan Villa (Hants) 112

Talbot, Fanny 115
Tamar Estuaries Historic Environment Advisory Forum 3
Tay Rail Bridge 33
Tay, River 31, 33
Tees Archaeology 23, 25, 27, 28
Tees Archaeology/NAS Rapid Response Register 25
Tees, River 25
Tentsmuir (Fife) 30
Tertiary period 5, 6, 86
Thames Estuary 6, 7, 10, 15, 70, 71
Thames Valley 6
Thames, River 1,3, 5, 7, 15
Thameside Marshes 71
The Seneshal's Quay (Ardkeen, Co Down) 62
The Stumble (Essex) 8
Thomas, Charles 82, 83
Thorrington (Essex) 10
Throsk (kiln site) 42
Thurrock 7
Tilbury 6
Tilbury Fort 15
Tillingham (Essex) 11
Titchfield (Hants) 112
Tollesbury parish (Essex) 14
Tomalin, David 1, 85-97
Tooley, M 25
Town and Country Planning Acts 85
Trenchmann, CT 25
Tresco (Scilly) 82
Turner, Joseph Mallord William 116
Twentieth century 15, 32

University of Southampton 86, 88, 92
University of St Andrews 29, 31

Varro, Marcus Terentius 107
Victoria County History 110
Victorian period 15

Wallasea Island (Essex) 8, 9
Walton on the Naze (Essex) 7, 8
Wangerland 17
Warren House Gill (Co Durham) 116
Warren, H 7, 51
Warsash (Hants) 112
Watering, John 109
Waughman, Mags 25
Wemyss Gas Works 32
Wentlooge Level 66, 67, 69
West Hook (Hants) 109
West Penwith (Cornwall) 116
West Porth, Samson 76
Westminster Abbey 71
Whitby (Yorkshire) 23
Wilhelmshaven 17
Williams, Brian 2, 61–63
Williams, Mike 118
Winnianton (Cornwall) 117
Wootton Creek (Isle of Wight) 88, 89, 94, 109, 112
Wootton Creek Project 1
Wootton Haven (Isle of Wight) 87, 91
Wootton-Quarr 86–8, 93–6
Wuppels (Saxony) 19, 20

Yeoman, Peter 32, 47